Preschool Readers and Writers

Additional Literacy Resources From High/Scope Press

General Reading Resources

How Young Children Learn to Read in High/Scope Programs: A Series of Position papers

Children Achieving: Best Practices in Early Literacy
S. B. Neuman & K. A. Roskos

Beginning Reading and Writing
D. S. Strickland & L. M. Morrow

Facilitating Preschool Literacy
R. Campbell

Learning to Read and Write: Developmentally Appropriate Practices for Young Children
S. B. Neuman, C. Copple, & S. Bredekamp

Much More than the ABCs: The Early Stages of Reading and Writing
J. Schickedanz

Starting Out Right: A Guide to Promoting Children's Reading Success
M. S. Burns, P. Griffin, & C. E. Snow

Preschool Reading

Educating Young Children: Active Learning Practices for Preschool and Child Care Programs (2nd Ed.)
M. Hohmann & D. P. Weikart

Fee, Fie, Phonemic Awareness—130 Prereading Activities for Preschoolers
M. Hohmann

High/Scope Preschool Key Experiences Series: Language and Literacy Video and Booklet

Helping Your Preschool Child Become a Reader: Ideas for Parents (Spanish version available)
A. S. Epstein

Letter Links: Alphabet Learning With Children's Names
A. DeBruin-Parecki & M. Hohmann

You and Your Child Parent Newsletter Series

Elementary Reading

High/Scope K–3 Curriculum Series: Language & Literacy
J. Maehr

Literature-Based Workshops for Language Arts—Ideas for Active Learning, Grades K–2
K. Morrison, T. Dittrich, & J. Claridge

Literature-Based Workshops for Mathematics—Ideas for Active Learning, Grades K–2
K. Morrison, T. Dittrich, & J. Claridge

Available from
HIGH/SCOPE® PRESS
A division of the High/Scope Educational Research Foundation
600 North River Street
Ypsilanti, MI 48198-2898
734/485-2000, FAX 734/485-0704
E-mail: *press@highscope.org*
Web site: *www.highscope.org*

Preschool Readers and Writers

Early Literacy Strategies for Teachers

Linda Weikel Ranweiler

HIGH/SCOPE® PRESS

Ypsilanti, Michigan

Published by

HIGH/SCOPE® PRESS

A division of the High/Scope Educational Research Foundation
600 North River Street
Ypsilanti, Michigan 48198-2898
(734) 485-2000, FAX (734) 485-0704
Web site: *www.highscope.org,* E-mail: *press@highscope.org*

Editors: Nancy Brickman, Holly Barton

Design and production: Judy Seling of Seling Design

Cover illustration, drawings: Robin Ward

Photography:

Gregory Fox—6, 10, 14, 15, 17, 21, 30, 31, 33, 34, 36, 37, 38, 43, 46, 48, 51, 56, 59, 64, 65, 69, 73, 75, 82, 88, 91, 92 (center & bottom), 94, 95, 96, 99, 103, 107 (lower left), 113, 114, 115, 119, 120, 124 (top center, lower left & right), 125 (top & center), 128, 131, 133, 134, 136, 143, 150, 153, 160, 164, 167, 169, 170, 172, 179, 184

Kevin McDonnell—3, 54, 67, 79, 90, 92 (top), 97, 102 (top), 105, 107 (upper left & right, bottom right), 108, 109, 125 (bottom), 139, 144

High/Scope Demonstration Preschool staff—29, 35, 41, 87, 102 (bottom), 126, 181

Patricia Evans—62, 117, 121, 124 (center)

Library of Congress Cataloging-in-Publication Data
Ranweiler, Linda, 1947-
  Preschool readers and writers : early literacy strategies for teachers / by Linda Ranweiler.
     p. cm.
Includes bibliographical references.
  ISBN 1-57379-186-5 (soft cover : alk. paper)
  1. Reading (Early childhood) 2. Language arts (Early childhood) I. High/Scope Educational Research Foundation. II. Title.
  LB1139.5.R43R36 2004
  372.4–dc22
                          2003022192

Printed in the United States of America
10 9 8 7 6 5 4 3 2

To my young grandsons Tayler, Matthew, and Jacob,
and to preschool-age readers and writers everywhere.
May the joy of reading surround you always.

Contents

Acknowledgments

Heartfelt thanks to the many people who made this book possible—

• The teachers, authors, and researchers of the past 30 years who have helped to illuminate the process of learning to read and write and produced a wealth of literature on early literacy

• The early childhood consultants and teachers who convinced me that this book was needed, and the many teachers and trainers who have generously shared ideas and resources over the years

• The High/Scope staff, past and present, who provided feedback, encouragement, and support during the writing and production of this book—Ann Epstein, Mary Hohmann, Andrea DeBruin-Parecki, Shannon Lockhart, Beth Marshall, Polly Neill, Sue Gainsley, Rosie Lucier, Pattie McDonald, Kevin McDonnell, Ursula Ansbach-Stahlsmith, Sue Terdan, Phyllis Weikart, and Libby Carlton

• My editors—Nancy Brickman, Holly Barton, and Lynn Taylor—without whose constant encouragement this book would not have happened

• And last but not least, my husband, Jack, for his support during the writing of this book—and especially for hauling all my resource boxes as we moved back and forth between Alaska and Mexico for three years

Preschool Readers and Writers

1

Introduction

Early literacy—how young children learn to read and write—is a subject that has fascinated parents, educators, and researchers alike. Because learning to read is such an internal process, it can seem to be almost magical, especially when it happens before the child is exposed to the formal teaching of reading in elementary school. How does a young child figure out that the written marks on a page in her storybook correspond to the words her mother is speaking when she reads the story out loud? Or that the marks on the store sign, the tube of toothpaste, and the fast food bag correspond to specific words? How does the ability to decipher the symbolic code of our alphabet develop? How does a four-year-old learn to write his own name? Is the whole process of learning to read and write as "natural" as the processes of learning to walk and talk? What part do adults play in helping children become readers and writers?

The answers to these questions are important to the many people who interact with preschoolers (children three, four, and five years of age), including parents and other family members, early childhood teachers, child care providers, and program administrators. Of late, the whole issue of early literacy has become important to a wider group: researchers and scientists, business executives, policymakers, politicians, and education professionals working outside the field of direct service to preschoolers. With the national spotlight on early literacy, the rest of society is finally beginning to recognize what preschool teachers have always known—just how

School success in later years depends heavily on language and literacy abilities, whose foundations develop in preschool experiences with both print and spoken language.

important the first five years of life really are. It is during these years that the foundations for literacy are laid and much of a children's potential for success in school (which depends heavily on language and literacy) may be determined.

This book was written primarily for adults who work with three-, four-, and five-year-olds in group settings, and for those that train and mentor them. It is designed to help teachers understand what they can do in their classrooms to foster early literacy, based on the latest research and literature in the field. The principles and strategies described are applicable in all kinds of preschool settings: private and public preschools and nursery schools, Head Start programs, child care centers, home-based child care programs, kindergartens, and special education programs.

In the first part of this chapter, we discuss what is now known and generally accepted about how young children learn to read and write. Next, we review eight dimensions of early literacy—what young children need in order to become readers and writers. Last, we explain some assumptions about learning that are a framework for the material presented throughout this book.

What We Know About Early Literacy

Much research on early literacy has been conducted over the past 10 to 15 years, and we now have a lot more knowledge about how young children acquire literacy. The "magic" has been explained, yet it is no less amazing.

- We know that the development of both language and literacy begins at birth and continues over one's lifetime.
- We know that the acquisition of language and literacy is developmental—that children go through various stages as they learn to listen, speak, write, and read.
- We know that there is much individual variation in language and literacy development, both in the paths that children take and in the rate at which they progress.
- We know that some children will pick up various literacy-related skills (such as phonemic awareness) quickly and easily, and other children will need more help.
- We know that the processes of language and literacy are intertwined and interdependent; that listening, speaking, reading, and writing develop concurrently rather than sequentially.
- We know that children's need to interact and communicate with significant others drives their ability to acquire language and literacy.
- We know that while much of language and literacy learning happens "naturally" or "informally" (meaning outside of formal schooling), it does not happen in a vacuum.

4

- We know that the acquisition of language and the acquisition of literacy can both be viewed as interactive processes: children are active constructors of their own learning, *and* they need supportive adults who provide what is needed for further development and learning.
- We know that children learn best when their experiences are relevant and meaningful to them.
- We know that children gain much of their literacy learning through playful activities, such as during dramatic play and exploring materials with print.
- We know that young children may enter preschool with many differences in their home languages and cultures, and that effective literacy instruction must respect, understand, and build on this diversity.

Beyond this current knowledge, these underlying principles, we also know many of the specific factors that contribute to young children's literacy acquisition. These are described in the following section.

What Young Children Need to Become Readers and Writers

In 1998, two professional organizations in the field of education—the International Reading Association (IRA) and the National Association for the Education of Young Children (NAEYC)—issued a joint position statement, "Learning to Read and Write: Developmentally Appropriate Practices for Young Children." This statement was subsequently published as the first section of a book by the same title, authored by Susan B. Neuman, Carol Copple, and Sue Bredekamp (2000). In the second section of their book, as they illustrate how the position statement translates into actual practice, the authors identify eight dimensions of early literacy development, and for each dimension provide many examples of teaching ideas for children from infancy through third grade. (This book is a valuable resource for all early childhood teachers.)

These dimensions provide a useful way to look at what young children need to become readers and writers, and are briefly described below:

- **The power and pleasure of literacy**—In order to *want* to become members of the "literacy club," children should see reading and writing as both useful and enjoyable activities. This usually occurs when children are read to frequently and find it pleasurable, when they see adults use reading and writing for many reasons in their own lives, and when they are encouraged to use literacy tools and props in their own play.
- **The literate environment**—The physical environment should be rich in *purposeful* print, such as labels and signs that children can see, interpret, and use.

There should be cozy, inviting places for both reading and writing to occur, a variety of readily accessible writing tools and materials, and books and pictures that reflect children's interests and their cultural and linguistic backgrounds.

- **Oral language development**—The development of speaking and listening lays the foundation for literacy learning, and cannot be overemphasized. Children should have many opportunities to hear and participate in meaningful conversations; to hear new words being used and explained; to learn rhymes, sing songs, and engage in word play; and to participate in dramatic play and small-group activities with their peers.

- **Building knowledge and comprehension**—A *language-rich* environment, where adults read to and talk with children and provide them with new experiences, promotes children's acquisition of knowledge and vocabulary. Children should be able to manipulate and use materials in a variety of ways, to go on field trips, to listen to informational books, to have meaningful conversations with adults, and to have many opportunities to assimilate knowledge from their new experiences through their play.

- **Knowledge of print**—When children grow up in a literate environment, *print awareness* begins to develop by the age of two to three years. To facilitate this development, adults should occasionally call attention to how print works (such as its top-to-bottom, left-to-right flow), help children to recognize and write their own names, point out the features of individual letters and words, and use the words associated with books (such as *title, author, cover,* etc.) when reading aloud.

- **Exposure to many types of text**—Being exposed to stories, nonfiction books, and other types of text (poems, letters, notes, lists, captions, invitations, newspapers and magazines, etc.) helps children to understand the kinds of language used and the elements involved in each genre. Adults should familiarize children with many different forms of text. Repeated readings of stories, related dramatic play, and story reenactments will also help children develop comprehension and understand the connection between spoken and printed words.

Pretend play can be an opportunity for children to develop vocabulary and comprehension and for adults to use new words and model the use of print. As a supporting player in the "doctor play" of these children, their teacher pretends to read a prescription they have given her.

- **Phonological awareness**—Children need to become aware of the *sounds* of language and its individual units, not just the meaning. To facilitate this awareness, adults should expose them to lots of language that contains rhymes (same ending sounds) and alliteration (same beginning sounds). Poems and songs, nursery rhymes and chants, tongue twisters and other forms of word play all help to make children aware of the sounds in words, which will later help them as they begin to link those sounds to written letters.
- **Familiarity with letters and words**—As part of print awareness, children need to be exposed to and become familiar with written words and the letters they are made of. They should have access to alphabet books, be able to play with three-dimensional letters, have many opportunities and materials for writing, see and use their own written names, and be exposed to letter-sound relationships.

Sometimes just four of these dimensions are emphasized as essential elements for learning how to read. The federal government's Early Reading First initiative, for example, focuses on oral language development, alphabet knowledge, print awareness, and phonological awareness.* In this book, however, we refer to all eight dimensions of early literacy, because children who have all of these elements in their lives before they enter kindergarten are much more likely to become *successful and enthusiastic* readers and writers. In high quality preschool classrooms, all eight of these literacy dimensions *are* present, and they are integrated throughout the day. (Note, too, that there are many other things that affect children's learning, not just their literacy learning, that this book does not cover—things such as their general health and nutrition, vision, motor coordination, the existence of special needs and so forth.)

Assumptions About Learning

A perspective on learning and development: The influence of High/Scope

This book reflects a general view of preschool learning and development as an active, constructive process. Adults support learning by providing diverse materials, by planning experiences designed to strengthen children's emerging abilities, and by interacting supportively with children during all classroom activities. The author's background as a teacher, teacher-trainer, and educational consultant using the High/Scope early childhood approach (see p. 8) has shaped this view. However, most of the suggestions for promoting literacy given here are not curriculum-specific. While these teaching ideas were

---

*Based on the recommendations of the National Reading Panel, the High/Scope publication *Fee, Fie, Phonemic Awareness* (Hohmann, 2002), offers 130 activities for preschoolers centered around these four components.

developed with High/Scope practitioners in mind, they should be equally useful for adults who work in other kinds of preschool settings, especially those following a child development approach to early learning.

Some readers may be unfamiliar with some of the High/Scope terminology used in the book. In particular, the phrase "key experiences" requires further explanation. The following six High/Scope **language and literacy key experiences** are viewed as essential to promoting literacy in the preschool years:

- Talking with others about personally meaningful experiences
- Describing objects, events, and relations
- Having fun with language: listening to stories and poems, making up stories and rhymes
- Reading in various ways: reading storybooks, signs and symbols, one's own writing
- Writing in various ways: drawing, scribbling, letterlike forms, invented spelling, conventional forms
- Dictating stories

These six learning experiences, referred to throughout this book, are part of a longer list of preschool key experiences (58 in all) that High/Scope has identified based on child development research and theory and the observations of teachers. The list con-

---

About the High/Scope Educational Approach

The High/Scope Curriculum provides a perspective on learning and development that guides many early childhood professionals. In "All About High/Scope" (2003, p. 1), Ann Epstein, Director of the Early Childhood Division at the High/Scope Foundation, describes the curriculum:

"High/Scope is an 'active learning' educational approach. Active learning means students have direct, hands-on experiences with people, objects, events, and ideas. Children's interests and choices are at the heart of High/Scope programs. They construct their own knowledge through interactions with the world and the people around them. Children take the first step in the learning process by making choices and following through on their plans and decisions. Teachers, caregivers, and parents offer physical, emotional, and intellectual support. In active learning settings, adults expand children's thinking with diverse materials and nurturing interactions."

In *Preventing Reading Difficulties in Young Children* (Snow, Burns, & Griffin, 1998), the High/Scope model is referred to as a high-quality preschool program "that had positive follow-up results in reading achievement for children with cognitive deficits" (p. 167). The High/Scope approach was initially developed for low-income, at-risk children, but has been shown to be effective with young children from all social, economic, and ethnic backgrounds, urban and rural, in the U.S. and around the world.

Readers may refer to Epstein's complete article (available online at *http://www.highscope.org/About/allabout.htm*) for more information, and are encouraged to read the High/Scope manual, *Educating Young Children: Active Learning Practices for Preschool and Child Care Programs* (Hohmann & Weikart, 2002), to learn more about the research and philosophy behind this approach, as well as how to put it into practice.

stitutes a comprehensive statement of the general kinds of activities that foster the social, cognitive, and physical development of children from the ages of two and a half to five years. Adults can support these key experiences by providing children with appropriate materials, by planning classroom experiences, and by building on key experiences when they occur in children's play and spontaneous interactions. The key experiences are organized in the following 10 categories or domains: *creative representation, language and literacy, initiative and social relations, movement, music, classification, seriation, number, space,* and *time.* While this book focuses on just one of the key experience categories—*language and literacy*—it is important to remember that all of these domains are developing during the early years, that they are *all* important, and that they often overlap and interact with one another. For example, counting out loud how many fish crackers are on a plate is an experience that strengthens both *language and literacy* and *number* abilities.

"Considering the total development of the child and not just the cognitive has been and always should be a hallmark in early childhood education."
—Leslie Mandel Morrow
(2001, p. 20)

In addition to the key experiences, other High/Scope terms that may not be understood are the names for the classroom interest areas (defined spaces for particular kinds of play) and the segments of the High/Scope daily routine. For more information on these High/Scope program elements and their connections to developing literacy, see Appendix A. Most teachers in non-High/Scope programs will see many parallels between standard High/Scope program elements and the organization of their own classroom spaces and daily routines.

Scaffolding and the zone of proximal development (ZPD)

While the glossary in Appendix B contains definitions for most of the terms used in this book, two terms need a bit more explanation: scaffolding and the zone of proximal development, or ZPD. These terms are often misused as well as misunderstood, so let's clarify what they mean, especially in the context of early literacy.

Lev Vygotsky (1896-1934), a Russian psychologist and social constructivist, coined the term **zone of proximal development,** or **ZPD.** The ZPD refers to the gap between what children can do independently (their "level of actual development"), and what they can do with help from an adult or more capable peers (their "level of potential development"). Vygotsky believed that learning occurs most effectively when a child is working within the ZPD, receiving appropriate assistance. He wrote, "What the child is able to do in collaboration today he will be able to do independently tomorrow" (1987).

The concept of **scaffolding** builds on Vygotsky's model of the ZPD, although Vygotsky himself never actually used the term. Wood, Bruner, and Ross (1976) were the first to use it in the educational sense; they defined it as "a process that enables a child or novice to solve a problem, carry out a task, or achieve a goal which would be beyond his [or her] unassisted efforts (p. 90)." They described how mothers use scaffolding as they read to their young children—offering lots of support initially, then gradually reducing it as the child takes over more of the task. Scaffolding is a way of referring to the assistance given to learners when they are in the "zone"—just like the wooden structure it is named for, it is temporary, adjustable, and gradually withdrawn as the need for it decreases. Another analogy often used to describe scaffolding is that of a set of training wheels on a bicycle: "It is adjustable and temporary, providing the young rider with the support he or she needs while learning to ride a two-wheeler. Without an aid of this sort, the complex task of learning to pedal, balance, and steer all at one time would be extremely difficult, if not impossible, for many youngsters. This scaffold—training wheels—allows the learner to accomplish a goal, riding a bicycle successfully, and then to happily pedal his or her way into a wider world" (Graves, Graves, & Braaten, 1996, p. 14).

Scaffolding is temporary support for children's use of developing skills that enables children to do things they could not do unaided.

Most teachers of young children already understand the concept of starting where the child is and building from there. Basically, "where the child is" is the child's independent level, what he can already do. Where we want to "build" is in each child's zone, offering assistance so that he can be successful in learning something new. If we try to introduce something new at a level above their ZPD, children often become frustrated or disinterested, because the skill or task is too hard and they are unable to do it. For example, it might be aiming too high to insist that a four-year-old who has little or no experience listening to stories sit quietly at group story time. And no matter how much assistance you offer, a three-year-old might not be able to print the letters of the alphabet, or even the letters of her own name.

The "zone" is where developmentally appropriate instruction aims: at a "challenging but achievable" level (IRA & NAEYC, 2000, p. 14). This level could very well be different for every child in a class, and to make the task of supporting children even more interesting, the zone for each child is always changing, gradually moving "up" as the child becomes able to do more and more things independently.

Scaffolding is something parents often do, informally and often unconsciously, with their young children. Parents initially do the whole job by themselves, then provide support as needed. They gradually withdraw their support as the child takes over more and more of

"One interesting and ironic characteristic of the construct of ZPD ... is that, like the construct of scaffolding, it is perhaps one of the most used and least understood constructs to appear in contemporary educational literature."

—Annemarie S. Palincsar
(1998, p. 370)

the responsibility for the task himself. Parents feed and dress their babies, carry them around, talk to and for them, and take care of their bathroom needs. Through scaffolding, children eventually learn (at different ages in different cultures) to feed themselves, choose and put on their own clothing, walk on their own, talk in complete sentences, and take care of pottying themselves.

Teachers using the High/Scope approach (or other approaches that encourage children's independence and initiative) also use the process of scaffolding, even if they are not familiar with the term itself. They observe children, see what they can do independently, provide the amount of support children need to get to the next level, and as the children learn how to do the task themselves, gradually withdraw their support. One example would be teaching children to wash out the paintbrushes. You might do the task yourself at the beginning of the year, then model for the children how it is done. You show the children how to soak the brushes, how to squish the paint out, how to rinse the brushes, and where to store them. You then let them try it, while you supervise, offering advice and assistance, until you see that they can do the job themselves. Early childhood teachers also frequently use scaffolding to support play: they observe children's play, then introduce materials they think will support and expand children's ideas; they talk with children about the materials and at times even model how to use the materials while taking part in the play at the children's invitation.

Sometimes what teachers do in the preschool classroom is just *part* of the scaffolding process. For instance, they use many different strategies to support children in step two of the scaffolded "learning-how-to-cut" process:

Step 1. Adults cut things for children.

Step 2. Adults help children learn to use scissors, through a variety of strategies:

- Provide opportunities for alternate activities (such as tearing).
- Provide materials that strengthen fine muscles (paper punch, tweezers, etc.).
- Provide scissors that work well.
- Provide opportunities for other children to model scissor use (small-group time).
- Model/demonstrate holding and using scissors.
- Provide materials that are easily cut with scissors (play dough, thin paper strips).
- Provide materials that are more challenging to cut (larger pieces of paper).

Step 3. Children cut things by themselves.

While scaffolding is not required for all learning (children learn much about the physical world, for example, through their own hands-on experiences with objects), all sorts of skills can be scaffolded. Below are examples of the scaffolding of physical, social, and literacy skills.

"IRA and NAEYC believe that goals and expectations for young children's achievement in reading and writing should be developmentally appropriate, that is, challenging but achievable, with sufficient adult support."

—International Reading Association and the National Association for the Education of Young Children (2000, p. 14)

Tying shoes (physical skill):

Amber (the adult) has always tied Leah's shoelaces. Then one day, Leah announces that she wants to tie her own shoes, so Amber begins teaching her how to do it. First, Amber shows her how to make an X with the laces, then lets Leah try. Soon Leah can make an X and pull the end of one lace through, to make the knot. After Leah does what she can, Amber completes the tying, always talking through the process: "Watch, now I'll make a tree with this lace, and then this lace, the rabbit, runs around the tree.…" Sure enough, Leah is soon wanting to do "the rabbit part" by herself. Little by little, Leah learns the steps. Amber does less and less of the work, until Leah is eventually able to tie her shoes by herself.

"Research supports the view of the child as an active constructor of his or her own learning, while at the same time studies emphasize the critical role of the supportive, interested, engaged adult (e.g., teacher, parent, or tutor) who provides scaffolding for the child's development of greater skill and understanding."

—International Reading Association and the National Association for the Education of Young Children (2000, p. 14)

Problem solving (social skill):

Josh (the adult) has always intervened when Michael and Caleb began fighting over a toy, solving the problem for them. At various times he has separated them, taken away the toy, or tried to distract one of them. Then one day (perhaps after attending a workshop on problem solving), Josh decides to teach the children conflict resolution skills. The next time a squabble starts, Josh approaches Michael and Caleb calmly, acknowledges their feelings, and asks each of them what the problem is. After they have both had a chance to identify the problem, Josh asks them to suggest some solutions, and they try one out. This process works successfully, so Josh continues to use it; over time the children know how to do more and more of the steps by themselves. As the children become more adept at this new skill of problem solving, they need less and less adult intervention.

Storybook reading (literacy skill):

Jeannette (the adult) has been reading books to her son Gregory since he was an infant. As a toddler he started choosing the books he wanted her to read; then he would insist on turning the pages while she read to him. Jeannette talked about the pictures with him, and she would relate objects and events in the books to their own experiences. She would often pause during familiar books, encouraging Gregory to chime in with words and phrases he knew. As Gregory became more interested in the words on the pages, she would often point to them as she read, occasionally pointing out letters and talking about the sounds they made. At times Gregory liked to read his favorite books (by memory) to Jeannette, and he soon began to figure out what certain words were. Gregory is now six years old, and he is well on his way to becoming a confident beginning reader.

You can see from these examples that the scaffolding process can take a long time for some skills (such as learning to read), or a relatively short time (such as learning how to clean paintbrushes). The common ingredients to these scaffolding examples are (1) scaffolding is a collaborative process between the child and adult (or another more competent person); (2) scaffolding operates within the child's ZPD; and (3) the scaffold is gradually withdrawn, as the child takes over more and more of the task.

The scaffolding process can involve individuals (the child's peers as well as adults), materials or tools (such as labels around the room, symbols and words on the message board, predictable books, training wheels), and techniques or strategies. Scaffolding strategies often involve language; some *verbal* strategies that are useful for preschool teachers include:

- Using encouragement
- Asking/answering questions
- Giving explanations
- "Thinking aloud" (verbalizing thinking)
- Providing feedback
- Using prompts or reminders
- Hinting, suggesting, and commenting
- Encouraging children to participate during storybook readings

Scaffolding strategies can also be *nonverbal,* such as providing play props or other materials, pointing to something, smiling or nodding encouragement, and modeling a process or task (sometimes modeling only part of the process, to allow for discovery and creativity).

Why is scaffolding so important to the whole issue of language and literacy? When young children learn how to talk, it is mostly a scaffolded process. Adults are constantly modeling the skills of speaking and listening. They explain, they provide feedback, they ask and answer questions, and they offer much encouragement to young language learners. Adults also often gear the way they talk to the developmental level of the child they are talking to. Parents and caregivers do more talking for a toddler who is not yet speaking, and much less by the time the child is five years old and can carry on a conversation.

Likewise, scaffolding is an important tool for literacy learning. Both reading and writing for various purposes are skills that are modeled by adults as they go about their daily lives. They also model these literacy skills specifically for children, writing words the children ask for, reading stories aloud to them. And just as they did when children were learning to speak, adults explain, provide feedback, ask and answer questions, and offer encouragement to young literacy learners. The gradual withdrawal of support applies to literacy scaffolding just as it does to language scaffolding: As children become more competent as readers and writers, adults tend to decrease the amount of reading and writing they do for children.

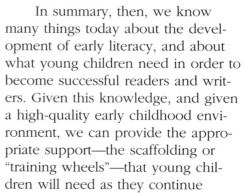

Children who have been introduced to the power and pleasure of literacy and have had plenty of scaffolded support in using print are eager to explore books on their own.

In summary, then, we know many things today about the development of early literacy, and about what young children need in order to become successful readers and writers. Given this knowledge, and given a high-quality early childhood environment, we can provide the appropriate support—the scaffolding or "training wheels"—that young children will need as they continue along their literacy journey.

The rest of this book gives the specifics teachers need to provide this scaffolded support for literacy in early childhood settings. The next seven chapters are organized around particular types of language and literacy experiences: speaking and listening (Chapter 2); word play, rhymes, and alliteration (Chapter 3); reading aloud and storytelling (Chapter 4); early writing (Chapter 5); alphabet learning (Chapter 6); reading in various ways (Chapter 7); and dictation (Chapter 8). Each of these "teaching practices" chapters describes materials, support strategies, and experiences to plan throughout the day relating to the chapter topic; the "whys" from research and theory supporting the recommended practices are also explored in depth. Following this, Chapter 9 discusses literacy assessment in preschool settings, Chapter 10 explores parent involvement in children's early literacy, and the Appendices provide additional resources.

2
Speaking and Listening: The Foundations of Literacy

In most early childhood classrooms, teachers are surrounded by children's words, day by day, hour by hour, minute by minute. When we are not talking to them (and many times even when we are!), children are talking—to us, to one another, to themselves.

"Teacher, teacher, c'mere and look! See what I found?"

"I want my Mama...."

"Hey, Tyler, y'know what I got for my birfday?"

"Gimme some of dose....I don't gots enough."

They talk about events in the classroom and at home, about people and animals they know and those they see on television or in books. They talk about the past, present, and future, about the real and the imaginary. They ask questions, and they answer questions. They tell others what to do, and they respond (in various ways!) to directions *they* are asked to follow. They talk seriously, and they talk playfully. Children also spend a great deal of time listening—to the sounds of the world around them, to adults, and to

Supportive early childhood classrooms are alive with the buzz of child conversations, because children have lots of interesting things to talk about.

other children. They listen to things that interest them: sounds and words, stories and poems, songs and conversations. Throughout the day, preschool-aged children use language—both speaking and listening—as they communicate and interact with others, carry out their intentions, engage in dramatic play, and figure out how things work.

It's truly amazing when you think about it—these little humans who came into the world just three or four years before, "who can't even add or tie their shoes, can understand and speak in full, complex grammatical sentences *without any training*" (Eliot, 1999, p. 351). Some children have much larger vocabularies than others, some are more talkative than others, but virtually all the children in our preschool settings have some language. And their language learning began long before these children came to our classrooms—it actually began the day they were born, perhaps even earlier.

Because it is such an important part of a child's development and a critical aspect of learning to read and write, all early childhood teachers should have a thorough understanding of oral language—what it is, how it develops, and how it can be nurtured at home and in a language-rich preschool classroom. The language-nurturing oral experiences that are most productive for preschool children are included in the first three of High/Scope's language and literacy key experiences: *talking with others about personally meaningful experiences; describing objects, events, and relations;* and *having fun with language: listening to stories and poems, making up stories and rhymes.* Note, however, that since oral language is the *foundation* of literacy, it is woven into the last three key experiences as well.

Although whole books have been written on the subject of oral language development, this chapter will lay out what is most important for *teachers* to know, especially as it relates to early literacy. Although the strategies for adult support later in this chapter will focus on preschool-aged children, we will trace the development of language from birth to age six years to better understand literacy at the preschool level.

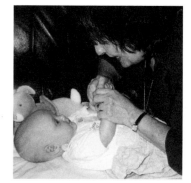

The foundations of literacy begin to develop long before children enter preschool.

What Is Language?

Before we discuss language, let's look at the larger concept of communication. Communication is the *exchange of information, the sending and receiving of messages.* Various modes of communication exist, and not just among humans—nearly all animals communicate, both with members of their own species and with other species as well: there are mating signals, warning signals, "This-is-my-turf" signals, and so on. Bees do a waggle-dance to tell other bees where nectar is to be found; canines and felines leave scents to mark their territory; primates use sounds, gestures, facial expressions, and other body language to communicate. We humans communicate in a variety of ways through both verbal and nonverbal means, including touch, gestures, facial expressions, body language, hand signs, pictures, symbols, vocal sounds, and words. The process of communication is a two-way interaction, requiring a message, a sender, and a receiver. The message is encoded by the sender, transmitted through a medium or channel, and then received and decoded by the receiver.

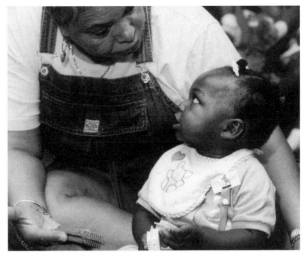

In infant-toddler settings, eye contact, gestures, and words are part of a communicative process through which the child learns language.

Children start communicating long before they start using language. Infants are great communicators. They cry when hungry or uncomfortable and fall back to sleep when their needs have been met. In their early weeks and months, they start making eye contact, cooing and smiling in response to an adult face. At about seven months, they bang with their fist or a spoon when they want attention, babble and laugh in response when an adult imitates their babbling. Around one year of age, they make known their desire for a cookie or toy by reaching or pointing, looking at a nearby adult, and making a noise. What starts out as purely *reflexive* communication (baby stops sucking when he or she has had enough milk) eventually becomes *intentional* communication (toddler pushes the spoon of strained peas away from his or her mouth). Young children are on the *receiving* end of communication even before birth. Always watching and listening, they are taking in the faces, the voices, and the sounds that surround them. As they attempt to make sense of all these experiences, they eventually figure out that certain sounds are words, and that the words have meaning and are linked to particular objects and actions.

> *"Research consistently demonstrates that the more children know about language...the better equipped they are to succeed in reading."*
>
> —M. Susan Burns,
> Peg Griffin, and
> Catherine E. Snow
> (1999, p. 8)

Language is one means of communication. It is a *shared code or system of communication used by a group of people*. This system consists of the meaning of words and the rules for how words are combined and how they are used to convey meaning. The primary purpose of language is for humans to communicate with one another, to give and receive information. Language can be spoken (oral), signed (with hand shapes, placements, and movements), communicated nonverbally (body language, facial expressions), or written. Language can also be expressive or receptive. *Expressive language* is the sharing of information with others. It can take the form of speaking, writing, signing, or making gestures or body movements (pointing, for example). *Receptive language* involves understanding the information that is conveyed by others: hearing and understanding spoken language, reading and understanding written language, watching and understanding signed language and body language.

Speaking, one of the two language skills discussed in this chapter, is an expressive skill. It involves both a mental process (formulating a thought or message) and a physical process (talking). Speaking is the production of sounds that make up words and sentences.

Listening, the other language skill we'll focus on here, is a receptive skill. Like speaking, it also involves both a physical process (hearing) and a mental process (interpretation or understanding). Listening is about making sense of oral language. It is the first language mode that children acquire, and one of the most used of the language arts throughout life.

The Subsystems of Language

There are five aspects or subsystems of language that young children assimilate during their earliest years, just by listening and responding to the adults around them. These aspects are like puzzle pieces that they put together as they acquire language—and they do it all without formal instruction, before they even get to kindergarten! These five subsystems encompass the mechanics of language **(phonology),** the meaning of language

> ### American Sign Language
>
> **Signing** is the use of hand shapes, placements, and movements that are used to express the words and sentences of various sign language systems, and **watching others sign** is the receptive mode. American Sign Language, a commonly used system, is a complete grammatical language, different than English but with all the same subsystems except phonology. There are many similarities between the acquisition of spoken language and the acquisition of signed language (as a first language). Deaf babies who are born to deaf parents and are exposed to fluent signing during their early months go through the same stages of language that hearing babies do (Apel & Masterson, 2001). They babble with sounds, which soon die out (due to lack of feedback from others as well as an inability to hear their own sounds), and they also babble with their fingers, making little gestures that are similar to signs but meaningless. About the same time hearing babies start saying real words, deaf babies start signing them, and the progression occurs in a similar order: first one word at a time, then two-word sentences, and eventually fully grammatical sentences.
>
> Because the sensitive time period for acquiring language is in the first four years, it is vitally important that parents make sure their baby can hear. A child who is not exposed to any language in the first year has much more difficulty learning it later.

(semantics), the rules of language **(syntax** and **morphology),** and the purposes of language **(pragmatics).** These subsystems of language are important not only for the development of *oral* language; they are also linked to children's later success in understanding and using *written* language.

Phonology refers to the *speech sounds* of language. An infant's phonological development begins very early (Apel & Masterson, 2001; Snow et al., 1998)—indeed, even in utero. Phonemes (the smallest units of spoken sound), pitch, stress, and intonation are all part of this system. Some interesting studies (Golinkoff & Hirsh-Pasek, 1999; Gopnick, Meltzoff, & Kuhl, 1999) have shown that infants pay attention to the sounds they hear and that they remember them. Infants can recognize (and prefer hearing) their own mother's voice, and can differentiate between the sounds and rhythms of their own language and other languages. Infants of course don't know which country they're going to be born into, so their brains are "programmed" to pick up whatever language the people around them speak. For the first six months these little "citizens of the world" can notice the differences among the sounds of *all* human languages, and even produce them when they start babbling. For example, babies born to Japanese speakers can (unlike their parents) hear the difference between /r/ and /l/ sounds, and babies born to English speakers can (unlike their parents) hear the three different /d/ sounds used in Hindi (Golinkoff & Hirsh-Pasek, 1999). But sometime between six and twelve months, the non-native sounds (those that are not spoken by the people they hear on a daily basis) fade away. Babies learn which sounds are important in their own language, and which are not. From then on, the sounds and intonation patterns in their babbling, jargon, and invented words reflect the distinctive sounds of their own community's language.

Semantics refers to the *meaning* of words, phrases, and sentences. Semantics involves both the types of words (for example, nouns, verbs, adjectives) and the meanings of words. Once babies have mastered the *sounds* of their language, they begin to figure out the *words* and what they mean. Children are learning semantics as they learn vocabulary—the words that name the objects, people, and actions in their environment. Under-

---

How the Subsystems of Language Relate to Literacy Development

+ **Phonology,** the mechanics of speech:

A child's *conscious awareness* of the sounds of spoken language—called **phonological awareness**—will start developing during the preschool years. This is the beginning of **phonemic awareness** (awareness of the smallest sound units that make up words), which plays an important role later in learning the **alphabetic principle** (understanding that words are made up of letters, and that there is a relationship between written letters and spoken sounds).

+ **Semantics,** the meaning of language:

The development of a large vocabulary—knowing a lot of words and what they mean—during the preschool years leads to better **listening comprehension, word** recognition, and **reading comprehension** later.

+ **Syntax** and **morphology,** the rules of language:

Children's familiarity with grammar helps them understand complex sentences, which will improve their **listening comprehension** and later their **reading comprehension.**

+ **Pragmatics,** the purpose of language:

An understanding of the unwritten social conventions that govern how people communicate with one another in both spoken and written language is another ability that contributes to children's **listening comprehension** and later to their **reading comprehension.**

standing of speech usually precedes production of speech by about five or six months. For example, a child who understands about 50 words at the age of 12 months (and has just produced his or her first word) may be saying 50 words by 18 months (and understanding 100–150).

Syntax is about word *order,* the structure of phrases and sentences. Word order is different for each language—for instance, adjectives come before nouns in English ("white house"), but in Spanish adjectives usually follow nouns ("casa blanca"). When children first start to speak, they really have no need to know the rules of syntax since they use only one word at a time. Nevertheless, studies have shown that they do understand about word order and the difference word order makes for sentence meaning. In one study with toddlers (Golinkoff & Hirsh-Pasek, 1999), video images of Big Bird and Cookie Monster were played on two television screens. On one screen, Big Bird tickled Cookie Monster from behind; on the other screen, their roles were reversed. The toddlers (who were familiar with these two characters) first heard the question "Where is Big Bird tickling Cookie Monster?" and they looked at the video scene depicting that action. When the question was changed to "Where is Cookie Monster tickling Big Bird?" they looked at the scene depicting *that* action. These toddlers were still at the one-word stage of speaking, yet they could understand the syntactical difference of sentences they heard!

When children do start speaking in two-word sentences, they already have an idea about grammar, and the word order they use is correct 95% of the time. "Mommy cup" could have various meanings, depending on the context: *Mommy, I want the cup; Mommy, take my cup; That's Mommy's cup; Mommy has a cup.* The child who starts saying "Mommy cup" will rarely reverse the order of those two words.

Morphology is about word *formation*—the structure of words. Whereas phonemes are the smallest units of sound in a language, morphemes are the smallest units of meaning. Morphemes may be a single letter or a group of letters, one syllable or several, a whole word or part of a word. *Flea* is a morpheme; so are *elephant, on,* and *run. Smiles* contains two morphemes, *smile* and *-s;* the final *-s* changes the word *smile* (noun) from singular to plural, and the word *smile* (verb) from first person (*I smile*) to third person (*she smiles*). The ending *-s* can also denote possession (*hers, Daddy's, the dog's*). The *-ed* that forms the past tense in most verbs (*they talked*), the *-ing* that indicates the progressive tense (*you are reading*), and the *-er* and *-est* used to form comparisons (*softer, happiest*) are all morphemes.

Syntax and morphology, two aspects of what is called *grammar,* seem to kick in between the child's second and third birthday, a year of "grammatical spurt." This is when children begin using morphological endings (*-ing,* the plural *-s,* past tense *-ed,* possessive *-s*) and adding function words—prepositions (*on, in*), articles (*the, a*), conjunctions (*and, but, with*), pronouns (*she, he, it, our*), and contractions (*I'm, he's*). You can tell when young children are internalizing morphological rules, as they will often overgeneralize them: they will use words like *goed, taked, mouses, feets,* and *goodest* before they learn the irregularities in our language for past, plural, and comparative

Pragmatics involves the social rules of language, like making eye contact, that children learn by listening to others and trying them out in their own conversations.

words. (This overgeneralization is one of the biggest pieces of evidence that children don't learn language merely by imitation, a theory that was once prevalent.)

How wonderful for us as parents and teachers that young children pick up almost all the basic grammatical rules of our language without our having to explicitly teach them. All they need is to live in an environment where they are surrounded by people who will talk, listen, and respond to the sounds they make. Just *hearing* language is not enough; there must be interaction. A child who grows up hearing language only on television or the radio, for example, will not learn to talk. What is important is that adults speak to and with the child, encouraging the child to communicate in return about the objects, people, and activities in his or her environment—the here and now.

Pragmatics involves the *social uses* of language as opposed to its structure. In every language and culture, there are specific social rules that people follow when they communicate with one another. In American culture, for instance, some of these rules include

- Making eye contact
- Taking conversational turns
- Rephrasing if your listener doesn't understand
- Modulating loudness and speed
- Staying on topic
- Not asking intrusive questions
- Talking differently around different people (to babies vs. adults, to family members vs. strangers), and in different situations (at home vs. at school)

Though children pick up many of these rules without formal instruction, just by watching what the people around them do, there are a few rules that many adults explicitly teach. In American culture, these are often rules about social conventions or politeness, such as saying *please* and *thank you,* not making unflattering comments about people within their hearing, and not using socially inappropriate language (swear words, for instance).

"Although unwritten rules for what is appropriate or inappropriate vary by culture, all cultures instruct children in these social uses of language, teaching children how to fit into the society in which they were born."

—Roberta Michnick Golinkoff and Kathy Hirsh-Pasek (1999, p. 204)

The Acquisition and Development of Language

Is it nature or nurture that plays the biggest role in children's acquisition of language? Over the years there have been various theories and much debate on how children learn to talk. The *behaviorist* perspective (led by B. F. Skinner) holds that language is learned through a process of conditioning involving imitation by the child and reinforcement from the adult. Proponents of this viewpoint believe that *nurture* plays the biggest role in language development.

The *nativist* view (described by Noam Chomsky and others) proposes an innate structure in the mind (a "language acquisition device") that enables children to learn language. Proponents of this viewpoint believe that *nature* plays the most important role in the development of language. (For a synopsis of the behaviorist and nativist perspectives, see Bruner, 1983.)

A theory that has many adherents today is the *social-interactionist* theory. This perspective is based on recent brain research and other studies of infants, toddlers, and preschoolers. Its basic premise is that language is both innate *and* learned, that nature and nurture are "inseparably intertwined" when it comes to language (Gopnik et al., 1999, p. 131). According to the social-interactionist view, the processes involved in language acquisition are

- *Biological:* A baby's brain is wired to acquire language; language is as instinctual to humans as spinning webs is to spiders.
- *Cognitive:* A baby has powerful inborn learning mechanisms that allow him or her to learn all the details of the language of the surrounding community.
- *Social:* The adults who live with and care for the baby play a critical role in his or her language development.

When we talk about language development, we're talking about the changes in children's language that occur over time—the stages they go through—from birth on. This development is only partly maturational: the musculature for speaking must mature before children can make cooing sounds, then babbling, then eventually all the sounds of their language. However, the role of experience and learning is considered much more significant.

The chart on page 24 depicts the stages of children's oral language development from birth through age five, including receptive language (hearing and understanding) and expressive language (talking). Keep in mind that although the order of these stages is virtually the same for each child, the time frame (the age at which children reach each stage and how long they remain in that stage) can vary enormously—in some cases by as much as a year.

"The child is certainly predisposed—indeed "wired"—to learn language. However, it is misleading to claim that language emerges spontaneously in a child or that being surrounded by talk is enough. Being included in talk and having talk adapted to your current level of talking are required for optimal learning of oral language."

—Judith Schickedanz (1999, p. 4)

22

The developmental stages on the chart refer to first language acquisition. According to Tabors (1997), children who acquire two languages *simultaneously* from birth (when each parent speaks a different language, for instance, or parents are bilingual) also follow this developmental path for each language. However, young children who acquire two languages *sequentially* (for example, when they come to a preschool where the primary language spoken is not their home language) follow a different developmental path for the second language. Researchers have noted that these children often go through four periods or stages:

1. Trying to use their home language in the second-language environment
2. Entering a nonverbal period when they discover that their home language doesn't work in the new environment. (Children are watching and listening to others during this period, and perhaps even experimenting with sounds and repeating words.)
3. Beginning to use words and phrases they hear others using in the second language
4. Beginning to use the second language productively (building their own sentences)

As in other areas of development, children learning a second language will often begin using techniques from the next stage before leaving behind the techniques of the stage they are in. Also, there are many individual differences in development in this area as well as in the rate of acquisition. Acquisition of a second language is affected by motivation to learn the new language, quantity of exposure to the second language, and the age and personality of the child (Tabors, 1997).

Although this chapter focuses on the preschool years, language development is really an ongoing process. School-aged children improve their pronunciation, use bigger and more words, construct more complex sentences, learn to think and talk metalinguistically (about language itself), segment and blend sounds in words, and write and read conventionally. Adolescents continue to build their vocabularies and use abstract concepts, metaphors, and analogies. As adults, we also continue to learn new vocabulary; the average adult understands around 50,000–60,000 words.

Now that we have briefly reviewed children's language acquisition, let's look at how to support it in the preschool.

Suggestions for Adult Support

In order to develop language, babies, toddlers, and preschoolers need lots of experience in listening—to sounds and music, to words and sentences, to songs and rhymes, to conversations and stories. In this section we'll discuss how adults can talk with children at different stages, suggest some ways to support children's listening skills, and finally, present language ideas for specific parts of the daily routine. Remember to consider both the developmental levels and the interests of the children you work with in deciding which of these experiences to offer.

How Does Your Child Hear and Talk?

Hearing and Understanding

Birth–3 Months
- Startles to loud sounds.
- Quiets or smiles when spoken to.
- Seems to recognize your voice and quiets if crying.
- Increases or decreases sucking behavior in response to sound.

4–6 Months
- Moves eyes in direction of sounds.
- Responds to changes in tone of your voice.
- Notices toys that make sounds.
- Pays attention to music.

7 Months–1 Year
- Enjoys games like peek-a-boo and pat-a-cake.
- Turns and looks in direction of sounds.
- Listens when spoken to.
- Recognizes words for common items like "cup," "shoe," "juice."
- Begins to respond to requests ("Come here," "Want more?").

1–2 Years
- Points to a few body parts when asked.
- Follows simple commands and understands simple questions ("Roll the ball," "Kiss the baby," "Where's your shoe?").
- Listens to simple stories, songs, and rhythms.
- Points to pictures in a book when named.

2–3 Years
- Understands differences in meaning ("go–stop," "in–on," "big–little," "up–down").
- Follows two requests ("Get the book and put it on the table").

3–4 Years
- Hears you when you call from another room.
- Hears television or radio at the same loudness level as other family members.
- Answers simple "who?," "what?," "where?," "why?" questions.

4–5 Years
- Pays attention to a short story and answers simple questions about it.
- Hears and understands most of what is said at home and in school.

Talking

Birth–3 Months
- Makes pleasure sounds (cooing, gooing).
- Cries differently for different needs.
- Smiles when sees you.

4–6 Months
- Babbling sounds more speech-like with *many* different sounds, including *p, b,* and *m*.
- Vocalizes excitement and displeasure.
- Makes gurgling sounds when left alone and when playing with you.

7 Months–1 Year
- Babbling has both long and short groups of sounds such as "tata upup bibibibi."
- Uses speech or non-crying sounds to get and keep attention.
- Imitates different speech sounds.
- Has 1 or 2 words ("bye-bye," "dada," "mama") although they may not be clear.

1–2 Years
- Says more words every month.
- Uses some 1–2-word questions ("where kitty?" "go bye-bye?" "what's that?").
- Puts 2 words together ("more cookie," "no juice," "mommy book").
- Uses many different consonant sounds at the beginning of words.

2–3 Years
- Has a word for almost everything.
- Uses 2–3 words to talk about and ask for things.
- Speech is understood by familiar listeners most of the time.
- Often asks for or directs attention to objects by naming them.

3–4 Years
- Talks about activities at school or at friends' homes.
- People outside family usually understand child's speech.
- Uses a lot of sentences that have 4 or more words.
- Usually talks easily without repeating syllables or words.

4–5 Years
- Voice sounds clear like other children's.
- Uses sentences that give lots of details (e.g., "I like to read my books").
- Tells stories that stick to topic.
- Communicates easily with other children and adults.
- Says most sounds correctly except a few like *l, s, r, v, z, j, ch, sh, th.*
- Uses the same grammar as the rest of the family.

Every child is unique and has an individual rate of development. This chart represents, on average, the age by which most children will accomplish the listed skills. Children typically do not master all items in a category until they reach the upper age in each age range.

➤ Talk to children in ways that are appropriate to their stage of development.

Children of all ages learn language best when they have a warm, loving relationship with the people who care for them. However, the kind of adult talk that is most beneficial for children is different at different stages in their language development. Below are several suggestions for the kind of talk infants, toddlers, preschoolers, and second-language learners need from us.

"What teachers need to know about language is important, but it is not as important as what they do with children."

—Sue Bredekamp (2000, p. 9)

Infants benefit from hearing the sounds of their language even when they cannot understand the meaning. Research shows that the best way to talk with babies is **child-directed talk,** sometimes called baby talk, motherese, or parentese because most parents around the world seem to intuitively speak this way to very young children. This type of talk is directed to the baby and involves exaggerated pitch swings and singsong, melodic intonations; slower speech; shorter, simpler sentences; longer, clearer pauses between utterances; new words placed at the end of sentences; lots of repetition; and animated facial expressions. Vowel sounds are lengthened and exaggerated in this type of talk, which makes them much clearer and easier to hear than in the ordinary speech we use when talking with adults. While it may sound silly to other adults, child-directed talk is apparently an "acoustic hook" for babies, enabling them to more easily learn the sounds and eventually the words and syntax of their language.

Another aspect of language babies tune into long before they can understand or speak any words is the **give and take of conversation.** When the adult makes a comment directly to the baby, watches the baby's physical reaction, then responds as if the baby had replied, the art of dialogue—the intimate social dance between baby and parent or caregiver—begins.

> Adult: *"Let's see if you're ready for a new diaper."*
> [Baby kicks legs and waves arms. Adult checks diaper.]
> Adult: *"Oh, you are! Let's go get a dry diaper for you."*

Babies live in the moment, so they learn words best when adults **speak to them about the "here and now,"** about the people and objects in their immediate environment. That way they can link what they are seeing and experiencing with the words they hear (*mommy, cup, fall down, kiss you*). Two useful strategies for helping babies make these links are parallel talk, or describing what the child is doing ("You kicked the ball!"), and self talk—describing our own actions ("Grandma is cutting the apple").

Once communication becomes intentional, it is helpful to use language that is slightly above the child's present level (within the child's zone of proximal development, as described in Chapter 1). So as babies and toddlers begin to communicate with gestures and sounds, interpreting their intentions in **single words and short phrases** will help them learn to speak the words connected to the objects and actions in their world.

[Tommy holds out his empty cup and grunts.]
Adult: *"Juice? More juice? Okay, I'll get you more juice."*

Toddlers at the one- and two-word sentence stage learn more words and longer phrases when we **repeat** their attempt and then **expand** it:

Sara [looking out the window]: "Daddy go."
Adult: *"Daddy go? Yes, Daddy is going, going bye-bye in the car. Bye-bye, Daddy!"*

Between 18 and 24 months, children's vocabulary explodes. During this period of growth, *toddlers* need **exposure to words**—lots of them. In a study by Hart and Risley (1995) comparing young children in welfare, working-class, and professional families, they found a vast difference in the number of total words children from each of these environments heard their parents speak. Over the course of a year, children from families on welfare heard 3 million words, children from working-class families heard 6 million, and children from professional families heard 11 million. When tested at age three, the children from professional families had larger vocabularies and faster vocabulary growth rates; at age nine, they still outperformed the other two groups on both IQ and language tests. Repeated hearing of a great number and variety of words seems to be critical to children's usage of those words.

As toddlers move into the preschool years, they become much more sophisticated language users. Whereas younger children benefit more from talk that is centered on the here and now, *preschoolers* should have many opportunities for **decontextualized talk** (also referred to as nonimmediate or nonpresent talk). This is talk about the "there and then," about things that happened in the recent past or will happen in the near future, about people, places, objects, and activities that, while familiar to children, are not readily observable when speaking about them. When a child wants to describe a new toy for his teacher, it is much easier if he can show it to her. There is little need for oral elaboration; the teacher can see for herself what the toy looks like and what it does. If the toy is at home, however, the child must use many more words to tell the teacher about it. In the same way, talking about past events is more challenging for children than talking about the present: they cannot rely on the physical environment to communicate what they did. Talking about last night or tomorrow involves thinking back and recalling what happened, or imagining what is going to happen. These kinds of longer conversations are referred to as **extended discourse**—talk that "requires the use of several utterances or turns to build a linguistic structure, such as in explanations, narratives, or pretend" (Dickinson & Tabors, 2001, p. 2).

Preschoolers need lots of extended one-to-one conversation with adults as well as with peers. This should include **cognitively challenging conversations**—talk that challenges children to think. Topics that encourage thinking include knowledge about the physical world ("I wonder where all those puddles went"), events ("What do you think we'll see at the farm tomorrow?"), human motivations ("Why do you think Goldilocks did

26

that?"), and ideas ("Who has an idea for solving this problem?"). Nonpresent talk ("What are you going to do this weekend?" "Tell me about that new puppy you just got!") also stimulates the thinking process.

As adults converse with children, answer their questions, talk about pictures together, go on excursions, and read books aloud to children, they should **expose children to rare words*** and their meanings. When children are exposed to novel words in the context of their own interests and activities, they have more of a reason to use the words themselves. In the Home School Study of Language and Literacy Development, it was found that "children's exposure during the preschool years to informative use of rare words...appears to be a strong predictor of their later vocabulary" (Tabors, Beals, & Weizman, 2001, p. 108). Building a large speaking vocabulary in the preschool years makes it that much easier for children to read and understand written text during their school years.

Many preschoolers are beginning to think and talk about language itself, which is a cognitively challenging skill called **metalinguistic awareness.** This skill, essential for the process of learning how to read, is encouraged when we talk to children about the sounds of words (as opposed to their meanings) and about syllables, words, and sentences (see Chapter 3).

When a child mispronounces a word or uses nonstandard grammar, it is not necessary (and is often counterproductive) to correct his or her speech. Instead, repeat the child's utterance, **modeling** the correct pronunciation and grammar:

Child: "Bwake won't gimme dem twucks!"

Adult: "Blake won't give you those trucks? Hmmm, let's talk with Blake, and see if we can solve this problem together."

Many of the communication strategies used with toddlers also work well with **children learning a second language,** regardless of their age (Tabors, 1997). Here are a few:

- Learn a few important words and phrases in the child's home language to use during the first few weeks. Ask parents or other family members to provide them for you.
- Use simplified language—both in terms of vocabulary and sentence structure.
- Always respond to children's communicative attempts, even if you don't understand their message.
- Use gestures, eye gaze, and/or actions to help children understand your words.
- Repeat and emphasize words you want children to learn; place those words at the end of your sentences.

---

*Rare words are words that are new to preschoolers, not words that are necessarily unusual for adults. For example, in the picture book *Shades of Black,* some of the words that would be new to most preschoolers are: *amber, brassy, corkscrew, ebony, gingery, luster, radiant, unique, wool.*

- Use language grounded in the here and now with second-language learners—talk about the objects, people, and actions they can see. Meaningful language in context is easier for them to understand than decontextualized language.

- Rephrase, repeat, expand, and extend children's language.

- When children have begun to use words and phrases, don't comply immediately with a nonverbal request if you think they may be able to use a word or two.

> *[Child hands adult a shoe.]*
> *Adult: "Oh, your shoe. What do you need?"*
> *[Child gives no response.]*
> *Adult [with actions]: "Hmmm, I could put it on my head…or on my foot."*
> *[Child giggles.]*
> *Adult: "Well, what should I do with this shoe?"*
> *Child: "My foot."*
> *Adult: "Oh, on your foot? Okay, I'll help you put the shoe on your foot."*

➤ Provide many opportunities for children to listen and respond to what they hear.

There are many ways to help develop children's listening skills in the preschool setting: call attention to sounds in the environment, play guessing games using sounds, and have children make and explore sounds (musical and nonmusical) in various ways. We can also help children learn to be aware of the sounds of language. Sometimes we may focus on the *meaning* of language (through our conversations with children, by reading aloud to them, and by playing direction-following games like Simon Says, for example); at other times we focus on the *structure* of language, helping children notice the various sounds in words.

In their book *Phonemic Awareness in Young Children* (1998), Adams, Foorman, Lundberg, and Beeler write, "Many of the activities involving rhyme, rhythm, listening, and sounds that have long been enjoyed with preschool-age children are ideally suited" for getting children to notice the sounds in words (p. 1). Try some of the activities below to help your children learn how to listen attentively. (For additional ideas, see Chapters 3 and 4.)

Listening to sounds in the environment

- At a time when the group may have to sit quietly and wait for a few moments, whether indoors or out, ask the children to listen for sounds that are all around. They may hear the wind blowing, leaves rustling, water dripping, birds singing,

28

dogs barking, insects buzzing; the sound of footsteps, voices, breathing, swallowing, their own heartbeat; cars, trucks, motorcycles, horns, sirens; a clock ticking or chiming.

- Put a variety of objects that make sounds in a large bag or pillowcase. Taking turns, children pull out one object where the others can't see it (behind the puppet stage or a blanket, for instance) and make noise with it. The other children guess what the object is.

- Hide a ticking alarm clock somewhere in the room, and have the children take turns locating it. After each child finds it, he or she hides it somewhere else for the next child.

- At any time during the day, call attention to sounds made by the children or by objects in the classroom or outdoors. Point out the similarities and differences in these sounds. Occasionally repeat sounds the children make.

- Play tape-recorded sounds and see if the children can identify them. Some sounds to try: blowing a whistle, clapping hands, coughing, crunching an apple, pouring water, ringing a bell, tearing paper, hammering, sawing, walking, whistling, snapping fingers.

- Give children rhythm sticks, beanbags, paper plates, or other sound-producing objects. Let children explore the sounds made when they hit or rub the objects together or shake them. Ask questions like "How are you making your sound?" "What makes a soft sound?" "What makes a loud sound?" "Who can make sounds that are the same?" "Who can make sounds that are different?" (Weikart, 1995, p. 213).

Listening to sounds in language

- Play Simon Says or a similar game with verbal directions. When children can follow single directions easily, give two-step and then three-step directions: "Simon Says, put your hands on your head and wiggle your tongue!"

- Ask children to point to various locations in the room with different body parts: "Can you use your *thumb* to point to the cub-

Games with verbal directions, like Simon Says, strengthen listening skills.

bies?" "Can you use your *knee* to point to the sand table?" "Point with your *elbow* to the ceiling!" Give directions verbally without demonstrating (Weikart & Carlton, 1995, p. 235).

- Sing songs often with the children. Singing helps to develop auditory discrimination, a foundation for phonological awareness.

- Read, tell, or sing a very familiar poem, story, nursery rhyme, or song, but change some of the words to make it nonsensical. Ask children to listen very carefully for the "mixed-up words." At different times, try these various changes (starting with the most obvious):

> Substitute a word: "Mary had a *hungry* lamb," "Humpty Dumpty sat on a *spider*."

Reading books to children introduces them to complex sentence structures, new vocabulary, and background knowledge.

> Switch the order of two words: "If you're happy and you know it *hands* your *clap*."

> Switch parts of two words: "There was a little *burtle* and he lived in a *tox*."

> Change the order of events: "When Goldilocks went inside the bears' house, the first thing she did was *go right to sleep*."

- Read aloud to children individually and in small groups every day (see Chapter 4). Children learn new vocabulary and background knowledge from listening to books read aloud; they also are exposed to more complex sentence structures; they learn how to sequence stories; and they experience participating in a group activity that involves talking and listening.

- During problem solving with the children, emphasize the importance of listening:

> *"We're going to listen to each of you so we can solve this problem. Rachael, we'll listen to you first…what's the problem?" "Now let's listen to Elana…Elana, what do you think the problem is?"*

- Find opportunities to have individual conversations with children whenever possible.

"Encourage conversation when children are in a comfortable setting. They're more likely to open up and talk when they are in a non-threatening situation, such as a one-to-one reading session, a walk outside, and during snack time. Perhaps the most effective way to converse with children is to take time to join in their play."

—M. Susan Burns et al. (1999, p. 51)

- Use a variety of vocabulary words as you converse with children, including a high percentage of novel words related to what the children are doing. Encourage children to use the new words, too.

- Share comments and observations with children. These contributions allow them to respond in a natural way.

- Ask questions from time to time rather than all the time. When you do ask questions, ask open-ended questions rather than those with one-word, right or wrong answers; try asking only questions you don't know the answer to. For example, while looking at a postcard reproduction of a still life, you could ask a question such as "What do you see in this painting?" instead of "Do you see the flower? Is the apple above or below the pear?"

Model good listening skills by actively paying attention to what children are saying.

> "We found better kindergarten performance when the children as 4-year-olds had teachers who limited their own talking and gave children more time to talk."
>
> —David K. Dickinson
> (2001, p. 250)

- Model good listening skills yourself. Listen actively to the children; get down on their level, and make eye contact; pause and allow wait time for children to respond when they are ready; invite them to repeat, clarify, or choose different words when they aren't understood; reflect their words back to them; expand on their meaning.

- Listen more than you talk.

➤ Support children's language development throughout the daily routine.

Opportunities for encouraging children to talk and gain new vocabulary abound throughout the day. Here are some suggestions to get you started.

Arrival

If the children in your program arrive more or less at the same time, **designate a certain area of the room** for them to meet in before the start of the program. The book area is a good place for this. If there is more than one classroom adult, have one greet incoming children and answer parents' questions. The other adult will then be free to **sit and converse or read with the children.** Conversations are more likely to occur when an adult is seated with the children rather than moving around "monitoring" the whole classroom. Encourage parents to sit and talk with children (their own and others) upon arrival, too.

Greeting time

Try to **add a new word each day** when discussing the morning message. For example, after the children read on the message board (see Chapter 7) that a teacher or child is out sick, you might be able to use the words *ill, fever, chills, vomiting, diagnosis, thermometer, temperature, medication,* or *prescription.*

Small-group time

Play **"Guess what I'm doing."** Have children take turns imitating animals or pantomiming actions or activities that they know, such as eating, cooking, sleeping, taking a bath, swimming, typing at the computer, playing soccer or baseball, or swimming. You could use pictures or photographs that illustrate the animal or activity to give children suggestions, or let children come up with their own ideas. The other children try to guess what the child is doing. When they call out their guess as a single word, expand it into a sentence and then encourage the children to do the same.

> Adult: *"Swimming—Toby is swimming. It doesn't look like he's swimming in the bathtub. I wonder where?"*
>
> Toby: *"No! I'm in the ocean."*
>
> Adult: *"Oh, Toby is swimming in the ocean."*

Play **"Name the parts"** as a vocabulary builder. Go on a walk, indoors or out, to play this game. When you come to something that has multiple parts, stop and see how many the children can name. For example, a chair has a seat, back, legs; a tree has a trunk, bark, branches, leaves, roots, flowers, seeds; a door has a doorknob, lock, frame, peek-hole, knocker, number. Expect to hear some names that may be unconventional!

Playing with puppets stimulates language from children, and more adult-child interaction can occur when they are used at small-group time rather than large-group time. Use a variety of puppets—ones you buy or ones you or the children make from recycled socks or mittens, paper bags or paper plates, or cut-out figures attached to tongue depressors or long cardboard tubes. When the puppets represent characters from favorite stories, children are inspired to retell the story in their own words and actions. Finding or making an impromptu puppet stage can be part of the small-group activity; a cardboard box will work, so will a table or a chair.

After introducing a basket of various puppets, you might mention how quiet they all are in the basket. "But the most amazing thing happens when you put the puppet on your hand or finger—it begins to talk!" Encourage the children to try different puppets and to have their puppet find another one to talk to. Participate yourself…your puppet can be a role model for both talking and listening.

Cooking and other food preparation activities at small-group time provide opportunities for children to learn new vocabulary words, to describe the ingredients and discuss the process, and to make predictions. A large recipe card (which may include pictures, symbols, and words) encourages language both during and after the activity, as children interpret the directions.

Find opportunities during small-group activities to **take dictation** from either individual children or from the group (see Chapter 8).

Opportunities to play with puppets encourage child language. Here children put on an outdoor puppet show with puppets made at small-group time.

Large-group time

Music and movement activities offer a good opportunity to **introduce rare words,** such as *stretch, sway, rock, leap, huddle, skate, twirl, relax, somersault, muscles,* and *floppy.* Many songs also introduce new and interesting vocabulary words. Be sure to discuss unfamiliar words with the children before you start singing.

Give movement directions verbally without demonstrating so that children must *listen* for what to do: "Reach your hands up high, then touch the floor."

Avoid long stretches of conversation with a single child during large-group times. Researchers have found that when teachers extend a topic with one child (which often happens during sharing and calendar times), the other children often tune out (Dickinson, 2001).

An alternative to the traditional sharing time (or show-and-tell) is the game of **"Mystery Bag,"** a simplified version of "20 Questions." One child hides an object (from home or from the classroom) in a pillowcase. The other children ask questions about the mystery item, such as the following (an adult can help them think of questions until they catch on): *Do you play with it? Wear it? Eat it? Look at it? Cook with it? Is it hard? Soft? How big is it? What color is it? Does it make a noise?* Another adult sits with the child who

33

is answering the questions, offering assistance as needed. If more obvious clues are needed, children can feel the object through the cloth or listen to whatever noise it makes. In this experience, *all* the children have an opportunity to talk, to ask questions, to think critically, and to offer their ideas.

Planning/recall time

Planning and recall times guarantee that children **use decontextualized talk every day.** During planning children think and talk about what they want to do (future); during recall they talk about what they have already done (past). Planning and recall actually support children as they transition from talking about the here and now to discussing the there and then, because these experiences occur in close proximity to work time, both in terms of time and space. So, when children plan, they can look around the room to see what they want to do and where they want to play; after work time, they can look at where they were or possibly at something they made to help them remember and talk about what they did.

Recall time, where children talk about what they did during work time, is an opportunity for "decontextualized talk." Having a microphone to talk into makes the experience more fun and stimulates child language.

Work and outside time

As children play and explore during work time and outside time, remain in one place long enough to **engage children in extended conversations.** Observe children's play first to decide if your entrance would be welcome or not, then comment on something they are doing or playing with.

Attractive props and interesting materials in each area of the room or playground **encourage dramatic play** during these child-initiated times of the day, resulting in both extended and decontextualized conversations. In the house area, for example, children transform a cardboard tube into a microphone and a shiny scarf into a magical cape. On the playground, the old bathtub becomes a getaway car for robbers. Children are experts at turning ordinary, everyday objects in their environment into symbols that stand for something else—and talking about these imaginary things.

Tahj picks up a block on the table and hands it to Zarius, saying "You have a phone call."

Charmaine stirs pine cones in a pot and yells, "Soup's ready!"

Madison stacks bottle caps and jar lids from large to small, then offers Molly a piece of "wedding cake."

As children show an interest in various activities, **provide prop boxes** that will extend their dramatic play ideas. For instance, gather items relating to a restaurant, seashore, campground, fire station, barber shop, or doctor's office. Props from familiar stories will also stimulate dramatic story play and language.

Provide **other materials that stimulate conversation** from children, such as pets, flannelboards, nature items (a snakeskin or bird nest, for example), wordless books, and photographs (those they bring in from home and pictures you take in the classroom or on field trips).

Having real telephones available for pretending encourages rich play conversations.

Snack/meal time

Make snack time a relaxing opportunity for children to talk to adults and to one another:

- **Sit with the children** rather than walk around as they eat snacks or meals. Have family-style meals, with a low adult-child ratio at the table. This provides more opportunities for one-to-one conversations between adults and children and among the children themselves.

- **Engage the children in discussions about nonimmediate events** or activities, both past and future.

- **Ask children to share personal experiences,** and share some of your own. When you talk with children about your own ideas and interests, you are modeling extended conversation.

- In your conversations, **use new words** the children have encountered recently.

- **Model polite forms of speech:** "Please pass the crackers, Carter." "Thank you for handing out the napkins, Toni."

This child's face reflects her delight in sharing an experience with a genuinely interested adult.

Transitions

Transition times offer natural opportunities for children to both listen and speak. For instance, when you let children know that the current activity will end soon, **give verbal as well as physical warnings.** As you flick the lights, you might say, "Five more minutes until the end of work time."

Announce the next class activity in the sequence of the daily routine ("After we finish this book it will be time to go to the planning table"). Children will be listening for these verbal cues, especially as they are developing a sense of the program day.

Remember to **give children choices** about what to do during transitions, such as finding a way to move backward to the next area, and to **describe their movements.** Encourage children to voice their own ideas for transitioning from one activity to another.

With so much focus currently on reading, reading, and reading, we must not forget where it all starts: with speaking and listening. Oral language is the foundation upon which literacy is built. If we want our children to become successful readers and writers, then one of the most important gifts we can give them in their first five years is to help them to be good speakers and listeners. In this chapter we have looked at what language is, how language develops in young children, and how it can be nurtured by parents and early childhood teachers. The next chapter will continue to focus on oral language, and show how *having fun with language* is related to learning to read and write.

3

Word Play, Rhymes, and Alliteration

Just as children enjoy playing with the more tangible objects in their world—play dough, Daddy's shoes, puddles of water— so, too, they enjoy playing with the sounds and words of our language. And just as exploring and experimenting with objects enhance children's cognitive development, so do language play and exploration contribute to children's language development and more specifically to their developing literacy. Children's own word play includes making various sounds; playing with real words; making up nonsense words; telling jokes, riddles, and stories; creating strings of rhyming words; and singing simple songs. Children also listen to the ways adults play with words—in books that have rhyming and nonsense words; in songs, chants, and fingerplays; in poems and nursery rhymes. This chapter discusses these playful experiences with *oral language,* and their role in children's literacy development.

As discussed earlier, we know that oral and written language development occur simultaneously in young children, beginning at birth. And as children explore and play with the sounds and words of their language, we can actually see one of the links between oral and

"Ideally, children begin at a very young age to relish language play. From nursery rhymes, fairy tales, and familiar stories children discover wonderful, fun ways to say things."

—Lucy Calkins (1997, p. 28)

By sharing stories, songs, poems, nursery rhymes, riddles, jokes, chants, fingerplays, and word games, children explore oral language and build a foundation for literacy.

written language learning: as children play with words, repeat stories, listen to and make up rhymes, they begin to become aware of the *sounds* in spoken language, not just the *meanings*. And according to researchers, "this ability to play with sounds in speech is the precursor to phonemic awareness," one of the understandings that are necessary for learning to read and write an alphabetic code (Bishop, Yopp, & Yopp, 2000, p. 41). These experiences with word play, books, and rhymes are included in the third High/Scope language and literacy key experience *having fun with language: listening to stories and poems, making up stories and rhymes.* However, as young children play with language, they are also using both speaking and listening skills, so the first two key experiences are also involved.

> *"Children's delight in jokes and riddles, silly verses, and all sorts of verbal play reflects their natural playfulness with language, which as teachers we want to actively nurture."*
>
> —Susan B. Neuman et al.
> (2000, p. 51)

Reasons for Encouraging Children's Word Play

Responsive adults encourage children's word play for a variety of reasons. Doing so shows that we are listening to them, and are interested in what they have to say. It affirms their attempts at communication, encourages them to continue talking, and thereby helps them to get better at communicating. It contributes to their learning of new words, and to their learning *about* words as well.

And now, because of the research in learning to read that has been conducted over the last 20 years and more recently analyzed by the National Research Council (Snow et al., 1998) and the National Reading Panel (2000), we know that playing with words and the sounds in words does something else for children. It helps to develop their **phonological awareness**—*the ability to perceive and manipulate various units of sound in our spoken language—words, syllables, parts of syllables (onsets and rimes), and phonemes (the smallest units of spoken sound).* The most advanced level of this understanding, which usually begins to develop in kindergarten and continues developing during the primary years, is called **phonemic awareness.** This is the understanding that every spoken word is made up of a sequence of individual speech sounds, or *phonemes,* and it includes the ability to *manipulate* those sounds.

Children often exaggerate and repeat word sounds as part of their play. This experimentation with language helps children learn to perceive the individual sounds within words as separate units.

The two "p-words" are often used interchangeably, but the first—phonological awareness—is the more encompassing term, and it is where most preschoolers are developmentally, as they become sensitive to the *various* sounds of their language.

Research tells us that being phonologically and phonemically aware facilitates learning to read when a child begins formal reading lessons in school. "Researchers and educators now know that a child's ability to think about language separate from its meaning is crucial in learning to read. In particular, it is a child's ability to think about the smallest building blocks of speech, the phonemes, that plays a key role in reading acquisition" (Bishop et al., 2000, p. 40).

"All teachers of young children need good, foundational knowledge in language acquisition, including second-language learning, the processes of reading and writing, early literacy development, and experiences and teaching practices contributing to optimal development."

—International Reading Association and the National Association for the Education of Young Children (2000, p. 5)

Primary-grade teachers, administrators, and even many parents are aware of the research. As adults who work with emergent writers and readers, preschool teachers also need to have some background knowledge and understanding of phonemes and other relevant aspects of language structure that are linked to the process of learning to read. The next two sections offer a summary of the sounds that make up our language and explain how children's developing knowledge of these sounds comes to play as they begin to read and write.

The Sounds of Our Language

Let's start with the smallest unit of spoken sound—the **phoneme***. As anyone who has ever struggled with the spelling of English words knows, ours is not a truly phonetic language with a one-to-one sound-symbol correspondence. While there are 26 letters in our alphabet, there are actually 40–52 phonemes (or sounds) in the English spoken language; even linguists don't agree on the exact number. (See Chapter 6, pp. 111 and 112, for charts of the phonemes in American English.) And it takes more than 250 graphemes (letters or letter combinations) to spell these phonemes (Moats, 2000). To illustrate the sometimes confusing relationships that our letters and sounds can have, consider the following:

- Some sounds need more than one letter to represent them, for example, /sh/, /ch/, /th/, /wh/, and /ng/.
- Some sounds can be represented in multiple ways: /ā/, for instance, can be represented by any of the following: *a* followed by a consonant and an *e* (as in *cake*), *ay* (as in *day*), *ai* (as in *wait*), *eigh* (as in *eight*), *ey* (as in *they*), and *ei* (as in *rein*).

---

*In this book, individual phonemes are represented by phonic or dictionary symbols (rather than the less familiar phonetic symbols) and are enclosed in back slashes to indicate that we are referring to a spoken sound rather than to a letter. For example, /b/ is the sound of the letter *B*.

- Some letters (including all the vowels) can represent more than one sound: the letter *C*, for example, can be a /k/ sound (as in *cow*), an /s/ sound (as in *cent*), or a /sh/ sound (as in *social*).
- Some letters consist of more than one sound: for example, the letter *X* is sometimes pronounced as /k/+/s/ (as in *fax*), and sometimes as /g/+/z/ (as in *exact*).

To illustrate these smallest building blocks of speech, the following chart contains several one-syllable words and the phonemes they consist of. Notice how the number of sounds does *not* necessarily correspond to the number of letters!

Although we are able to write down these sounds as separate units, when we speak we do not pronounce phonemes separately—we actually fuse or blend the sounds together into a syllable. We do this without even thinking about it, and so do young children— they've been doing it ever since they uttered their first word. But in order to read and write, one needs to think about the individual sounds, and to be able to pull them apart. It turns out that "pulling apart" individual sounds is a difficult task, however—especially for a young child, who is used to attending to the *meaning* of words rather than the *sounds* of them. When asked what sounds they hear in the word *cat*, preschool-age children might (quite logically!) respond, "Meow."

Word	Number of phonemes
ice	2: /ī/ + /s/
know	2: /n/ + /ō/
though	2: /th/ + /ō/
choose	3: /ch/ + /o͞o/ + /z/
baby	4: /b/ + /ā/ + /b/ + /ē/
fax	4: /f/ + /ă/ + /k/ + /s/
straight	5: /s/ + /t/ + /r/ + /ā/ + /t/

Adding to the difficulty of hearing these abstract, individual phonemes is the fact that what we hear when someone speaks isn't even separate words, but whole phrases and sentences—*heardasastreamof-continuoussounds.* The "spaces between words" in our written language do not exist in most of our spoken language; our minds perceive breaks that our ears don't actually hear.

Indeed, young children are used to hearing language as whole ideas (phrases and sentences), because they have always attended to the *meaning*. As we help them pay attention to the *sounds* of language, they gradually learn that ideas (sentences) are made up of individual **words.** This process of acquiring the **concept of word** is aided by their developing print awareness—it is easier for children to see written words as separate units because of the spaces that separate them.

Children eventually become able to hear that words are composed of smaller units called **syllables.** Syllables, which are clusters of phonemes containing a vowel, are easier for young children to identify than individual phonemes, because syllables (unlike phonemes) are pronounced separately: *air-plane; class-room; Mad-i-son; mom-my; hel-i-cop-ter.*

Onsets and rimes are the smaller units within syllables. An **onset** is the consonant sound or sounds that come before the vowel: /b/ is the onset of *base* and *ball*; /bl/ is the onset of *blue* and *black*.

"Most youngsters enter kindergarten lacking phonemic awareness. Indeed, few are conscious that sentences are made up of individual words, let alone that words can be segmented into phonemes."

—Hallie Kay Yopp
(1995, p. 20)

A **rime** is the vowel and what follows it: the *-all* in *ball,* the *-ack* in *black.* All words have rimes (because they all contain vowels), but some words do not contain onsets (for example: *at, each, is*). When words end with the same rime (*b-at, c-at, s-at*), they rhyme; when words begin with the same onset (*b-ig, b-all, b-ounce*), they alliterate.

Constance Weaver (1996) writes, "Research shows…that at first, it is much more difficult for children to hear separate sounds [phonemes] in words than to

Listening to adults read books with alliteration (such as "seven, silly") or rhymes helps children become phonologically aware.

hear the beginning of a syllable (the 'onset') as a unit and to hear the vowel plus any following consonants (the 'rime') as another unit…Therefore, it is helpful to focus first on elements that alliterate and that rhyme, before focusing on individual sounds" (n.p.). So it is through the use of **rhyme** and **alliteration** that we can best support the preschool child's emerging phonological awareness.

Rhyme and alliteration activities are one of the most important ways early childhood teachers help preschoolers learn to read, because such experiences help children become *phonologically aware.* If you regularly include rhymes and alliteration experiences in your preschool program, you are helping children learn how to pay attention to sounds—first, to environmental sounds in general, and then to the specific sounds in words, in our spoken language. You are helping them develop awareness of the sounds in words through books, stories, songs, rhymes, games, and classroom materials that focus on rhyming and alliterative words. And best of all, your children are *having fun with language* while they are learning!

Linking Sounds and Letters: The Alphabetic Principle

It is important to remember that phonological awareness is an "ear" skill; it has to do with the *sounds* of oral language, not with the *letters* of our written language. But "when adults help draw children's attention to the individual sounds of spoken language, we begin to build the foundation for later understanding of how letters represent sounds that build words" (Bishop et al., p. 41). Once children become aware that words are made up of a sequence of sounds, they also begin to "get" the **alphabetic principle**—that each sound can be represented with its own alphabetic symbol or symbols. And as they make this sound-symbol connection, they begin to be able to map the spoken sounds onto the written letters, enabling them to encode (write) and decode (read) words. This is what **phonics** is all about.

Phonological and phonemic awareness continue to develop as children make the connection between letters and sounds, and as they begin to write and read in preconventional and conventional ways. Weaver (1996) advises teachers of young children to help children develop phonological awareness in the context of *meaningful* reading, writing, and language play. She also points to the research showing that while phonemic awareness facilitates learning to read, learning to read also facilitates phonemic awareness.

When preschool-age children begin to show an interest in letters and words, it is appropriate to draw their attention to the letter-sound connection. Children may show their interest in various ways, such as by asking specific questions about letters and words, trying to sound out the words on a label, inventing a matching game that involves letters, and so on. Teachers should follow cues from the child, and build on this interest. For example, when a child asks you, "What letter is this?"—whether they're pointing to a letter in a book or on a classroom label, or to one of the sponge letters at small-group time—you would say both the name of the letter *and* the sound it makes: "That's the letter *C*, Toni, and it has a /k/ sound in this word, which is *corn. C-c-corn.*" If the child seems interested in continuing in this vein: "That's a *B*, the letter that makes the /b/ sound, like in *B-B-Ben*'s name….Yes, like in *book* area, too—you found another *B* with a /b/ sound. Can you find any others?" Other brief, enjoyable activities that build on this interest can be initiated by the adult at various times throughout the day.

There may also be times when you briefly point out letter-sound connections to the whole group. For example, when taking group dictation, you could occasionally "stretch" a word out orally as you write it, helping children to hear the sound of each letter: "You want me to write 'I **ran**'? Let's see, that's *rrrrr* [writing *r*]…*aaaa* [writing *a*]…*nnnn* [writing *n*]." Or you might point out all the similar letter sounds in a story or song: "Listen to all these /m/ sounds when we sing 'Miss Mary Mack, Mack, Mack.'" (For more details on **alphabet learning,** including the relationship between phonemes and graphemes, see Chapter 6. For more on **dictation,** see Chapter 8.)

While this chapter is largely focused on phonological awareness in the context of word play, rhymes, and alliteration, we should keep in mind the following words from

Learning to Read and Write (Neuman et al., 2000): "Phonemic awareness…is a key skill but by no means the only language skill that is critical for success in reading" (p. 118). There are at least seven other dimensions that support children's emerging literacy, which are listed in Chapter 1 and discussed throughout this book. Incorporate the activities that follow into your daily routine, but remember to balance them with others. Children need to be immersed in the sounds of *natural* language as well as enjoying the nonsense of playing with words.

When a child points to a letter and asks "What letter is this?" you can build on this interest in letters by saying both the letter name and the sound the letter makes.

Judith Schickedanz (1999) has written, "Conscious awareness of language at the phoneme level is learned. It does not develop spontaneously with maturation." She believes that "specific experiences are necessary to help children begin to notice and think about this aspect of language" (p. 63). Neuman et al. (2000) would agree: "Few young children spontaneously acquire phonemic awareness. But when teachers plan activities and interact so as to draw attention to the phonemes in spoken words, children's awareness develops" (p. 81).

As J. Brewer (1998) has written, "Phonemic awareness is not a skill that children either have or do not have; it is a complex behavior that develops over time" (p. 128). And in the context of natural interactions with words and the sounds of words, children in a language-rich preschool setting begin to develop and expand their phonemic awareness.

Suggestions for Adult Support

There are many ways that adults can support and extend children's interest and emerging skills in literacy as they play with words and have fun with language. Sometimes children will initiate word-play activities; at other times adults will initiate them. Here are some support strategies to use at these times.

"Phonemic awareness may be critical for a learner linking the oral to the written coding of language, but it is one of several types of awareness that can be observed as children learn literacy, all of which are necessary for literacy performance."

—Marie Clay (1998, p. 61)

➤ **Support children as they spontaneously play with words.**

At any time of day, in a setting where child talk is valued, children will spontaneously play with language—make silly sounds, create nonsense words, tell a joke, chant their own version of a line from a familiar story or poem: "Run, run, as fast as you can, You can't catch me, I'm Kristin!" During greeting time, at small- or large-group time, during work time, at snack or lunch time, on the playground, while on a field trip, and during transitions, children often initiate language play. There are many ways that adults can follow the children's lead. Using responsive interaction strategies, an adult may

"Activities that involve playing with language—singing, doing fingerplays, playing rhyming games, listening to poems, and reading books such as those by Dr. Seuss—need to be a regular part of the preschool day for all children."

—Susan B. Neuman et al. (2000, p. 118)

- **Repeat** what the child says:

    While washing the table, Miranda chanted, "Dribbles, chibbles, dribbles." Rosie, the teacher, joined Miranda in the chant. Then Eli started chanting, "Fibbles, fibbles, fibbles."

- **Join in playing** with language and sounds, adding variations:

    When Eli said he felt silly and "I think I'll wear my bippers" as he reached for his slippers, his teacher Sue said, "If you're going to wear your bippers, maybe we should call you Beli."

- **Listen** appreciatively:

    In the book area at work time, Cory rocked in the small rocking chair, singing to himself "Boat and coat, boat and coat." Hearing him, Rosie, his teacher, looked over and smiled, swaying her head to keep time with his song.

- **Encourage the child to share** it with others:

    As the children made up ideas for rhyming phrases while singing "The Ants Go Marching One by One," Rosie said, "Zach says, 'skinned his knee' to rhyme with three. Let's sing it Zach's way."

- **Call the child's attention to what he has done** with the words:

    "Hey, I just heard you make a rhyme, Jared—funny and sunny sound the same!"

- **Encourage the child to continue:**

    "I wonder what other words we could think of that sound like funny and sunny?"

- **Write down children's words,** as an anecdote to add to their literacy portfolio and to share with their parents:

11/13—At outside time, when Rosie asked, "Do you hear something the same when I say Madison *and* mitten?" *Irene said, "They both start with /mmm/."*

➤ Initiate word play.

Adults can support and extend child-initiated word play in the moment, and they can follow up as well by planning brief and playful experiences with words. Choose an activity from the suggestions that follow, then see where in the daily routine you might introduce it. As with all teacher-initiated activities, remember to look at both the *developmental levels* and the *interests* of the children you work with in deciding whether to try any of these experiences. And be prepared for a variety of responses, as your children will no doubt be at many different levels of phonological awareness.

Rhyming games

The following playful activities focus on rhyming. (Note: When playing rhyming games with preschoolers, the children will often generate "nonsense" words rather than real ones. This is fine—the point is to see if they can attend to the sound of the word and generate rhymes by changing the onset, not to see if they can create "real" words.)

- **Substitute a word at the end of a line** in a familiar song or chant and see what word children choose to rhyme with it. For example:

  Hey diddle diddle, The cat and the fiddle,

  The cow jumped over the *house*.

  The little dog laughed to see such a sight,

  And the dish ran away with the_____.

- **Play "Let's Think of Words That Rhyme."**

  "Let's think of words that rhyme with sat." *(Any rhyming word or nonsense word will do:* hat, bat, that, crat, jat, mat.)

  Let children be the leaders. When children are familiar with this game, try making up rhyming phrases with them:

  "I saw a goat sailing in a _____." (Any rhyme will do: boat, moat, coat, zoat.)

- **Play rhyming "I Spy"(or "I See"):** After children get the idea of rhyming words in the above activity

> *"Rhyming is considered an important indicator that a child is developing good skills that are prerequisite to learning to read, and a first step toward awareness of speech sounds. In order to be able to hear that two words rhyme, a child must attend to the way the ends of words sound (not their meanings), and ignore the different beginning sounds."*
>
> —Susan L. Hall and Louisa C. Moats (1999, p. 173)

(where there are multiple "right answers"), introduce this game (where there is usually only one right answer).

"I spy (or "I see") something that rhymes with _____. What do you think it is?"

Initially, the adult leads; eventually, children are able to take the lead. Start with the most concrete form of this game: children do not have to search for the objects, because you have them right in front of you and the children:

"I spy something I am holding that rhymes with call."

"I spy something next to me that rhymes with fox."

"I spy something we are sitting on that rhymes with bug."

When children can play that form of the game easily, expand the area where the objects can be found:

"I spy something in the book area that rhymes with willow."

"I spy something in the block area that rhymes with star."

"I spy something in the room that rhymes with label."

"I spy something on the grass that rhymes with hug. *Does anybody know what it is?"*

Alliteration games

Here are some helpful ways to help children notice the sounds at the beginnings of words:

- To familiarize children with the initial sounds in their names, play **"I Know Someone,"** using the names of the children in your group:

  "I know someone, right here in this room, whose name starts like this: /shhhhhhh/. Who do you think it is?"

  "There are two children in our room whose names begin with this sound: /t/.../t/.../t/. Who are they?"

  "I know three children whose names starts with a /j/ sound."

  "I'm thinking of a person whose name starts with the same sound as monkey."

- As the children become more familiar with the initial sounds in one another's names, play **active group name games.** Stress the matching initial sound in each action word as the children call out the names that begin with that sound:

  *"If you see someone whose name begins with a /b/ sound, **b**ounce on your **b**ottom…Yes, we're **b**ouncing with **B**rianna!"*

  *"If you see someone whose name begins with a /j/ sound, **j**ump up and down….Now we're **j**umping with **J**oey and **J**essica!"*

  (Think of actions for all the children's initial sounds: /l/ sound, **l**ie down; /k/ sound, **c**rouch down low; /s/ sound, **s**wing your arms; /sh/ sound, **sh**ake your leg, etc.)

- When children are familiar with the sounds their own names begin with, make up alliterative phrases together, using their **names:**

  ***B**en **b**ouncing **b**all, **A**nna **a**pple **a**nts, **K**ara **c**andy **c**up, **Y**vonne **ee**ple **e**ater, **T**aylor **t**en **t**oes, **J**uan **w**isher **w**ood.*

- Play **"Let's Think of Words That Start Like This."**

  Introduce a word or a sound, then let children come up with other words that begin with the same sound. Once the children catch on, they can take turns leading this game:

  *"Let's think of words that start like **b**ig, **b**aby, **b**ottle…"*

  *"Let's think of words that start with /**m**/, like **mmmommy!**"*

  *"Let's think of words that begin with a /**b**/ sound."*

  Repeat children's responses.

- Play **alliteration "I Spy."** Find objects in the room, and add descriptive or non-sense words to make an alliterative phrase:

"Not by the hair of my chinny-chin-chin. Hey, whose name starts with the same sound as chin?*"*

> *"I spy a ball—a **big, big ball.**"*
>
> *"I see a pencil—a **pippity-poppity pencil.**"*
>
> *"I see a mirror—a **magic mouse mirror.**"*
>
> *"I'm looking at Benjy—**be-bop Benjy, a boy.**"*

Once children have the idea of the initial sounds of words, try this version:

> *"I spy (or "I see") something that starts with a /**d**/ sound. What could it be?"*

Initially, the adult leads; eventually, children are able to take the lead. Again, start with the most concrete form of this game, with objects that are right in front of you and the children.

> *"I spy something on the floor in front of us, that starts like this—/**t**/…/**t**/. What could it be?"*
>
> *"I see something on this table that begins with a /**l**/…/**l**/…/**l**/ sound. What is it?"*

When children can play that form of the game easily, expand the area where the objects can be found (and where there might be multiple objects that begin with that sound):

> *"I spy something on the easel that begins with a /**p**/…/**p**/…/**p**/ sound. What could it be?" (paper, paint, paintbrush, etc.)*
>
> *"I spy something out on the playground, that starts like **Sssssssarah.** What do you think it is?" (slide, swings, scooter, sidewalk, snow, etc.)*

• Substitute new sets of alliterative words in familiar alliterative phrases:

> *"**Mee Millie Minkie** ran through the town."*
>
> *"Three cheers for outside time. **Bip-bip booray!**"*

- At snack time (or during transitions), a child or adult chooses a sound. Everyone changes key words to begin with that sound (this is done very informally):

  *"It's **back** time. Whose turn is it to pass out the **bapkins?**" "I didn't get a **bup!**" "Please pass the **buice.**" "Can I have more **bapples?**"*

  *"It's time to go **routside** now. That's why we're putting on our **rackets.**" "Did you look in your **rubby** for your **rittens?**"*

- If your children have really caught on to this and enjoy playing with initial sounds, you might suggest:

  *"What if we change the /**m**/ in **mittens** to a /**k**/ sound? Then we'd be putting on our...**kittens!** And if we change it to a /**s**/ sound, we'd be putting on our...**sittens.**"*

Note: For many more activities with rhyming and alliterative words, see the book, *Fee, Fie, Phonemic Awareness* (Hohmann, 2002).

Picture cards for sound matching (rhyme and alliteration)

These cards are available commercially, but can be teacher-made as well. Some four- and five-year-olds may choose to use these cards during work time, alone or with a partner. The advantage of making your own cards is that you can use pictures of things the children are familiar with. You could draw the pictures yourself or cut up workbooks meant for matching initial consonants. Back each set of cards with a different color of paper, and store the sets in separate containers (perhaps in the book or writing area). Begin with only a few rhyming pairs or letter-sound sets at first, and observe how the children use them. You can add more cards later. (Note: Don't be surprised if children make up their own games—like variations of Memory or Snap—that have little or nothing to do with rhymes and alliteration!)

Here are some examples of sets to make:

- Set #1: Pictures of words that have the same **initial consonant sound.** Examples:

  carrot, cow, cup, crayon
  dog, doughnut, dress, doll
  fish, feather, fork, fire
  table, TV, two, tail

- Set #2: Pictures of words that **rhyme.** Examples:

duck/truck	spoon/moon
fox/box	king/ring
star/car	rake/cake
mouse/house	bed/bread

fish/dish	sock/clock
goat/boat	tree/key
kitten/mitten	cat/hat
plate/skate	bear/chair

Before adding these cards to your room, introduce them to the children, perhaps at greeting time. Here is a playful way to show how the rhyming words (Set #2) can be matched: You pick up the kitten card, "walk" it over to the bear card, and say, "Meow, meow, I'm a little *kitten,* looking for my *mitten.* Can you help me find it?" When the children point out the mitten card to you, set the two rhyming cards together. Then "walk" the bear card over to the goat card and say, "I'm a big brown *bear,* and I want to sit in my *chair.* Can you help me find it?" Continue with the other animal cards in the same manner, showing the children how each card has a "matching" one that sounds the same, or rhymes.

"As long as children have many authentic literacy experiences— experiences in which literacy is used for a purpose and all of its various aspects are brought together in the acts of reading and writing—some use of specific practice materials will do no harm. In fact, they provide an opportunity for children to do something they like: repeat a skill or action over and over until they master it."

—Judith Schickedanz (1999, p. 145)

Books and stories with rhyme and alliteration

Here are some ways to use the many wonderful preschool-level books and stories that are filled with rhyme and alliteration (see the list in Appendix D):

- When reading or telling stories with rhyming phrases, occasionally ask the children to identify the rhyming words they hear. Or **pause at the end of a line** so children can fill in the rhyming word.

    "Hickory, dickory, dock. The mouse ran up the ____."

    Then point out,

    "Clock sounds like dock—clock and dock rhyme!"

- **Read stories and rhymes** to children that include alliterative phrases such as

Fee, fie, fo, fum	Clickety-clack, clickety-clack
Miss Mary Mack	Wee Willie Winkie
Clip, clop, clip, clop	Fine feathered friends
Peter, Peter pumpkin-eater	Snip, Snap, Snurr

- When reading familiar stories and rhymes that include alliterative phrases, **pause so children can say them with you or fill them in.**

    "The first billy goat started across the bridge, [pause] trip-trap, trip-trap."

Songs, chants, fingerplays, and jingles

Using **creative variations on familiar songs** is another way to focus on beginning or ending sounds in words:

- Change the words in familiar songs and fingerplays to **add more rhymes.** The traditional song, "This Old Man," is a great rhyming song, and it can have many variations:

  This old man he played *red* (continue with other colors)

  He played knick-knack in his *bed* (anything that rhymes, even nonsense words)

  or

  This old man he played *up* (continue with *down, in, out, over, under*, etc.)

  He played knick-knack on a *cup* (anything that rhymes)

- Change the words in familiar songs by **substituting sounds:** for example, the chorus to "I've Been Working on the Railroad" ("Someone's in the kitchen with Dinah") can be changed by substituting various initial consonant sounds (Yopp, 1992):

  I know a song that we can sing

  I know a song that we can sing

  I know a song that we can sing

  It goes something like this:

  Fee-fi-fiddly-i-o

  Fee-fi-fiddly-i-o-o-o-o

  Fee-fi-fiddly-i-oooooo

  Now try it with the **/k/** sound!

  Kee-ki-kiddly-i-o

  Kee-ki-kiddly-i-o-o-o-o

  Kee-ki-kiddly-i-oooooo

  Now try it with the **/b/** sound!

  Bee-bi-biddly-i-o

  Bee-bi-biddly-i-o-o-o-o

  Bee-bi-biddly-i-oooooo

  Now try it with the **/z/** sound!…etc.

Change the words in familiar chants and songs to highlight word beginnings or endings, and encourage children to do the same.

Other familiar songs can be used for practicing sound substitutions. In "Old Mac-Donald Had a Farm," the "E-I-E-I-O" line becomes "bee-by-bee-by-boh," "see-sigh-see-sigh-so," etc. In the "Happy Birthday" song, initial consonants can be substituted ("Bappy Birthday boo boo") or repetitive syllables ("Ta-ta ta-ta ta ta") can replace the words.

- Change **whole songs**; use the familiar tunes to create your own. For instance, sing these words to the tune of "If You're Happy and You Know It" or "Put Your Fingers in the Air"; let children choose other rhyming words:

  Did you ever see a (bear) in a (chair)?

  Did you ever see a (bear) in a (chair)?

  No, I never, no, I never, no, I never, no, I never

  No, I never saw a (bear) in a (chair).

- Sing **songs that have been recorded for young children**—without the recording—so that you and the children can change the rhyming words and play with the sounds. Raffi, a popular performer of children's songs, has recorded these:

  "Down By the Bay": "Did you ever see a *whale* with a polka-dotted *tail?*" Name another animal and something it might wear or do that rhymes: "Did you ever see a *fly* baking a *pie?* Did you ever see a *duck*, driving in a *truck?*"

  "Willoughby Wallaby Woo": "Willoughby wallaby *wee*, an elephant sat on *me*; willoughby wallaby *woo*, an elephant sat on *you*." Substitute a rhyme for a child's name: "Willoughby wallaby *Wary*, an elephant sat on *Mary*."

  "The Corner Grocery Store": "There were plums, *plums*, twiddling their *thumbs*, at the store, at the store...corn, *corn*, blowin' on the *horn*..." Name a food and think of a rhyme for it: "There was cheese, *cheese*, walkin' on its *knees*..."

  "Apples and Bananas": The vowel sounds are changed in this simple tune: "I like to eat, eat, eat apples and bananas...I like to ate, ate, ate *ay*-ples and ba-*nay-nays*...I like to oot, oot, oot *oop*-ples and ba-*noo-noos*." (The melody is available online; search the *musiclegacy.com* Web site.)

Poems

What kind of poems are appropriate for preschoolers? Many kinds—poems that rhyme and those that don't; poems that are silly and poems with beautiful language; poems that are written for children, and some that are not; poems that are written by other children. Choose poems you know and love, poems the children know, and poems that you and the children make up.

- Read or recite at least **one poem a day** to the children, more if you can. In some programs, greeting circle is a good time to share poetry; in others, just before lunch or at naptime might work better. Don't forget to mention the author's name, if you know it.

- Display a **favorite poem on the wall** where children can see it.

- Include some of the children's **favorite poems in any newsletter** that you send home to parents—along with the rationale for immersing children in poetry and other rhymes.

- Encourage children to create **their own poems and rhymes.** Creating poetry often happens spontaneously, when the children say that they notice rhyming words:

  "Billy's being silly. Hey, listen, I made a rhyme!"

  "I went to the store last night and got a new kite. Night *sounds like* kite, *doesn't it?"*

You could support this orally, by continuing to play with the words ("His name is Billy and he likes to be silly, my name is Linda and I'm not a pinda!" etc.).

> *"Nursery rhymes are rather like a very special kind of toy which children can take over and play with—sometimes to bounce and dance to, sometimes to muck about with the language, and sometimes to explore ideas about what is forbidden, naughty, frightening or just plain puzzling."*
>
> —Marian Whitehead
> (1999, p. 41)

- You could also support children's poetry by writing their **spontaneous poems** down, and underlining the rhyming words *if* they have the same spelling pattern. (Explaining why *night* and *kite* sound the same but look so different is a bit beyond the preschool level. If a child notices and asks about it, you might answer, "Well, the same sound can be spelled using different letters—you know, like Karla and Casey's names both start with a /k/ sound when you say them, but one is spelled with a *K* and the other with a *C*.")

- Be tolerant of **nonsense words** when children create poems. As discussed earlier, getting the rhyme is much more important than coming up with a real word.

- Write down **children's words when they sound poetic** to you, even if they haven't asked you to.

Nursery rhymes

Nursery rhymes may be used in both traditional and nontraditional ways:

- **Read and recite** nursery rhymes daily.

- **Stock the room** with nursery rhyme books, audiotapes, puppets, and pictures.

- **Make a nursery rhyme "big book."**

- **Send home copies** of the children's favorite nursery rhymes, stapled into a book format. Children could decorate their books before taking them home.

- **Recite appropriate nursery rhymes with cooking activities** or snacks:

  "Humpty Dumpty"—scrambled eggs

  "The Queen of Hearts"—fruit tarts

  "Peter Peter Pumpkin Eater"—carving pumpkins

- **Make up nursery rhyme riddles;** encourage children to do the same, once they are familiar with the rhymes.

  "I'm under the haystack, fast asleep. Who am I?"

  "I lost my sheep, and I don't know where to find them. Who am I?"

Nursery rhyme books are an important resource. Read and recite nursery rhymes daily, and look for opportunities to incorporate them throughout the day.

- **Record the children's nursery rhyme riddles** on chart paper as a dictation activity (see Chapter 8).

- **Encourage children to act out nursery rhymes** (or to recite them while other children act them out). Provide props when possible (a candlestick for Jack; a stool, bowl, and spoon for Little Miss Muffet, etc.).

- **Make a set of sequence cards** for favorite nursery rhymes, and store them in the book area. Children can "read" the pictures and put them in proper sequence...or mix them up and create silly new stories ("Humpty Dumpty fell off a wall...and Little Miss Muffet ate scrambled eggs for breakfast!"). Pictures that can be used for sequencing cards can be found online; try the *enchantedlearning.com* Web site, or search "nursery rhymes" and "sequence."

- **Read the book *Each Peach Pear Plum*** and look for all the nursery rhyme characters.

➤ Incorporate word-play activities into the daily routine.

Greeting time

Sing a **rhyming song** when it's time to put away the books and puzzles:

It's greeting time, it's greeting time,

Let's put the books away.

It's time to read the message board,

And see what's new today!

Planning/recall time

Here are some ideas for **rhyming chants:**

- Chant a rhyme as the marked **hula hoop** is turned around:

    Around and around at planning time,
    Tell us your plan when we finish this rhyme!

    When the chant ends, whoever is holding the part of the hoop that is marked with tape relates his or her plan.

- Try patting the beat to a rhythmic chant that uses words that rhyme with the **children's names:**

    *Willoughby wallaby **wared**, it's recall time for **Jared**.*
    *Willoughby wallaby **weesa**, it's recall time for **Lisa**.*

Cleanup time

Start a **rhyming game** as you help children clean up the room:

*"I'm putting away the **truck**, which sounds like...**duck**!...Cory's picking up **blocks**, which sounds like...?" (Wait for children to respond.) "What are you putting away, Alicia? The **dishes**, which sounds like...?" "Donnie's washing the **table**, which sounds like...?"*

Expect children to respond with nonsense words (and celebrate it when they do!); if they can make rhymes, it shows that phonemic learning *is* taking place!

Large-group time

Most teachers are already doing rhyme and alliteration activities at this time. These ideas will enhance what you are already doing:

- As an opening activity to "lure" children over to large-group time, start chanting or singing **"The Name Game."** (The Shirley Ellis recording of this song was popular in the '60s, and has been recorded more recently on several compilations of children's songs.) "Shirley, Shirley, bo-birley, banana fanna fo-firley, fee fi mo-mirley, Shirley!" You can substitute any child's name—the number of syllables doesn't matter. The initial onset of the name is replaced by /b/, /f/, /m/, as in

    "Jenna, Jenna, bo-benna, banana fanna fo-fenna, fee fi mo-menna, Jenna!"
    "Dirk, Dirk, bo-birk, banana fanna fo-firk, fee fi mo-mirk, Dirk!"
    "Christopher, Christopher, bo-bistopher, banana fanna fo-fistopher, fee fi mo-mistopher, Christopher!"

- Sing **songs with alliteration,** such as "Thumbs go Wiggle Waggle" (Weikart & Carlton 1995, p. 229):

  Thumbs go wiggle waggle,
  wiggle waggle, wiggle waggle,

  Thumbs go wiggle waggle, then they stop!

  Have children choose other alliterative words to substitute for *wiggle waggle (jiggle jaggle, sneaky snakey,* etc.).

- As well as enjoying various forms of language play, you can also occasionally **talk** about them, drawing children's attention to the rhyming and alliterative words. For instance, an adult may remark at large-group time, "The song 'Willoughby Wallaby Woo' reminds me of our books *Mrs. Wishy-Washy* and *Wacky Wednesday*—all those /w/-/w/-/w/ sounds." Before long, they will be noticing the sounds of words and pointing them out to you.

Chant a rhyme as a marked hula hoop is passed around at planning time. At the end of the rhyme, or on a particular word, the hoop stops and it's that child's turn to plan.

Small-group time

Plan a small-group activity using objects gathered from around the classroom whose names have the **same initial sound.** Let the children explore and talk about the materials first; when they begin naming them, see if they notice that many of the words start with the same sound. If not, call attention to two or three of the words: "Ball... baby... block. Boy, I hear a lot of /b/ sounds!" Be aware that children might identify some objects with different words than you had in mind—*rabbit* instead of *bunny,* for instance. Also be prepared for some children choosing to use the objects in their own way, rather than thinking or talking about the words!

To carry out the activity, plan to have about twice the number of items as the number of children in your group. You may want to hold this small-group time on the floor, so there is plenty of space. Some possible materials:

Objects with names that begin with /b/: block, baby, ball, bead, book, box, bag, bear, barn, bat, bread, bunny, boot, bucket, boat, bus, basket, bowl, baby bottle, broom, brush, belt, button, bone, bug, bell, bolt, beans, Band-aid box.

The *Berenstains' B Book,* or a Dr. Seuss book with lots of alliteration, would be a good back-up material for this activity.

If children enjoy this activity, you could vary it by giving them objects with **two different initial sounds,** and have them sort the objects into two groups as they figure out what the sounds are. Some possible materials:

Objects that begin with /m/: marker, mitten, marble, map, mouse, mop, mirror, magnet, maraca, magazine, mask, menu, motorcycle, money.

Objects that begin with /p/: paper, pencil, pen, pegboard, pine cone, puzzle, puppet, plate, paintbrush, paper punch, potholder, pail, pillow, pan, plane.

Transitions

Once children are familiar with the **initial *sound* of their names** (see the game, "I Know Someone," on page 47), you could try this as one of the ways to move them to the next activity:

*"You can go to your small-group table when you hear the sound your name begins with. Whose name begins with this sound—/**k**/, /**k**/, /**k**/, /**k**/?"* (Do Christopher, Carlos, and Karina all respond?) *"Whose name begins with /**mmmmmm**/? Next, whose name begins with /**shhhhhhh**/?"*

If you've waited a while and a child does not move in response to his or her name, you might then say something like

"Karina, you can also go to your table, because Karina *begins with the sound /**k**/, /**k**/, /**k**/."*

Preschool teachers have always known that children learn much about the world and the people in it through their play. And now research has shown that much of what children need to learn about language, both oral and written, is also learned through play. In this chapter we have seen how playing with words—having fun with language— is so easy to do with three- to five-year-olds: by playing rhyming and alliteration games with them, reading books and telling stories that focus on rhyme and alliteration, and engaging them in songs, chants, fingerplays, poems, and nursery rhymes. In the next chapter we will take a closer look at the whole process of reading books and telling stories to young children.

4

Reading Aloud and Storytelling

Listening to stories—whether they are being read aloud or told—enables children to have fun with words and learn more about language. It is a pleasurable experience that starts with a focus on oral language and leads eventually to an understanding of written language.

Reading aloud and storytelling are two related but different literacy activities that adults in preschool classrooms should engage in daily with children. The first part of this chapter is devoted to the art of reading aloud, and the latter part to the art of storytelling. When young children listen to stories being read or told, they are *having fun with language,* the third of High/Scope's language and literacy key experiences. And because we encourage them to become engaged and participate in the story, the first two key experiences, which involve speaking, are also involved.

"The most valuable preschool preparation for school learning is to love books, and to know that there is a world of interesting ideas in them."

—Marie Clay (1991, p. 29)

Listening to a story takes children to another world.

Reading Aloud

Reading aloud has been found to be one of the most important ways adults can foster children's emerging literacy. Indeed, points out read-aloud expert Jim Trelease, research shows that "reading aloud to children improves their reading, writing, speaking, listening—and, best of all, their *attitudes* about reading" (2001, p. xvii).

More specifically, reading to children supports all eight dimensions of literacy learning discussed by Neuman et al. (2000):

1. When we read with enjoyment to children, we demonstrate the **power and pleasure of literacy.**

2. Books that children listen to (as well as look at) are a prominent part of the **literate environment.**

3. Reading aloud enhances children's **language development** through the introduction of new words, concepts, and language structures.

4. Reading aloud builds children's **knowledge and comprehension** of the world.

5. When children are read to regularly, their **knowledge of print** is enhanced.

6. When we read a variety of books, not just storybooks, children learn about the many different **types of text.**

7. Children's **phonological awareness** is increased when we read aloud to them and talk about the *sounds* in the words.

8. Reading aloud supports children's developing interest in and knowledge of **letters and words.**

> *"The single most important activity for building [the] understandings and skills essential for reading success appears to be reading aloud to children."*
>
> —International Reading Association and the National Association for the Education of Young Children (2000, p. 6)

When educators talk about "reading aloud" or "reading to children," they can mean different things. There is reading *with* children, sometimes referred to as shared reading (see p. 121 in Chapter 7), and reading *to* children—when we want to just "snuggle around the warm glow of a story" with children (Calkins, 1997, p. 32). In preschool classrooms, we typically use both practices. Sometimes we read a story mainly for enjoyment, reading straight through but accepting children's questions and comments throughout. At other times we may stop the reading to point out various features of the book, the print, or individual words; we may ask questions or make comments about the story; we may pause at appropriate places for the children to chime in or complete a rhyme. Preschoolers who are already beginning to read conventionally may even want to read some words, phrases, or sentences themselves.

We read many things to and with children throughout the day: symbols, words, labels, signs, notes, posters, and child-dictated words and sentences. Most of the reading aloud we do in preschool, however, involves reading books. In the following section, we'll first discuss why we read books aloud to children—what are the benefits?—and then we'll look at where, when, what, and how to read aloud.

Why read aloud to young children?

The benefits of reading aloud to children are so many and so powerful that, as Trelease writes, "When you look at all the arguments in its favor, how could we *not* read aloud to children?" (2001, p. 12). These benefits include learning about reading and books, learning about stories, learning about language, and learning about the world.

What children learn about reading

One of the most important discoveries children make when adults read to them is that reading can be an enjoyable activity, for if children are to become good readers they must find pleasure in reading. Reading aloud presents a positive reading role model to all children, thereby "instilling the habits and values of a literate life" (Weaver, 1996, p. 75).

By listening to adults read, children also become familiar with the reading process itself. They begin to see how the written words on a page are matched to the reader's spoken words, and the print-to-speech connection is gradually established. When adults point to the words as they read them or talk about various features, children begin to learn some of the concepts about print: in English one reads a book from front to back, words and lines from left to right, and lines from top to bottom; quotation marks mean somebody is talking; a period signals the end of the sentence; and so on. Being read to also affords children the opportunity to hear what fluent reading sounds like, which is especially important for beginning readers.

What children learn about books

Children learn much about books as we read to them. They discover that books hold new worlds, new friends, and new knowledge, as well as familiar and comforting themes. When we read a wide variety of books to children, they also learn that text comes in different genres: fiction and nonfiction, poetry and prose. Because it is mostly picture books that are read to children when they are young, children first learn to "read" (interpret) the pictures; with more experience they begin to understand that the print carries the meaning and is supported by the pictures. Finally, reading aloud exposes children of all ages to books that they might not choose on their own.

What children learn about stories

Through listening to storybooks, children begin to develop an understanding about the shape and structure of stories: how they work, what kinds of things can happen in stories, how plots are structured, and how events can be anticipated. They learn that stories have a beginning, a middle, and an end. They also begin to understand important cognitive concepts that are embedded in stories, such as time and sequence or cause and effect.

What children learn about language

The language of books is different than conversational language. Book language is more formal, more descriptive, and more rhythmical, with longer, more complex sentences. The language patterns in books are "more carefully structured and beautifully balanced than those of everyday speech" (Kropp, 2000, p. 88). Hearing these rich language patterns read aloud prepares children to understand them when they learn to read themselves. Children are also exposed to a range of new vocabulary when we read to them;

they learn far more new words from books than from either conversation or television. The English language contains 500,000 words, yet only 15,000 words are used in everyday speech, and only 7000 words on television (Kropp, 2000). In addition to learning about language, children are learning *to think about language.* Their sensitivity to the individual sounds of language can be heightened when adults call attention to those sounds during read-alouds. Reading aloud exposes children to good grammar, and to what Trelease refers to as a "second language—the *standard* English of books, the classroom and most of the workplace" (2001, p. 50).

> *"Of all the literacy experiences children can have during their preschool years, storybook reading seems to be the most powerful in helping them learn language and gain knowledge about the world."*
>
> —Judith Schickedanz
> (1999, pp. 42–43)

What children learn about the world

Along with new vocabulary, children acquire knowledge about a variety of topics when they are read to. Both fiction and nonfiction books extend their ideas about life's daily routines. Children learn about people of both similar and different backgrounds—their family compositions, their interaction patterns, their homes and jobs, their cultures and belief systems. They see how others deal with feelings and conflicts and how they solve problems. Books also expand children's skills in basic academic areas. They introduce children to information about how things work, about the natural and physical sciences, art and architecture, sea and space, life in different times (history) and places (geography). Through books, children's store of background knowledge increases as they learn about the world, both the world outside and their own inner world—their emotions, ideas, and values. This background knowledge—along with the knowledge children acquire from their everyday experiences—is critical to later comprehension when children begin to read for themselves.

Other benefits children receive from being read to

Reading aloud to children stimulates their imagination, as evidenced when their dramatic play includes elements from various stories they have become familiar with. Being read to also stretches their attention span, improves their listening comprehension, nurtures their emotional development, and can build a sense of community in the classroom.

As they are read to, children aquire background knowledge of the world outside as well as of the inner world of emotions and values.

62

Children love to hear their favorite stories again and again, sometimes to adults' dismay. However, re-reading has many benefits for children's learning. Repetition

- Immerses the child in the language of the story, making it easier to learn
- Helps to build children's confidence (they know what's going to happen next)
- Strengthens and reinforces the neural connections in children's brains
- Improves children's vocabulary, sequencing, and memory skills
- Increases the possibility that children will be able to read the book on their own afterwards
- Encourages children to reenact their favorite stories

"Once we have enjoyed the same stories, we have a base for shared dialogue, play, and reenactment. We belong to a community where stories matter."

—Linda Torgerson
(1996, p. 95)

Suggestions for Adult Support—Reading Aloud

Reading aloud might seem like such a natural activity to do with young children that adults wouldn't need any suggestions on how to do it. However, studies have shown that "reading stories as an act in itself does not necessarily promote literacy" (Morrow & Gambrell, 2000, p. 568)—that what makes a read-aloud session effective includes environmental factors (such as the type and quality of books, the size of the group, and the physical setting), as well as the adult-child interactions that occur before, during, and after the reading. Following are some ways that adults can make read-alouds more enjoyable, interactive, and beneficial.

➤ **Read throughout the day in a variety of settings.**

In preschool classrooms, children should be read to every day, throughout the day, in different settings. Reading aloud should be a regular part of the daily routine, so that each child is read to at least once or twice a day. For instance, you might read to one or more children before all the children have arrived for the day. At greeting time, share a poem or very short story with the group before or after reading the message board together. Also, read to a few children at work time at their request. Studies show that more children will be attracted to the book area at work time if an adult is present there on an intermittent basis than if there is no adult there or if an adult is always there (Schickedanz, 1999).

At small-group time, you can introduce an activity with a related story. You can also read as the children are having snack, after lunch as they prepare for naptime, or as children begin to get up from napping. *Have at least one time of the day be a consistent time for reading aloud;* it gives children something to look forward to if they know, for instance, that they *always* get to hear a story at snack time.

Having a regular book-sharing time at the beginning of the day encourages parent participation and eases the transition for both children and parents.

Reading aloud one-on-one, in pairs, or in small groups has been found to work best with children. That way, they can see the words and engage in meaningful conversation. Reading in intimate groupings rather than the traditional large-group setting makes it a warm and personal experience and offers children more opportunities to develop the skills of literacy. As Schickedanz writes, "If teachers rarely read books or read them only during large group story time, children may not receive the individual scaffolded experience they need to launch independent retellings of favorite books" (1999, p. 91). This "scaffolded experience" happens most easily during what is sometimes referred to as lap-reading, when the child sits on the adult's lap or nestles against the adult—the way parents often read to their children.

Whenever you read to children, choose a comfortable spot. Sit on the floor, on a couch, or in another cozy place in your room where children can cluster around you. On a nice day, take your small group outside to read on a blanket under a tree.

➤ Read a wide variety of books.

Select a wide range of books to share with children—some books that relate to the children's current activities and interests, that will be personally meaningful to them, and others that will open up new worlds to them. Strive for a balance between new and familiar books—between those *you* introduce and those the children pick out. Read fiction (narrative text and stories) as well as nonfiction (expository books, informational and reference books, concept books). Read published books as well as books you and the children have made. Read traditional stories (like folk and fairy tales) as well as contemporary ones. Occasionally read easy-to-read books designed for beginning readers, and read high-quality children's literature often.

Be aware that not all picture books written for children are ideal for reading aloud. In making your selection, consider your children's cultures, languages, interests, background knowledge, developmental levels, and attention spans. There are many lists of recommended read-aloud books for young children; one excellent source that is updated about every four years is *The Read-Aloud Handbook* (5th Edition) by Jim Trelease (2001). *Ready for Reading* (Bishop et al., 2000) presents 60 "book-sharing experiences," designed for use with preschoolers. However, since thousands of new children's books are published each year, don't rely solely on lists published in books (not even in this one!). Use them as a starting point, and look for more recently published books as well. Up-to-date lists can be found online; search "read-aloud book lists," or look at the links on Jim Trelease's own Web site (*www.trelease-on-reading.com*). You might also contact your local library to request an up-to-date list of good children's books available there.

Select a wide variety of books and place them in an accessible location so children can explore them and include them in their story requests. Change the selection periodically.

Here are some ideas for the types of books to read aloud; see Appendix D for lists of specific titles.

- **Books that contain rhyme and alliteration.** These books allow you to draw children's attention to the fact that words are made up of various sounds, helping them to develop phonemic awareness. Books with rhyme and alliteration can be stories, poems, songs, or nursery rhymes. (Refer to the ideas in Chapter 3 as you read these books with children.)

> *"In the teaching of reading, there are only a handful of things that everyone agrees are essential. Perhaps the most important of these is the fact that children need to listen to the best of children's literature read aloud to them."*
>
> —Lucy Calkins (2001, p. 51)

- **Predictable books.** These books, which help children think of *themselves* as readers, use various literary devices to make them predictable—repetition (*The Three Little Pigs*), rhyme (*Is Your Mama a Llama?*), refrain (*Chicken Soup With Rice*), cumulative text (*The Napping House*), sequential patterns (*The Very Hungry Caterpillar*), interlocking patterns (*If You Give a Moose a Muffin*), text closely matching the illustrations (*Goodnight Moon*), or one idea or thought per page (*Brown Bear, Brown Bear*) (Schickedanz, 1999; Bishop et al., 2000).

- **Books with easily remembered phrases or lines** for the children to chant, such as *Millions of Cats, Caps for Sale, The Little Red Hen, The Story of Ping, The Gingerbread Man, Tikki-Tikki-Tembo.*

- **Books that invite physical as well as verbal participation.** For example, children can mimic the "trip-trap, trip-trap" of *The Three Billy Goats Gruff;* they can shake their fists and stomp their feet with the monkeys in *Caps for Sale;* they can be the animals in *The Mitten* by crawling into a large bag (made from a sheet folded in half and sewn up like a sleeping bag).

- **Books that reflect the identities, home languages, family structures, and cultures of the children** in your class. Choose books that avoid stereotyping.

- **Wordless books.** Demonstrate to children how they can make up the story as they "read" the pictures. (These books are also excellent for recommending to low-literacy parents, as well as to parents who speak little or no English. They can read them to their children by talking about the pictures.)

- **Big books** of familiar stories or poems. Point to the words as you read them; children will often chime in and read along with you. Many will begin to notice the print-to-speech connection.

- **Alphabet books.** There are a myriad of ABC picture books on the market; according to Rhoten and Lane (2001), more than 175 were published in the 1990s alone. These authors believe that quality alphabet books "invite the response or involvement of the child in the read-aloud experience, and they also provide teachers with a rich source of ideas for extended activities in the early childhood setting" (p. 42). Once they are familiar with ABC books, children can also help to create their own. (Refer to ideas in Chapter 6.)

> *"Predictable books are designed to make their text memorable. Their structure specifically encourages children to chime in as the adult reads and helps them recall chunks of text during independent retellings."*
>
> —Judith Schickedanz (1999, p. 73)

> *"If a book makes children laugh, cry, squeal, shiver, or wriggle and jiggle in some way, it takes up residence in their hearts and stays there."*
>
> —Mem Fox (2001, p. 130)

➤ Involve children before, during, and after the reading.

An important aspect of reading aloud is *how* you do it; the way you read to children can significantly affect their literacy learning. Here are some tips for how to read aloud to the children in your classroom; some points are more applicable for small-group read-alouds than when you are reading to individual children.

Ahead of time

When you, rather than the children, are choosing the book, do a little "homework" before you read:

- Choose an appropriate book (see previous section).
- Check the illustrations: Are they large enough for all to see? (If not, consider reading the book *without* showing the pictures. Used occasionally, this strategy can actually improve children's listening and visualization skills and increase their comprehension.)
- Read the book yourself to become familiar with it, and to see how long it takes to read without conversation. (Double that for the actual time that may be needed to accommodate comments from you and the children.)
- Decide if there are any words you want to explain to the children. (Pick only a few at any one reading.)

"It is extremely important to make multi-cultural literature integral to read-alouds. Children need to see themselves and others in our diverse society reflected in the selections read by the teacher."

—William H. Teale and Junko Yokota (2000, p. 15)

Before the story

- Introduce the book. Draw children's attention to the cover: "What do you think this book will be about?"
- Read the title, author, and illustrator (using those terms) to the children.
- Ask if the children are familiar with this story, this book, or any other books by this author or illustrator.

During the story

As you read, use a natural voice with appropriate inflections and modulations. Read slowly and clearly, making sure your voice is loud enough for all to hear, even when you need to lower it or whisper as appropriate. Look at the children frequently, and point to illustrations at key times—especially when they add to the meaning of a word.

Read interactively and with pleasure. Reading interactively involves input from both you and the children:

- Respond to children's questions and comments.
- Add a brief explanation or synonym for a new word when you read it (do this with only a few words each time you read a book).

You can introduce a new story to children by showing them the cover, reading the title, author, and illustrator, and asking them to guess what the book is about.

- Occasionally ask children to predict events: "What do you think is going to happen next?"
- Ask for the children's opinions: "I wonder why she did that?"
- Repeat or expand what the children say: "Yes, he *does* look angry, doesn't he?"
- Verbalize your pleasure in reading, as well as your feelings about the story: "I just love to read books!" "This part of the story always makes me feel sad."
- Invite children to make comments, ask questions, respond to your questions, chime in, make sound effects, add actions or other movements, read along with you, and fill in words or phrases at the end of sentences.

The first time you read a new story to the children, you may want to read it straight through, without many side comments or explanations, to "let the words work their magic" (Calkins, 2001, p. 53) and allow children to get caught up in the story. So for a first-time reading, the following strategies work best *after* the story. Otherwise, these are appropriate to use throughout the read-aloud:

"Merely reading the book aloud from cover to cover is not nearly as helpful to emergent readers as predicting from the cover picture and title what the book might be about, stopping periodically to make further predictions from text and illustrations, talking about the pictures and making connections between pictures and words and their own lives, and perhaps noticing other aspects of the print as adult and child read and reread favorite books."

—Constance Weaver (1996, p. 72)

- Help children make connections between story events and their own life: "Have you ever done that—had a sleepover at someone else's house?"
- Go back to a page or two and talk specifically about an illustration or a word. "Let's look at that picture again. What's happening here?"
- Ask open-ended questions about the story, using *what* and *why:* "What do you think Abiyoyo is going to do now?" "Why do you think those monkeys threw all their hats down on the ground?"
- Discuss the characters, their feelings and motivations: "How do you think Susan felt when her baby brother kept crying?"
- Comment on rhyme or alliteration found in the book: "Hmmm, *munch* and *lunch* sound the same—they rhyme, don't they?" "*Green* and *grass* start with the same sound. What other words in this story start with a /gr/ sound?"

After the story

- If you read the story through without much comment, use some of the discussion strategies outlined above when you finish the story.
- Ask children which parts of the story they liked best.

- Try to make your transition to the next activity connect to the book in some way. For example, after you have read *Freight Train* to them, the children could form a train and chug over to the cubbies to get their jackets on.
- Put the book into the book area (or another area where books are available to children) so they can read it themselves later (look at the pictures, retell the story).

"The more adults talk with children about the stories they read, the more the story reading helps the children's language development."

—Judith Schickedanz (1999, p. 54)

➤ Be sensitive to children's disinterest in story time.

If you follow the suggested strategies when you read to small groups of children, it is very unlikely that you will lose their interest. If the whole group becomes restless, it is wise to discontinue reading the book—and then try to figure out the cause. Was the problem the particular book you were reading (not interesting or understandable to these children), the timing (the children were tired of sitting or were anxious to go outside), or perhaps something about the delivery (you were tired at the end of the day, or didn't like the book they chose)? Perhaps this particular group of children is more active overall. Whatever you feel is the cause of the children's disinterest, remedy the situation so they have a more positive experience the next time.

All children sometimes need to be read to individually, on your lap or nestled on a shoulder. This is especially important for children who have difficulty attending to stories.

If one particular child is causing the disruption, and it happens repeatedly, try to find out about the child's home experience with being read to. Many children who have had little or no experience with books or with being read to at home are often restless or disruptive during group story times. "No experience," writes Trelease, "means no attention span" (2001, p. 41). Here are some hints for helping these children learn to enjoy listening to stories:

- Read to these children individually as much as possible. Let them experience lap-reading with an interested adult. Parents, grandparents, and other volunteers can be helpful in this capacity.

- Even listening to stories in a small group may be difficult for some children at first. Having another adult sit next to them may help some children; others may initially need an alternative quiet activity during group story time.
- Start with short, easily understood books, such as simple predictable stories and alphabet or counting books.
- Keep read-aloud times quite brief at first. As children are able to listen for longer periods of time, you can lengthen the story times.
- Read books that build on the children's interests.

"Read-aloud sessions offer an ideal forum for exploring many dimensions of language and literacy. This is especially important for children who have had little storybook experience outside school."

—Catherine E. Snow et al. (1998, p. 179)

With time and positive experiences, children will come to enjoy story time!

Storytelling

Storytelling is a universal, age-old art. All around the world, people have been telling stories to one another far longer than they have been writing stories down and reading them out of books. As we tell stories to children rather than read aloud to them, we weave a special kind of magic. Young children become entranced by our words and by the images that the stories create inside their minds.

Storytelling can be a highly satisfying experience for adults and young children alike. It is a skill worth adding to your repertoire of ways to support children's early literacy.

The benefits of storytelling

There are almost as many benefits from *telling* stories to children as there are from *reading aloud* to them. Storytelling benefits children in the following ways:

- Functions as a bridge between children's language development and their literacy development
- Helps children learn to listen and concentrate and increases their attention span
- Exposes children to new words and language patterns
- Helps children develop an appreciation for literature
- Helps children develop a sense of story; acquaints them with the elements of character, setting, dialogue, and plot
- Fosters a relaxed and intimate atmosphere in the classroom; children begin to connect the telling of stories with enjoyment and comfort
- Encourages children to tell stories themselves, especially when familiar stories have been told again and again

- Enhances children's interest in reading and writing stories on their own
- Stimulates the imagination of the listeners as they bring words to life in their minds
- Encourages listener participation: children make predictions, contribute ideas, and add sounds and motions to the story
- Encourages children's thinking and comprehension
- Can nurture a sense of humor in children
- Provides a safe, nonthreatening context for exploring both positive and negative feelings
- Helps children develop social abilities, such as listening to others, understanding the feelings of others, and contributing to a group effort
- Enhances children's understanding of community and self
- Helps children appreciate their own cultural heritage
- Increases children's knowledge of and understanding of other places, cultures, and beliefs

"Listening to stories that are being told rather than read is a slightly different but excellent preparation for literacy learning."

—Marie Clay (1998, p. 45)

Storytelling actually has several advantages over reading aloud. It is "portable" literature; it can be done anywhere, at any time, without any materials. Unlike stories in books, the stories we tell can easily be personalized to fit the children in our classrooms. Also, because the children are not simultaneously looking at pictures, storytelling improves their listening and visualization skills.

Suggestions for Adult Support—Storytelling

Everyone is a storyteller—we tell stories informally all the time, to children and adults, to our friends and family, to the people we work with daily and sometimes even to strangers. We call it sharing personal anecdotes—the "mishaps and wonders of our day-to-day lives" (National Council of Teachers of English [NCTE], 1992). For example, when we sit at the dinner table and tell our family about an incident that happened at work or school, we are telling a "story" about our day. When children beg a parent or grandparent to "tell me a story about when you were growing up," they are not asking for a plotted series of events, they just want to hear about a time and a place and the people who matter to them. If you have previously shied away from storytelling with your children because you thought you couldn't do it, think again! If you look at storytelling as *sharing* rather than *performing,* it may be easier for you to try it.

Storytelling is a flexible activity. It can be planned in advance or spontaneous, initiated by the adult or done at the children's request. You can *tell* stories to children at the same times of day that you would be likely to *read* to them: as they arrive for the day, at greeting time, work time, small-group time, before or after lunch, before or after naptime. You can also tell stories to children at times when there are no books available, for example, on car or bus rides, on the playground, or while waiting during a field trip.

Some storytellers prefer telling stories that they've learned from books; others like to start with stories that they themselves learned as children and know well by heart. Still others like to make up stories, either preparing them ahead of time or making them up as they go along. Whatever feels most comfortable to you is a good place to start. The children in your classroom will respond best when you are enjoying yourself and the story.

In this section are several strategies to help you select stories to tell and perfect your storytelling techniques.

"Telling tales, as distinct from reading books to children, is an ancient and central human activity and still has the power to enchant audiences of any age. The ability to tell a story, no matter how short, is the educator's and carer's best life-saving kit!"

—Marian Whitehead
(1999, p. 34)

➤ Adapt children's books for storytelling.

Storybooks provide a wealth of material for storytelling. Folk and fairy tales, myths and legends, tall tales, and stories from children's literature all lend themselves to a storytelling format. When choosing a story from children's picture books, it's best to choose one that is matched to the interests and needs of your children, that has an interesting plot, and that you enjoy—one that speaks to you personally.

As you choose a story and prepare it for telling, consider these ideas:

- Read the story several times; think about it in your spare moments.

- After the story is familiar to you, lay the book aside and tell the entire story without looking at it. You will know if and where you need more work.

- Feel free to make some changes, but keep the original story line. Children should be able to recognize the story when they hear it read from a book at another time.

- Do not memorize the story; tell it in your own words, using some of the author's language and key phrases. Memorize only chants and refrains that are essential to the story, such as "Run, run, as fast as you can. You can't catch me, I'm the gingerbread man!"

- Ask the children to help you tell some stories, chanting the recurring phrases or joining in with motions. Some stories that work well with this technique are *Caps for Sale, The Carrot Seed, Koala Lou, The Little Red Hen,* and *Millions of Cats.*

- Some stories are perfect for using with a flannelboard and felt cutouts. *Polar Bear, Polar Bear, What Do You Hear?, The Napping House, Frederick,* and *If You Give a Mouse a Cookie* all work well as flannelboard stories. (Storyteller Cathy Ivins has created an online handbook with directions for making a flannelboard and story pieces: search *flannelboard + handbook* on the internet.)

Tell a story with a flannelboard and felt cutouts; then let children retell your story or make up their own with individual flannelboards.

- Try telling some stories as if you were the main character. Put on a blond wig to tell the story of *The Three Bears* from Goldilocks's point of view, don long ears to tell *Mr. Rabbit and the Lovely Present,* or make a paper bag dress to wear as the *Paper Bag Princess.*

- Record your storytelling (on audiotape or videotape); if you hear a lot of *uh's* or *you know's,* work on eliminating them.

- Prepare a short introduction connecting the story to your children: "I know how hungry you all are just before lunchtime, so I'm going to tell you the story of *The Very Hungry Caterpillar* while we're waiting for lunch."

➤ Tell stories you've heard.

Sometimes it is easier to retell stories you've heard than those you've learned from books, because you're less concerned with reproducing the exact wording and because the language of stories passed down orally is less formal than the language in written stories. Here are some ideas:

- Recall stories that you remember from *your* childhood.

- Ask friends and family members to tell you their favorite childhood stories.

- Listen to children's stories on storytelling audiotapes, and practice telling them until they become part of your repertoire.

➤ Make up your own stories—ahead of time or on the spot.

Another good source of stories is your own imagination. Come up with stories about real or imaginary people, animals, places, and things; stories about your childhood and other personal experiences; made-up stories using the names of the children in your class. You can even make up your own "fractured fairy tales"—traditional stories retold with different characters, a different setting, or a different outcome.

Following are some ideas to consider when making up your own story **ahead of time.** These suggestions are adapted from an article by High/Scope field consultant Ursula Ansbach-Stahlsmith (2001, pp. 2–3).

- Identify the basic parts of the story—the *who* (characters), *what* (plot), *where* (setting), and *when* (time).

- Develop each character; form a mental picture of each one. Different characters have different voices, gestures, and ways of doing things. Know your characters well.

- Develop the events of the story. Write out a skeletal structure of the plot—the beginning, middle, and end. Learn the sequence, but don't memorize the story word for word.

- Bring the story as close to the children's own lives as you can. Build the story around their names, with at least a few places or experiences that are familiar to them.

- Think of ways to stimulate the children's senses. Include details like smells, textures, sounds, and visual images to make the story come alive. Think carefully about your "special effects"—the sounds and gestures you'll use.

- Introduce props as applicable to involve the senses or imagination.

Sing a Story!

Stories have probably been told in song for as long as people have been singing. There are medieval ballads and folk ballads, modern-day rock and pop music ballads; even many spirituals and carols are stories set to music. Words and stories that are sung rather than recited are more easily learned and remembered by both children and adults. (How many advertising jingles of the past, cute or annoying, are floating around in your memory today?!)

Davy Crockett, Froggie Went A-Courtin', There Was an Old Lady Who Swallowed a Fly, and *Abiyoyo* are all stories that are told in song. Besides singing many of the traditional children's story-songs with your class, try setting some stories they know from books to simple tunes they are familiar with. Some preschool children enjoy singing *Brown Bear, Brown Bear, What Do You See?* to the tune of "Twinkle, Twinkle, Little Star"—and can accurately recall the entire sequence. One advantage of children's memorizing a story this way, of course, is that when they follow along in the book, and say or sing the words that are written on the page, they begin to make a connection between how the words sound and how they look.

- Keep the story line brief, clear, and simple. Though it's important to add a rich range of specific details as described above, it's also important not to overdo it and make your story too complicated.
- Practice your story ahead of time, including gestures, sounds, voices, and dialogue.

When you choose to make up an **impromptu story,** consider these ideas:

- Ask the children for a story starter, and build your story from there.
- Use real situations in the classroom as topics for stories—anything from problem solving ("The Week No Toys Were Put Away") to everyday routines ("While the Children Were Taking a Nap") to current events ("The Adventures of the Runaway Hamster").
- Any object can become part of a story: add the word *magical* or *invisible* to it (as in "this magical bowl"), then talk about where the object came from and what it can do, and you're off!

➤ Set the stage for your story.

Whether you are telling a story from a children's book or from your memory or imagination, it's important to let children know that something special is about to happen. Sit on a special chair; wear a special hat, shawl, or pocket apron to signal that it's storytelling time. Make sure the children are secure, comfortable, close to you, and feel invited into the story. Here are some additional ways to set the stage for your story:

Distribute props or puppets so children can participate as you tell the story.

- Make the break with everyday reality with a special routine—dim the lights, sing a repeated phrase, ring a bell or triangle, or pat your knees to the steady beat of a chant. One storyteller asks children to close their eyes and take three deep breaths; another uses the following chant with a wave of her "story wand":

  > This magic wand can take us
  >
  > To a land far, far away.
  >
  > Where will we go? What will we do?
  >
  > Who will we be today?

- If you have props or puppets that are or could be associated with the story, involve the children in using them by passing the props around in a basket for the children to choose from. When telling the story of *The Mitten* (Jan Brett), for example, you could prepare a set of stick puppets by copying and laminating the animal characters from the book and attaching them to tongue depressors. Make sure there are enough props for each child to have one.

- If the story comes from a picture book, show the cover of the book briefly as you introduce the story, so the children will know how to find the story afterwards.

- If you find yourself searching for a good way to introduce your story, remember that "Once upon a time…" can't be beat for an attention-getting opener!

Are Folk and Fairy Tales Too Scary for Young Children?

Katherine Grier, a Canadian storyteller, suggests that when choosing folk and fairy tales to tell, you should make sure they address the concerns and interests of small children—not all of these tales were meant for young audiences. But she, like Bruno Bettelheim (1989), believes that many of these traditional stories are satisfying and not usually troubling to children three years of age and older, especially when told without the use of visuals. "One of the advantages of telling a potentially frightening story without props or illustrations," Grier writes, "is that children seem to have an internal editing device that allows them to make the images in their heads only as frightening as they can handle" (1997, p. 3).

➤ Deliver!

As you tell the story, enjoy yourself. Be enthusiastic and animated. Get excited about the characters and events, and the children will, too.

- Have fun with the language. Use lots of repetition, exaggeration, jokes and nonsense, songs, alliteration, rhymes, foreign words, and playful mispronunciations.

- Use variety—in the tone, pitch, and volume of your voice; in your pacing; in your rhythm. Variety helps to keep the children's attention.

- When telling a story the children are familiar with, accept their comments and build them into the story. "Yes, that's what she did next, Danielle, she went right into the bears' bedroom."

- With impromptu stories, let children add their input and sometimes control the direction of the story. "And when they peeked s-l-o-w-l-y [stretch out the word *slowly*] into the box, what do you suppose they saw in there? [pause] Yes, it *was* a monster, Hannah, a giant hairy monster. And he was crying big, wet tears. Why do you think he was so sad?"

- Be flexible; with preschoolers, expect unexpected reactions!
- Add colors, sounds, and other sensory images to your story. "The mud was thick and soft, and their boots went 'bloop, bloop, bloop' as they walked through it."
- Add dramatic pauses and emphasis to build interest and suspense. "And thennnn ....the rabbit **popped** out of the box!"
- Change the pace as needed to match the action. Dialogue usually occurs at a slower pace, narrative a bit faster.
- Again, enjoy the telling of the story—have "the courage to make a fool of yourself!" (Whitehead, 1999, p. 35).

➤ End the story and bring children back to the present.

Endings should be clear so the children know when the story is over. Try one of these story-ending techniques:

- Make a comment such as "And that's the story of *Caps for Sale.*"
- Slow down and emphasize three beats in the final phrase: "...and they lived **hap**pily **ev**er **af**ter," "...and **that** was the **end** of **that,**" "...and they **nev**er **saw** him a**gain.**"
- Bring the children back to reality by reversing the strategy you used to take them *into* the world of story (such as a song, an instrument, a rhyme, or a "spell").

> Our magic wand will bring us back
> As we chant this simple rhyme,
> We'll go to story land again—
> But now it's [outside] time.

When you use the above storytelling strategies, it is very unlikely that you will lose the attention of the group. Stories have a way of mesmerizing even the most active of children. If a child does become disruptive, however, you could first try using his or his name in the story, involving the child personally in some way, or asking the whole group to do something physical ("Let's get up and stomp around the rug like these elephants were stomping through the jungle"). If those methods don't work, you could say something like "I can't tell the story when you're doing that, Jesse." That may be enough. If not, and there are other adults in the room, one of them should place herself near the disruptive child. In fact, any other adults in the room should be modeling good listening skills—not talking together or cleaning tables while you are telling the story.

➤ Encourage children to be storytellers.

Children are storytellers from a very young age. Even toddlers are often seen acting out their own stories in play, long before they can add words to what they are doing. During the preschool years, young children tell stories in a variety of ways, in both home and school environments. This section describes some of these ways along with suggestions for encouraging children to be storytellers.

"Very young children will not always tell their stories verbally, although they certainly talk to themselves a great deal. They act stories and dance them, they draw or paint them, they mold them in mud, sand and clay, or even beat up a favorite teddy!"

—Marian Whitehead
(1999, p. 28)

Young children tell **personal narratives** that are sometimes real, sometimes not. They talk to themselves and to others. They talk about their day, about past and future significant events, about the people close to them. Relating these personal narratives contributes to children's ability to tell stories when they are older. Susan Engel describes a narrative as "an account of experiences or events that are temporally sequenced and convey some meaning....Unlike a story, which is told or communicated intentionally, a narrative can be embedded in a conversation or interaction and need not be experienced as a story by the speakers" (1999, p. 19).

Young children also **create and act out stories in their pretend play**—sometimes alone, sometimes with others. Their early stories are acted out more than told, as children rely more on physical props and action than words. As children's language skills develop, their pretend play "relies increasingly on ideas, imagination, and language," bringing it "closer to the experiences of storytelling, writing, and reading" (McLane & McNamee, 1991). The increasing use of language allows children's play to extend beyond the immediacy of what they are doing. Children can add words independent of action, such as "what if…" and "let's pretend…." They can add imaginary actions that occur before or after the events they are acting out.

Young children **retell and act out stories they've heard,** either formally or through play—stories from favorite picture books, oft-heard fairy and folk tales, and family stories of people and events. Sometimes children **dictate stories,** either to an interested adult to write down or into a tape recorder for later listening (see pp. 148–151).

There are a variety of strategies you can use to encourage children's storytelling, including the following:

- Converse often with children. Extended conversations with an adult often contain the seeds of a story, long before children can construct a story on their own.
- Talk about the past and the future with young children, even if they are not yet doing this themselves.
- Talk with children about their lives, and about your own.
- Be an attentive listener. Your facial expressions, gasps of surprise, or laughter let children know they are being heard.

- Respond to children's narratives or stories with genuine interest; ask questions that reflect your interest. Occasionally respond with a story of your own.

- Take dictations of children's words and stories (see Chapter 8).

- Provide access to a tape recorder so children can tape stories on their own.

- Collaborate with the storyteller. You might ask a question that shapes the child's input; you might add a piece to his or her story, you might include the child's contributions in a story of your own.

- Tell and read all kinds of stories to children, so that they experience what Engel calls a "multiplicity of voices and genres" (1999, p. 214). Involve children in the storytelling and story reading.

- Support and encourage pretend play, which very often becomes cooperative storytelling. Nigel Hall writes, "What students of literacy and play know is that sociodramatic play is a literate activity; it is authorship in action" (1998, p. 98). Storytelling is "play put into narrative form" (Paley, 1990, p. 4).

- Place props in the classroom that lend themselves to reenactment of favorite stories: a boat and plastic farm animals with *Mr. Gumpy's Outing,* hats in several colors with *Caps for Sale,* doll bed and stuffed animals with *The Napping House.* Some teachers call these "paper bag stories," as the props and book are stored together in a large paper bag, labeled with a picture from the book.

- Use a prop to pass around during cumulative storytelling at small-group time. Wearing a fishing hat, one teacher began a story this way: "One day an old man went down to the sea to fish. He cast his fishing pole into the water and..." Then she handed the hat to the child sitting next to her, who put it on and added an idea. The story continued around the circle in this manner. Teachers supported the children by frequently summarizing the story, commenting on plot changes, and clarifying. (Preschoolers' story ideas do not always make sense or follow one

> *"The more children engage in telling stories, the more command they get over language. With more language, they can understand more detail in the stories they hear. That gives them a better idea of how stories hang together. So the better their own storytelling and retellings get, the more experience they'll bring to reading stories and to writing them."*
>
> —Marie Clay (1998, p. 40)

A bag containing a popular storybook and props for reenacting it can be stored in one of the interest areas for children to use during play.

79

logical train of thought!) "Oh, so the fisherman caught a shark, the shark ate the fisherman, and a dinosaur jumped into the sea and ate the shark. Then the fisherman went into a boat and went to dinosaur land. What happened next, Jamal?"

Reading aloud and storytelling can be pleasurable experiences for adults and young children alike. Preschool children not only enjoy listening and joining in, they also learn much about language, both oral and written. They learn about how books and stories work, and they learn more about the world and the people in it. As you read and tell stories to your children daily, you are giving them a head start on their journey to literacy.

5
Early Writing

While learning how to read and how to write are complementary and interrelated processes, it makes sense to discuss writing first because, as Marie Clay has noted, "Children are drawing and writing before they are reading" (1998, p. 186). According to Clay, preschoolers attempt to write before they attempt to read because "writing is easier to attend to than reading when you are little. In the act of writing, somehow, what you look at, and how you do it, and what people around you do, are more apparent…than the more mystical act of reading" (p. 104).

Marilyn Adams has defined writing as "a system for conveying or recording messages through constellations of visual symbols" (1996, p.13). However, when we talk about young children writing, we could be referring to any of several different actions of representation:

"Growth in writing precedes and supports growth in reading."

—Lucy Calkins
(1997, p. 52)

- Recording a message or idea, for oneself or for others
- Performing (or imitating) the physical act of handwriting
- Forming letters of the alphabet (or letterlike forms)
- Tracing or copying letters or words
- Generating words, spelling in various ways
- Combining words into sentences to express complete thoughts; composing stories

The purpose of writing is to communicate, either with others or within ourselves (to clarify our thinking). Children come to understand the purpose of writing quite early, when they interact with supportive adults who model the act of writing while talking about what they are doing. And they learn to write by writing—in a variety of ways. Since writing in any of these early forms is an essential learning experience for preschoolers, *writing in various ways* is included as the fourth language and literacy key experience in High/Scope's early childhood approach.

Early writing supports the development of reading.

The Developmental Continuum of Writing

Writing is a developmental process. Children proceed from representing things with objects (using a block for a telephone, or making a train out of chairs) to using more abstract representations such as drawing, pretend writing, symbols, and ultimately, conventional writing. We can say a child is a writer as soon as he or she begins to communicate ideas or messages in pictures, scribbles, or symbols and identifies these as writing. "This is about my doggie." "Look, I made a card for Mommy and it says, 'I love you'!" "Here's my list—I'm gonna get sugar, milk, and peanut butter."

The following forms of writing are the different ways children might explore writing along their journey of learning to write conventionally. Not all children will use all of these writing forms, nor go through stages in this order. Also, children will sometimes switch from one form of writing to another, depending on the task. (See pp. 84–85 for examples of these stages.)

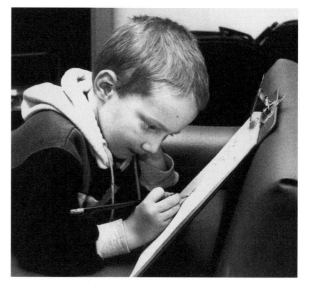

Children become intently involved in writing when they are creating a message that is important to them—a birthday greeting, a love note to a parent, a "get out" sign.

Early writing forms

Drawing

The first two-dimensional symbols children use for communicating are usually drawings. Very young children create scribble-drawings, while older preschoolers often create pictures that are recognizable to others. When young children have had many picture books read to them, they come to associate pictures with meaning, with the stories. Since pictures are much more concrete than written words and letters, it is quite natural for children to create stories by drawing pictures.

Scribble-writing

Children eventually realize that there is a difference between pictures and writing, and that the words tell the story, not the pictures. This realization can occur as early as two to three years of age, and is often signaled by the addition of scribble-writing to children's drawings, which they may identify as "my name," "just words," "the story about my picture," or something similar. While not all children engage in this form of early writing, many do. Scribble-writing often has the same graphic features as adult forms of written language. For example, children who grow up where an alphabetic, horizontal writing system is used often produce scribble-writing that is linear, horizontal, and made up of wavy, loopy, or zigzag lines—much like cursive writing.

Letterlike forms (mock letters)

Before children begin to reproduce the letters of the alphabet, they often make up their own written symbols, using lines, arcs, and circles in various combinations. This indicates that they are beginning to attend to letters in the print around them and to notice how these letters are formed.

Actual letters

The first letters a child usually masters are those in his or her first name. These are the letters a child probably sees most often and most consistently, especially if they are used to label his or her belongings. Besides, what could be more *important* to write than one's own name? Children learn to write alphabet letters in a variety of ways; see Chapter 6 for more on alphabet learning. As their ability to write letters develops, young children use various configurations.

Random arrangement of letters. As children explore and experiment with the writing of letters, they often write letters they know over and over again, sometimes covering an entire page (and often mixing in some mock letters, as well).

Patterned arrangement of letters. As their *print awareness* (see Chapter 7, pp. 119–120) develops, children begin to write letters in linear patterns, similar to those they see in the environmental print around them. They may write letters from left to right or right to left; they may write in vertical as well as horizontal rows; they may group letters with spaces in between or write them in one long continuous string.

Preconventional and conventional spelling*

Children's concept of what a word is can take a long time to develop. Some young children believe for a while that each letter on a page is a word. Another commonly held belief is that the bigger the object, the bigger the word should be: Cats are bigger than kittens, so the word for a cat should be bigger (have more letters) than the word for a kitten.

As children begin to learn that a word is a cluster of letters (which doesn't happen just by hearing adults say this once or twice), their writing takes on another dimension. Instead of just writing letters, they now begin to write words, phrases, and whole sentences. They may or

"Trying to spell words presents children with one of the best opportunities to learn to segment words into their constituent phonemes."

—Judith Schickedanz
(1999, p. 125)

---

*The stages of preconventional spelling have been referred to (since the 1970s) as *invented spelling,* to indicate that children invent how they think a word should be spelled. Although this term has fallen into disfavor in some areas, the concept is alive and well. Children's preconventional spelling can also be referred to as *developmental spelling,* if one prefers.

Early Writing Forms

Drawing

Children often write messages and stories in the form of pictures. Their early picture-writing may be simply be scribbles, like Madeline's "rainbow" on the left. Later, their pictures become more recognizable, like Tahj's on the right, "a dragon's mouth with fire coming out."

Scribble-writing

Brian's writing, "I miss my dad," is mostly scribbles, but shows horizontal marks that suggest he is beginning to notice some of the patterns in writing.

Letterlike forms

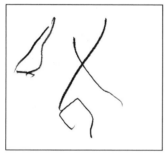

Rosita's note ("It says, 'Dear Mom, I love you'") includes letterlike forms, both curves and lines.

Actual letters: Random arrangement

Often the first letters children learn are those in their names. Tahj wrote his T's over and over on this sheet.

Christopher wrote most of the letters of his name in a random arrangement. Included in the mix is his letter-linked symbol, a cat.

Actual letters: Patterned arrangement

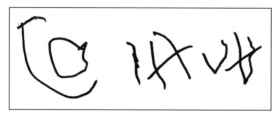

This sample includes actual letters in a conventional pattern. Joshua wrote the letters of his name in the right order, with some letters positioned backwards or upside down.

Prephonemic spelling

Nate's *"Get out and stay out!"* sign is an example of prephonemic spelling. Although it includes real letters, they have no relationship to the word sounds in his message.

Early phonemic spelling

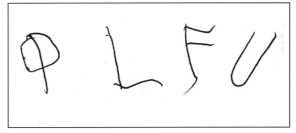

Anna's message to her Mom, *"iLFU"* (I love you), illustrates early phonemic spelling, because it includes letters that roughly correspond to the sounds of beginning and ending consonants in the message.

Later phonemic spelling

DeWan's retelling of *"The Gingerbread Man"* includes an example of later phonemic spelling. He wrote the alligator's words ("These will be good, yum") as they sounded to him, including letters for both vowel and consonant sounds.

Conventional spelling

Madeline spelled her name conventionally (followed by her symbol), then copied the names of Nya, Anna, and Tahj from the coat hook area.

may not include "white spaces" between the words. Words are run together in our speech, so it is not surprising that young writers often run written words together on the page.

Children sometimes like to copy words, or even trace them. When they begin generating their own words, some children will ask adults how to spell them "the right way," and some will prefer writing words in their own way.

Young children's spelling development typically goes through several stages, lasting from the time they start writing actual letters well into the primary grades. These stages—prephonemic spelling, early and later phonemic spelling, and finally, conventional spelling—are described next.

Prephonemic spelling. At the prephonemic spelling stage, children know that print represents spoken language. But the letters they write do not correspond to the sounds of the "words" they say they are writing. When a child writes long strings of random letters, the best response, says Lucy Calkins, is "to act as if they are meaningful, and with all the faith in the world, ask, 'Will you read it to me?'" (1997, p. 61). Even though there may be no apparent match between the written letters and the spoken words, the fact that the child intends a specific communication becomes evident when the child "reads" back the same or similar words each time he or she is asked to decode this string of letters.

Early phonemic spelling. Children using early phonemic spelling "get" the alphabetic principle—the understanding that words are made up of letters, and that there is a relationship between written letters and spoken sounds. They are able to write the letters that correspond to the first and sometimes the last sound of a word: "Happy birthday" is often written as "H B"; later it may become "H P B D." There may be some unrelated letters mixed in at this stage as well. Instead of correcting children's early phonemic spelling, adults should give them lots of encouragement when they begin to write words this way—it is evidence of their growing phonemic awareness. As children try to sound out more and more letters in their *writing,* they are paving the road that leads to *reading.*

Later phonemic spelling. At this later stage, children gradually become able to identify all the sounds in a word, including those in the middle of a word and vowel sounds. They spell words phonetically: *lik* for *like, majik* for *magic.*

Conventional spelling. The conventional spelling stage is typically reached when children are in the early elementary grades, although some preschoolers are able to write a few words conventionally—usually their own names, the names of some important people in their lives (*Mom, Dad*), and perhaps

"It is important for parents and teachers to understand that invented spelling is not in conflict with correct spelling. On the contrary, it plays an important role in helping children learn how to write. When children use invented spelling, they are in fact exercising their growing knowledge of phonemes, the letters of the alphabet, and their confidence in the alphabetic principle. A child's "iz" for the conventional "is" can be celebrated as quite a breakthrough! It is the kind of error that shows you that the child is thinking independently and quite analytically about the sounds of words and the logic of spelling."

—M. Susan Burns et al. (1999, p. 102)

a few frequently used or encountered words (*no, yes, love, exit*). Some children enjoy copying conventionally spelled words that they see in the classroom, such as other children's names and words that are on classroom labels or area signs (*art, book, house, toy, block*).

This section has described the many forms that children's early writing typically takes. It is important to anticipate and value all these forms of children's writing, and to encourage children to write throughout the day. Some teachers even occasionally demonstrate the various ways that children write— this shows children that all of them are *already* writers, and that they are on the path to writing the way grownups write. Some suggestions for supporting children's early writing follow.

Suggestions for Adult Support

The following ideas for encouraging children to write build on those already published in curriculum materials from the High/Scope educational approach (for example, see Hohmann & Weikart, 2002, pp. 361–364).

➤ Provide materials for early writing.

Writing area materials

If there is enough space in your room, consider setting up a writing area. It could be near the book area (to encourage book-making), the computer area, or the art area, where additional writing supplies can be easily provided. Add a few chairs, a table for children to write on, a shelf for the materials, perhaps individual mailboxes so the children can send letters to one another. Now you have created a place where children will find many reasons to write. Some materials to include in the writing area are listed at right.

Writing/drawing materials in all areas of the room

Materials to encourage writing should not be limited to the writing and art areas. Create a classroom environment that invites children to write, wherever they are and whatever they are doing. Writing, like reading, can naturally accom-

One classroom's writing area is stocked with writing supplies handily arranged in baskets.

Materials in the Writing Area

Paper of all colors, shapes, and sizes
Blank books (have parents make them)
Memo pads, notebooks, folders
Multicolored pencils, pens, markers, crayons
Necklace pens
Pencil and crayon sharpeners
Chalkboard, chalk
Dry-erase board and markers
Stickers, stamps, cards, and envelopes (recycled junk mail)
Rubber stamps and ink pads
Movable alphabets (letters made of plastic, cardboard, wood, sandpaper, laminated paper, tiles, etc.)
Flannelboard and felt letters
Cookie sheet (or other metal surface) and magnetic letters
Letter and design stencils
ABC picture charts or strips
Name (and other word) cards
A sturdy, working typewriter
Computer and age-appropriate writing software

Writing Materials Throughout the Room

Materials for drawing and writing

Art area: Markers, crayons, pencils; paper; paint and brushes; paint in roller-type deodorant bottles; chalk and chalkboards (also with water and paintbrushes); glue and glitter; Wikki (wax) sticks; clay and toothpicks; pipe cleaners; finger paint

Block area: Markers, 3" x 5" cards, popsicle sticks, and tape (for making signs), stored in a small basket

House area: Notepads, checkbook registers, receipt books, order forms; recipe cards; calendar, stationery, and envelopes

Computer area: Computer with age-appropriate writing software, printer (for printing out stories and other writing samples)

Outside: Water buckets and paintbrushes; thick colored sidewalk chalk; sticks in the sandbox

Materials not specific to one area: Message board; white board and dry-erase markers; chalkboard and chalk; easel paper for group dictations and shared writing; clipboards with attached pencil and paper (stored around the room and taken outside as well); file box for children's journals.

Materials to encourage literacy play

Props for office play, restaurant play, post office play, grocery store play, doctor's office play, library play, transportation play.

Materials for small-motor development

Water table: Nerf balls, sponges, small pieces of chamois cloth; turkey baster; squeeze bottles (from catsup, detergent, etc.), plastic eyedroppers

Art area: Play dough, clay, "goop"; tools: garlic press with play dough, scissors with play dough and paper; paper punch; stapler

Book area: Tiny books; finger puppets

Toy area: Small balls: golf, rubber, and ping-pong balls; marbles; tiddly-winks, large buttons, poker chips; plastic worms, popsicle-stick "tweezers"; geoboards with rubber bands; pegboards and pegs; beads and laces; lacing cards; squeezie balls, Etch-a-Sketch

House area: Old-fashioned squeeze sifter, spoon tongs

Materials for letter-making, letter play, and word-making

Alphabet charts (letter/picture/keyword), ABC puzzles, letter-matching games

Wooden ABC blocks

Picture-letter matching cards, flash cards

Old magazines (for cutting up)

Wood, plastic, or laminated tag board letter tiles

Flipcards and dial-a-word materials (change initial letter with various rimes)

pany any type of play and work for children, just as it does for adults. Besides the obvious category of materials for drawing and writing, remember to provide materials for small-motor development (preparation for handwriting); materials for letter-making, letter play, and word-making; and materials to encourage literacy play. See the list at left for suggestions for all these kinds of materials.

➤ **Encourage children to write in their own way throughout the day, anticipating and supporting a range of early writing forms.**

The following are ideas for incorporating writing activities into each part of the daily routine. As with all teacher-initiated experiences, remember to look at both the *developmental levels* and the *interests* of the children you work with as you decide which of these activities to try.

Arrival

Sign-in sheet. Keeping in mind that you will get a variety of responses along the writing continuum, try introducing a sign-in sheet to be the children's first writing experience of the day. Set out a copy of a list with the children's names and symbols on it (printed in a large font with plenty of room for the children's additions). As they come in each morning, the children find their own name and next to it write their symbol, letter, or name. While a child's name is often the first word he or she comes to recognize and is able to write conventionally, children who do *not* know how to make their symbol or letters are encouraged to make any kind of mark that will indicate that they are present.

    With this activity, you are showing the children that you value *all* kinds of writing, that writing is a progression, that they are already writers, and that by practicing whatever kind of writing they can do now, they will get closer and closer to the kind of writing that adults do. It is important to talk about this with the children *and* with the parents, to make sure that no child is made fun of or teased or pressured about how they choose to write their name.

"Preschool teachers typically accept the ways children draw and build. They understand children's need to explore and experiment. A similar attitude of acceptance coupled with supporting development is also appropriate at the writing center."

—Judith Schickedanz
(1999, p. 131)

On a daily sign-in sheet, children can write their names in various forms. In this sample, Anna, Kara, Madeline, Nya, and Tahj wrote their names conventionally, Julius wrote his first initial, and Drew and Lee made scribble marks to indicate they were at school that day.

Note to parent who is missed. When a child is having separation problems after the parent leaves, encourage him or her to write a note to Mom or Dad. This might involve drawing, dictation, and/or shared writing. (In shared writing, the child and adult write the note together, with the child doing as much as he or she can and the adult adding whatever words the child requests.) It is amazing how talking and writing about strong feelings ("I miss you so much, Mommy—I wish you would come get me") works to dissipate them.

Greeting time

Children's additions to the message board. When a message board is used as part of the morning routine (see Chapter 7), preschool children are quick to catch on to the idea of written communication. While it is teachers who initiate the idea (and usually write the daily messages), children's own message-writing can be encouraged in several ways:

After greeting time, the teacher provided wipe-off message boards for children to write their own messages. This child's message let people know that the sand-and-water table was filled with water that day.

- Provide a large sheet of unlined paper nearby, or a second whiteboard.

- Provide a box of clipboards (with paper and pencils attached) so that many children can write messages at the same time.

- Leave room on the board for them to add their own messages.

> *As he was coming into the building one morning, Zach found a mitten on the playground. He taped it to the message board and drew a question mark. At greeting time, he read his message, asking whose mitten it was.*

Small-group time

This teacher-planned part of the day is an ideal opportunity to introduce writing-related experiences. Here are some activity ideas for particular kinds of experiences.

Activities to develop small muscles for writing. Provide the small-motor tools listed on page 88; and introduce a possible activity using them. Here are a few examples:

- **Ping-pong balls and spoon tongs.** Have children use the tongs to transfer balls to different-colored bowls or transfer balls from a wide container to a tall container. A variation might be to have children play a game of beating the one-minute timer or sand timer as they transfer the balls.

- **Teacher-made popsicle-stick "tweezers."** Provide one set of tweezers for each child, and offer a variety of interesting objects for children to pick up and put into containers or into water, for example, plastic fishing worms, cotton balls, biodegradable packing peanuts, etc. (To make popsicle stick tweezers, take two popsicle sticks—often sold as "craft sticks"—and wind a rubber band around one end of one of the sticks. Place the second stick on top of this one, and wind the rest of the rubber band around the end of it to hold the two sticks together. The bulk and tension of the rubber band will hold the tweezers in an open position; show the children how to hold them in one hand and "pinch" the sticks together in order to pick things up.)

- **Various small-motor materials.** Have your small group sit on the floor in the toy area, and set out a variety of small-motor materials: small balls to roll back and forth, tiddly-winks to play with, rubber bands to stretch on geoboards, beads and cards to lace, etc. Invite the children to play with these materials with a friend, by themselves, or with you. If any of the materials are new to any of the children, demonstrate how they might be used.

Drawing and writing activities. When you have children who seldom choose to work in the art area at work time, small-group time affords the opportunity for them to use drawing and writing materials and to practice their emerging writing skills. (Note— avoid restricting children who choose to use the materials for other purposes.) Here are some ideas:

- Provide **paper** in a variety of colors, sizes, shapes, sometimes folded into a "book."

- Provide a variety of **drawing/ writing tools:** crayons, thick and thin markers, pencils.

- Provide an **idea:** "Let's make a book [or individual books] about our trip to the zoo." "Let's write stories about our new classroom fish." "What would you like to draw or write about today?" "We need some labels for the new toys we just got."

- Encourage children to add a **caption** to their pictures (in their preferred way of writing) and to write their **name** (or symbol) somewhere on the paper.

Working with small eyedroppers and colored water at small-group time helps children develop strength and coordination in their hands and fingers.

- Vary the **"paper"**: use individual slates (with chalk) or small whiteboards (with dry-erase markers).
- Encourage children to draw and write with **fingers or sticks** in individual trays of sand or cornmeal.
- Give children buckets of water and paintbrushes to "paint" with on **outdoor surfaces.**
- Take paper attached to individual **clipboards** (made of stiff cardboard and large metal clips) outside for children to draw/write about something they see: a critter, a plant, the playground, etc.

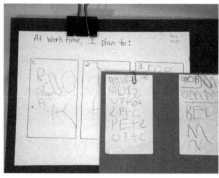

Teacher-made clipboards for children's use encourage writing both indoors and outside.

Message-sending activities. Provide folded paper and a variety of drawing/writing tools, and encourage children to make

- Cards for a sick classmate or adult
- Notes home to parents about an upcoming event
- Thank-you notes after a field trip or visitor

Alphabet letter activities. In the following small-group times children have hands-on experiences with letters:

If large sheets of paper and markers or chalk are available to take outside, children include writing and drawing in their outdoor activities.

- **Manipulating letters.** Provide letter sets plus some similar, non-letter materials for children who have not yet begun to be interested in letters. These children will still benefit from the discussion about letters that will inevitably occur. Some possible combinations of materials are

    Sponge letters and shapes, paint, and paper

    Magnetic letters, numbers, shapes, and animals, with metal cookie trays

    Letter (and other) stamps with paper and stamp pads

    Letter (and other) cookie cutters with play dough

    Letter and picture lotto cards, with photos of children and name cards for matching

- **Constructing letters.** Provide one of the following materials, and after children have had a chance to explore it, encourage them to construct things: objects, animals, letters, their name, etc.

Teachers supplied pipe cleaners and encouraged children to make letters and add them to a "letter tree" created with branches from outdoors.

Moldable materials: play dough, clay, edible dough (bread, pretzel, or cookie), pipe cleaners, wax sticks

Cooked spaghetti noodles on dark construction paper or cardboard

Plastic alpha-shapes (straight and curved interlocking plastic pieces)

As children explore and construct with the materials, make connections: "Look, Tania made a **nest** with her play dough, and Nathan made an **N.**" Wait to see if children point out the connection; if not, you could say: "Hey, I hear a /n/ sound in *n-n-n-nest!*" Be sure to notice and comment on *all* the children's creations, not just the ones who make letters.

Planning and recall time

Use a variety of planning and recall strategies, occasionally having children plan or recall by writing on paper:

- Using a prepared planning sheet illustrated with symbols and words, children circle the area they plan to (or did) work in.

- Children trace around an object they plan to (or did) use.

- Children show their plan (or activity) using drawings and/or words.

Recall time is another opportunity for writing. On his recall drawing, Tony copied the word "rocketship," to indicate what he had made at work time. Nya wrote about her experience on a prepared recall sheet by copying the words "block area" and drawing a picture of what she did. She then read her writing: "We put blocks on a stage and we had pretty dresses."

Work time

Because there are writing materials in each area of the room, adults who are partners in play with the children can easily encourage them to use the materials during work time. Following are some examples of ways to encourage writing as you join in children's play in various areas of the classroom. (Be careful not to push children to write. Your encouragement to write should be a natural part of the play that helps children further their play aims and does not interrupt the flow of the play.)

Block area. Encourage children, writing in their own ways, to make signs or nametags for roads, buildings, animals, or people. "Hmmm, how will my car know that this is a one-way street?" "Could somebody make a STOP sign for this policewoman to hold up when the children cross the road?" Unfinished structures may need a sign stating "Work in progress" or "Please save!"

House area. Encourage children to write out shopping lists, restaurant orders, recipes, letters and envelopes to mail, doctor prescriptions, directions for travel, etc. "This stew is yummy, Marco. Here's a recipe card—could you write down what you put in it so I could make it for my family tonight?" "Oh, Blake, I think the passengers will need tickets to get on your bus. How could we make some?" "Thanks for fixing me up, Doctor Amy. Could you write down what medicine I should buy at the pharmacy?"

Art area. Encourage children to label their drawings, paintings, and constructions with titles, captions, and/or descriptions of how they were made. Show them examples of how artworks are labeled in museums and galleries with the artist's name, the title of the work, and the materials used. If children have taken a field trip to an art exhibit, they might want to set up their own display with written labels for their work.

Toy area. Encourage children to add words they know to the picture labels on classroom shelves and storage containers (*LEGO, bears*).

Writing area. Encourage interested children to play games with letter tiles, matching lotto games, etc. Having premade blank books available encourages children to make their own books.

"Writing often emerges naturally as children incorporate it into their pretend play....As they assume adult roles in their play, they will imitate that aspect of adult behavior."

—Renée Casbergue (1998, p. 211)

Work-in-progress signs (which include a NO symbol) are available for children's use in some classrooms. Children use them to warn others not to dismantle their block structure or artwork.

Large-group time

Large-group time presents another opportunity for teacher-initiated writing experiences. Some ideas are described below.

"Wall writing." Attach ribbon or yarn to the wall (with spray adhesive) in both curved and straight pathways, about 3 feet from the floor, and show children how to follow the ribbon or yarn with their two hands joined. (The teacher does not make actual letters, just curved and straight lines.)

Writing letters in the air. Using big arm strokes, with your hands together, demonstrate how to make several letters (an *O,* an *M*). Ask children to try writing letters in the air, too. See if you can guess one another's letters.

Other parts of the day

Helper charts. Children may add their own names to a specific chart when they are chosen for or volunteer for a job. In one classroom, for example, the snack chart lists four jobs, and the children write their names or symbols in the appropriate box as their names are chosen.

Waiting for turns. Children may write their names on a waiting list when something they want is being used by another child—a computer or the tape recorder, for instance.

➤ Display and send home samples of children's writing.

Just as you display children's artwork on your classroom walls, do the same with their writing samples: drawings, scribble-writings, letter approximations and explorations, notes, lists, cards, stories, and dictations.

Helping parents to understand the developmental continuum of writing is crucial to encouraging children's writing. At the beginning of the year, share the information in this chapter with parents: through workshops, handouts, home visits, parent conferences, and/or informal chats. Throughout the year, send home examples and anecdotes of each child's writing, with comments pointing out the progress he or she has made.

A snack chart shows whose turn it is to pour juice, pass snacks, etc. Children write their names in their own ways next to their chore.

➤ Model, model, model!

Model what it means to be a writer—let children see you write often, for different purposes: to communicate with them, to communicate with their parents, to communicate with your coworkers, to make notes for yourself. Let them know why you are writing anecdotal notes about them (to help you remember what they said or did). Write notes to yourself during the day (for example, a reminder to buy apples for tomorrow's snack), then show and talk about what you are doing. Write notes and letters to your children, and encourage them to write notes back to you.

Just as you often *read aloud* to the children, *write out loud* with them as well. Writing aloud is when the adult writes in front of the children, verbalizing what he or she is thinking while writing (Routman, 1994). This makes both the internal and external processes of writing more visible to young children. For example: One morning, instead of preparing the message board ahead of time, you might write the morning messages while the children are watching and talk aloud to yourself as you write: "Well, the first message—I'll write down number one right here—is that Julie is out sick today, so I'll draw her lying in bed, and I'll write her name and symbol underneath. And Kathy is going to be the teacher for Julie's group. I wonder how I should draw Kathy on our message board?"

Shared writing, a form of modeling the writing process, "encourages and invites students to participate in and enjoy writing experiences they might not be able to do on their own" (Routman, 1994, p. 60). Sometimes the teacher initiates the experience ("Let's make a list of all the things we saw on our walk this morning"), sometimes the children do ("I miss Lisa—I want to send her a letter"). Shared writing is different than taking dictation, in that the teacher doesn't do all the work. Children are asked to contribute to the process ("Okay, Kari remembers seeing squirrels. Where should I write *squirrels,* the next word on our list?") and sometimes to the actual writing itself ("I wonder what letter we should write first, for the word *Dear?*").

While you are taking dictation or doing shared writing with children, occasionally talk about the various aspects of print, such as left-to-right directionality: "Let's see, I'm going to start over here on this side of the paper; this is where we always start writing." "That's the end of your sentence, Taylor, so I'm going to put a period, right here at the end."

➤ Respond to children's questions; offer information.

When a child asks you how to write something, a letter or a word, how do you respond? It all depends on the child, his or her background knowledge, and where he or she is currently. A few of the possibilities for children who are just beginning to show an interest in writing:

When writing has been modeled for children, they soon begin to initiate their own writing projects. Here, a child uses word and name cards as she creates a valentine for a classmate.

- *"Why don't you write that in your own way of writing."*
- *"Let me see how* **you** *would write it first."*
- *"Do you remember what a* K *looks like?"*
- *"How do you think* love *is spelled?"*
- *"I bet Carly can help you; she wrote that very same word this morning!"*

Some children know that scribble-writing and letter approximations and invented spellings are *not* the conventional ways that adults write, and they really want you to show or tell them the "grown-up way." To show respect for these children, your answers might be something like these:

- *"Let's look at the alphabet chart to see how to make that letter."*
- *"Here, I'll write it on this piece of paper [sound out the word aloud as you write it] and then you can copy it."*

- *"Can you find that word somewhere in the room/the writing area?"*
- *"Well, cute is spelled like this: the /k/-/k/-/k/-/k/ sound is the letter* **c**...*/u/-/u/-/u/—right, the letter* **u***, just like it sounds...* /t/-/t/-/t/-/t/—*yep, that's a* **t** ...*and then there's a letter at the end of this word that doesn't make any sound at all: an* e!"

If a child insists that you read what he or she has written, *KPLF*, for example, you could do so by saying, "Hmm, the letters in this word make these sounds: /k/ /p/ /l/ /f/. So this says, 'Kplf!'"

> *"Most preschoolers need the adult to sound out the word— to isolate its phonemes— before they can do so independently."*
>
> —Judith Schickedanz
> (1999, p. 126)

➤ Encourage experimentation and risk-taking.

As Connie Weaver (1996, p. 175) points out, "experimentation is essential for learning to speak, read, and write." She makes the following points (p. 173):

- "Permitting 'incorrect' forms in the early stages is no more harmful than letting toddlers utter approximations for single words."
- "We need to help children view writing as a multiphase process—not a process that requires getting it right the first time."
- "By encouraging risk-taking and approximations in writing, we promote increasing skill in writing."

Children who are afraid to take risks for fear of being criticized or labeled as "wrong" will have a difficult time learning to write and read.

➤ Expect children to write, and they will!

According to Marie Clay (1991), "a class environment which creates the assumption that children will write will have writers" (p. 244). Lucy Calkins (1997, p. 58) agrees: "The single most important element children need to grow as writers is the belief that they are writers." You show children what your expectations are through all the other support strategies:

- By providing, throughout the classroom, materials that encourage writing
- By encouraging children, throughout the day, to engage in writing activities

Anna arrived early at school one day and asked the teacher if she could help write the messages on the daily message board. In Anna's messages, she used some of the same symbols and words the teacher had been using on the message board. The photo shows Anna's version of the picture symbol the class uses for the song book with the word SONG underneath.

- By accepting the various forms of writing that children are already capable of, and by helping them develop new ones
- By displaying their written work and helping their families to understand and value it
- By acting as a writing model throughout the day and providing a scaffold for children
- By responding to children's questions and offering them information
- By encouraging experimentation and risk-taking

Through all their early writing experiences, young children learn many things that help them as well as they learn to read. They develop print awareness, letter knowledge, and phonological awareness. Writing is one path to literacy that young children can travel successfully and joyfully.

6

Alphabet Learning

Concern about young children learning the ABCs—the symbolic "code" used to write down our language—is nothing new in the early childhood field. Over the years, approaches to alphabet learning have swung back and forth between total avoidance of letters in the preschool and formal teaching of them. But as Barbara Wasik, researcher and director of the Early Learning Program at Johns Hopkins University, writes, "Research and experience point a middle way, a playful approach grounded in children's background knowledge and interest, one that enables children to build and apply alphabet knowledge in meaningful contexts" (2001, p. 39).

Judith Schickedanz writes that she has a "considerably higher regard for the ABCs" now than she had back in 1986, when her book, *More Than the ABCs,* was published. In her 1999-updated *Much More Than the ABCs,* she writes, "I learned from the children that it is not necessary to choose between nurturing children's love of learning and curiosity, on the one hand, and teaching them about letters or other literacy-related information and skills, on the other" (1999, p. xi).

The Benefits of Knowing About Letters

The shift in attitudes about alphabet learning at the preschool level has come about because the observations of researchers and teachers are confirming its benefits for children. Research has found that young children's knowledge of letters and letter names is a good predictor of the success they will have in learning to read (Adams, 1990). Letter knowledge plus phonemic awareness leads children to the alphabetic principle: understanding that there is a relation-

Exploring and playing with letters helps children learn to recognize them.

ship between spoken sounds and written letters. In fact, alphabetic knowledge has been identified by the Early Reading First initiative of the U.S. Department of Education as one of the four skills needed to prepare preschool children for school (and reading) success. (The other three are oral language, phonological awareness, and print awareness.)

Connections between letter knowledge and specific skills involved in reading were noted by Adams (1990) in her review of the research. It has been found that learning letter names often causes children to be more interested in their sounds and in how words are spelled. Conversely, when children *don't* know letter names, it is much more difficult for them to learn letter sounds and to recognize words.

Interestingly enough, several studies have found that just teaching children letter names does not seem to help them learn to read. "When young children are taught the alphabet using rote memorization or other methods devoid of context, they do not benefit from this instruction" (Wasik, 2001, p. 35). As Adams writes in explanation, "It is not simply the *accuracy* with which children can name letters that gives them an advantage in learning to read; it is the ease or fluency with which they can do so—it is their basic *familiarity* with the letters" (p. 62) [emphasis added].

Because children are surrounded by letters in their environment, the ABCs are neither meaningless nor too abstract for all preschool-age children. In fact, many young children are fascinated by the alphabet, and because it is such a big part of the adult world, they want to explore it, understand it, and use it, just as they want to do with other adult tools. So the challenge for early childhood teachers is in finding developmentally appropriate ways to support children's interest in the alphabet, in an active learning environment.

How Letter Knowledge Develops

There are multiple ways for children to "know" the letters of the alphabet; many of these are listed below. The list is *not* a sequence of stages—some children never learn the ABC song, and others can produce some letters long before they even know what those letters are called. Clay (1998) states that most children "will be reading text long before they can identify the entire set of symbols" (p. 52). The development of letter knowledge may begin as early as age two and last well into the primary grades. Any class of preschoolers (ages two and a half to five years) could very likely include children who have no knowledge of letter shapes, names, or sounds, as well as children who can already identify both uppercase and lowercase letters. The following are some ways preschoolers show us their developing letter knowledge (keep in mind that for each of these accomplishments, there is a continuum from knowing a few letters to knowing all):

- Child can recite the names of letters (sings part or all of the ABC song).

- Child can recognize letters by their shapes (points to or picks out a *B* when asked "Where is the letter *B*?").
- Child can identify (name) letters (points to a letter and says its name: "That's a *B*").
- Child can identify letters in various shapes and contexts (uppercase and lower-case, and in different fonts).
- Child can identify the sound(s) a letter makes ("This letter says /b/.../b/.../b/").
- Child can produce letters in various ways: for example, forms letters out of materials (play dough, pipe cleaners, or own fingers), prints letters (traces them in sand or in the air, draws/writes them with writing tools), types them on a keyboard (typewriter or computer).
- Child can recognize and use letters embedded in text (composes words out of magnetic letters; reads some words, by sight or sounding out).

Children acquire these aspects of letter knowledge at different rates and in different sequences. Some children learn to recite the names of the letters first, when they learn to sing the ABC song. This can happen as early as ages two or three years. Learning to recite the ABCs is fairly easy, as the *names* of the letters are a constant—unlike their shapes and sounds, which are variable. For example, **A**, **a**, and *a* are some of the shapes the letter *A* can take. And it can make the various sounds heard in *apple, bake, all, any, father,* and *car.* But we always call it (in English) the letter *A*.

After children learn to recite the names of letters, it is easier for them to attach these names to the shapes of the letters they encounter—to identify letters by appearance in various contexts. (This is when many children discover that "ellemenohpee" actually stands for *five* letters!) Some children then proceed to learn what sound is associated with each letter; others learn to write the letters in various ways; still others learn a little of both simultaneously.

Some children may come to you with little or no experience with literacy and the alphabet. These children, especially, need lots of exposure to and experiences with print to help them become familiar with the *function* of letters and print—as well as the names of letters.

Suggestions for Adult Support

Following are some strategies that help children to build letter knowledge. Many of these strategies also contribute to overall literacy learning, and are discussed in other chapters as well. Since letter learning is integral both to children's early reading *and* to their early writing, it is an aspect of two High/Scope language and literacy key experiences: *reading in various ways* and *writing in various ways*.

➤ **Provide a print-rich environment that exposes children to letters in meaningful contexts.**

Because the goal of learning the alphabet is not just for children to know the letters but for them to be able to use them to read and write, it is important to surround children with meaningful print in their environment, not just isolated letters. This way, you can find opportunities to talk about individual letters in a more meaningful context ("Look at that—*lunch* and *lasagne* both begin with the letter *L*"). This does not mean putting labels on everything in sight: the door, walls, windows, tables, etc. It does mean including "text that holds meaning and value for their immediate community" (Hohmann, 2002), such as children's names with their personal symbols—on cubbies, group lists, and individual artwork. It means using both symbols and words on the message board, and wherever you have pictorial symbols: labels (for areas of the room, storage containers, and shelves), the daily routine chart, song cards, planning charts, etc. It also means occasionally drawing children's attention to the print—just because it's there doesn't mean they notice it. And, it means making sure there are objects with print (including books) in each area of the room:

The availability of maps and small road signs in the block area adds a print dimension to road-building and travel play.

> **Book area:** Magazines and books (see pp. 126–127 for different types of books to provide)

> **House area:** Cereal boxes and other food containers, calendar, menus, recipe cards, grocery bags with print, coupons, catalogs

> *Books:* Cookbooks, phone books

Children use maps as they go on a pretend trip.

> **Block area:** Miniature road and construction signs, photos of local stores and buildings (with their signs visible), vehicles with print (*SCHOOL BUS*), maps

> *Books:* Books about construction and vehicles

> **Art area:** Magazines and newspapers, catalogs, junk mail, cards; art reproductions (available on postcards) with the name of the work and the artist; labels on the children's displayed artwork

Books: Books about art, handicrafts

Toy area: Puzzles, board games, and cards with words on them

Books: Activity books (such as *Where's Waldo?*), concept books

Music area: Tapes, records, and CDs (all labeled with symbols as well as words); song cards (each with picture and title); songs written on chart paper; cards with movement positions in words and stick figures (*walk, jump, arms up, tiptoe,* etc.)

Age-appropriate letter recognition software is available in the computer area.

Books: Children's songbooks, books with audiotapes

Computer area: Appropriate reading-related software for children, such as interactive stories, children's word processors, letter recognition programs, and sound-matching programs. (For recommendations, see the online newsletter *Children's Software Revue,* available at *http://www.childrenssoftware.com.*)

Sand/water table: Plastic food containers and lids, measuring cups

Woodworking area: Tool catalogs, home repair magazines

Outdoor area: Seed packets, gardening catalogs

Books: Nature guides (of birds, flowers, trees, insects)

➤ Provide and use three-dimensional letters and other alphabet materials with children.

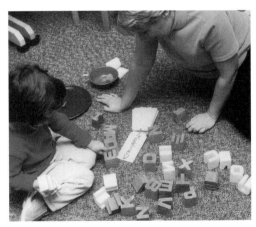

Experiences with environmental print are a valuable source of letter knowledge for children; children's letter knowledge also develops as they work directly with various kinds of alphabet manipulatives and other letter-related materials. There is no shortage of alphabet materials that are both useful and fun for children to play with. They can be found in discount department stores like WalMart and Target, in many grocery stores, and in teacher supply stores and catalogs. In addition, many alphabet materials can be teacher-made. Even

A girl makes her name with movable letters, following her name card.

beginning alphabet and phonics workbooks can be put to good use in making manipulatives—you can duplicate, laminate, and cut apart the alphabet letter "tiles," picture-word cards, initial consonant word wheels, or any other letter manipulative that might be helpful for a child in your class. Some of the most useful kinds of alphabet materials are described in the next section.

Three-dimensional movable alphabets

Children like to handle, explore, and manipulate objects. A set of colorful plastic magnetic letters that can be arranged and rearranged in endless combinations or a set of large wooden letters that can be held in both hands and traced around are much more appealing—and therefore more likely to be used by children—than a paper alphabet chart high up on the wall. And when children are working with alphabet letters, there is likely to be discussion about them, both with peers and with adults, thereby increasing children's familiarity with the names (and sounds) of those letters. Therefore, equip your classroom with many different kinds of letters that children can handle, explore, work with, and talk about, and store some in each area of the room. (For storage ideas, see pp. 106 and 108.)

Children benefit from "information about print coming to [them] from both hand and eye. [They] may be able to discriminate better the shapes that [they] can handle or make movements with, rather than the ones [they] can merely look at."

—Marie Clay
(1991, p. 285)

Three-dimensional letters (or movable alphabets) are available commercially in various forms—wood, plastic, tag board, sponge, and metal. You can also make your own sets, from laminated construction paper. Some letters are magnetized and can be used on metal boards (like cookie sheets or metal cabinet doors). Other three-dimensional letters are larger, and designed to be used as templates for children to trace around. Still others are designed as cookie cutters: these work well with play dough.

One advantage of movable alphabets is that children are learning the letters through another sense, by the *feel* of their curves, straight lines, and angles. This kinesthetic experience helps to increase children's awareness of differences in letter shapes and segments. Another advantage is that children can use the letters to create words and messages, before they have mastered the more difficult job of actually writing letters.

Textured letters. You might consider including a set of *textured* letters among your alphabet sets. These letters can be made from sandpaper, velvet, coarse paper—any textured material—and mounted on small rectangles of tag board or cardboard. (Some teachers even mount the consonants on one color, the vowels on another.) Children can run their fingers over these letters, using their sense of touch to aid learning.

"Big *A*, little *a*" sets. Alphabet sets can be bought and/or made in both uppercase and lowercase letters, although you may want to start the year with only uppercase, and add the lowercase letters later. Uppercase letters (which many children learn to write first, if they learn to write their names at home) are more distinguishable, and therefore harder to confuse or reverse. (Compare *c-e* with *C-E*; *p-q* with *P-Q*.) On the other hand, when children start reading, most print they encounter in books will be in lowercase letters. In addition, in many preschool environments, adults write labels (children's names, and labels for materials and room areas) using lowercase letters. So children need to become familiar with both—and indeed, some children will already be.

Other alphabet manipulatives

Teacher-made letter match-up cards. These easy-to-make cards can be used by children in many ways. (See below for ideas for using these.)

To make a set, draw a vertical line down the middle of 26 white index cards, and print one letter of the

Movable alphabet letter sets are available in many sizes and materials.

Activity Ideas for Letter Match-up Cards

Children can try any of these ideas at work time, or when you introduce the cards at small-group time and demonstrate these games.

+ Single-letter half cards can be matched to the corresponding double-letter whole cards.

+ The set of half cards can be used by itself, matching uppercase and lowercase letters.

+ Cards can be categorized in various ways by children:

  Whole cards into two groups: Letters that have the *same* shape in uppercase and lowercase (*Cc, Oo, Pp,* etc.), and letters that are different (*Aa, Bb,* etc.)

  Half cards into three groups: Letters with only straight lines (*A, E, H*), letters with only curves (*c, o, s*), and letters with both (*b, D, G*)

  Lowercase letter cards into two to three groups: Tall letters (*b, d, f*), short letters (*a, c, r*) and possibly, letters with "tails" (*p, q, y*)

+ Children draw a card, and see if they can find an object in the room that begins with that letter (or sound).

+ Children match letter cards with corresponding picture cards (commercial or home-made).

+ Children form simple words out of the letters, then "swap" one letter to change the word: *c-at* becomes *h-at* becomes *s-at* becomes *r-at.*

+ A child might notice (or you could point out) that some letters look like other letters when their orientation changes (*M* becomes *W, N* becomes *Z, d* becomes *p*), some stay the same (like *O*), others are recognizable but not "conventional."

Teacher-made letter match-up cards can be used in a variety of ways.

---

alphabet on each card—uppercase on one side, lowercase on the other. On a set of *colored* index cards, do the same thing, then cut the colored cards in half.

Laminate the cards to make them more durable. Store these card sets in a box or basket in the toy area, for children to use at work time. They will discover various ways to use them, and you can suggest others as you interact with children (either during work time, or when you first introduce the cards as a new material).

Teacher-made letter families. These are another kind of letter match-up cards. To create a set, make more half cards (see previous item) on a third color of index card, using large letters cut from newspapers and magazines or computer-generated letters. Try to find both types of printed lowercase letters (**a**/a and **g**/g), and a variety of fonts.

Children can use these cards to look for all the letters that belong to the "family of *A*'s," etc. Introduce only two or three letter families at a time.

Letter-keyword-picture charts. A commercial or teacher-made alphabet picture chart can be posted at children's eye level in the writing area, so children can refer to it when writing. (To prevent confusion, check to make sure the pictures represent the most common sounds—for the letter *X*, a picture of an X-ray makes more sense than one of a xylophone (/z/); *E* is better represented by an eagle or egg than by an eye.)

You can also make a manipulative using this idea for pictures and initial sounds: Divide a piece of construction paper or tag board, or even a box lid, into four or six sections, label each with a different letter, and add a set of picture cards with objects that begin with these initial sounds. Children sort cards into the letter-sections that correspond with the beginning sounds of the objects in the pictures (see opposite, lower right).

Where to store letter-related materials

Movable alphabets and other letter-related materials may be stored in various places in your classroom. Wherever possible, include sets of numerals with these alphabet materials, as familiarity with both sets of symbols is important. As they explore and talk about numerals and letters, children will gradually learn to understand the difference. Consider placing numbers and letters in the following locations:

Art area: ABC stamps (with stamp pads); ABC sponges (with paints); ABC cookie cutters (with play dough); alphabet templates and stencils (wood, metal, plastic); ABC markers; letters and words cut from magazines and newspapers (large type size)

Writing area: Alphabet stencils, sandpaper letters, laminated die-cut letters, felt letters (with flannelboard), alphabet strips and picture charts, letter guides, name cards and photo boards

Toy area: ABC puzzles; alpha-shapes (straight and curved plastic pieces that can be snapped together to form letters); alphabet cards, picture cards, board games; alphabet tiles and dice with letters (from games like Scrabble and Boggle, or homemade versions)

Letter families show a letter and its "relatives" in various forms.

A large alphabet keyword chart shows pictures corresponding to each letter.

Letter stamps can be introduced at small-group time, then placed in the art or writing area.

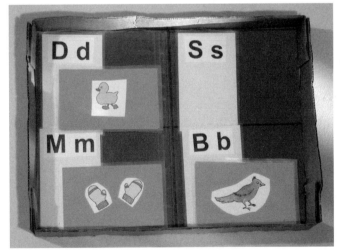

A teacher-made game encourages children to match pictures of objects with their initial letter-sound.

Block area: Wooden ABC blocks

House area: Magnetic letters and board, plastic placemats with letters printed on them, alphabet ice cube trays

Book area: Alphabet books

Computer area: Alphabet picture chart

Water table: Vinyl bathtub letters (they stick to wet surfaces)

Music area: Large laminated letters to be used in movement activities

➤ Continue to encourage children's early writing in all its forms.

As discussed in Chapter 5, children often progress from drawing to scribble-writing to let-terlike forms before they begin to make "real" letters. It is important to avoid putting too much emphasis on letters—children may think you value the stage of writing real letters more than the earlier stages. There should be samples of *all* kinds of writing displayed on classroom walls and sent home to parents. Referring to all the children as "writers," no matter where they are developmentally, is another way to encourage them along their road to writing conventionally.

When children begin to write real letters, there are many informal ways you can help them—it is not necessary or desir-able to provide structured writing "les-sons." According to Schickedanz (1999), there are several aspects of letter knowl-edge that children need in order to learn how to form letters. First, they need a good **visual image** of each letter, an understanding acquired through experi-ences like these:

- Playing with matching games and puzzles, where letters can be com-pared to each other
- Seeing the letters in familiar words like their names
- Exposure to alphabet books

In addition to this knowledge of what each letter looks like as a whole, children also need to be aware of the **line segments** used to form each letter. This aspect of letter knowledge may develop through various activities:

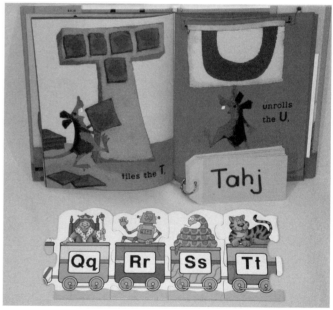

Various letter materials encourage children to develop a good visual image of each letter.

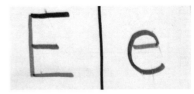

- **Experiences with letter-matching materials:** When making some letter-matching materials (described on page 105), consider making each line segment of the letters in a different color, so children can see where each continuous segment ends.

- **Demonstrations:** Occasionally play guessing games like the "alphabet clue game" described on page 115, where the adult forms a letter segment by segment, and children try to guess what letter it will be.

- **Dictation:** When taking dictation from children (group or individual), occasionally draw attention to a letter's formation as you are writing it.

If you are making letter-matching materials, consider making each line segment in a different color, so children can see where each segment ends. The letter E might have a green vertical line and black, blue, and red horizontal lines.

Knowledge about the **sequence** and the **direction** in which to draw the lines is a third key aspect of letter knowledge, according to Schickedanz. This develops as children work with the following:

- **Small alphabet picture charts:** Place one at eye level in the writing area; laminate a few others to carry to other areas when needed.

- **Letter guides:** Laminate several letter guides, and store them in the writing area. These can be used independently or when a child requests help in letter formation. Teachers may also want to refer occasionally to a letter guide to make sure their own printing is clear and consistent when they are writing for children.

The pictures on alphabet picture charts remind children of the sound each letter makes.

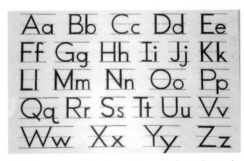

Demonstrations and dictation, as above, will help children learn the sequence and direction of line segments as well.

Clay (1991) has pointed out another important dimension of letter knowledge: the **physical orientation** of letters. Letter orientation can be a difficult concept for young children to grasp. Other things in their world keep their identity no matter how you hold them—a block is a block in any position, a cookie is always a cookie. Letters have a specific orientation: even though we can *recognize* an *F* when it is backwards, upside-down, or on its side, we always write it in an upright position, pointing to the right. In their writing, and in their play with a variety of alphabet manipulatives, children will explore and experiment with letters in a variety of positions, and will eventually (usually by second grade) learn to make them conventionally.

Children can refer to a letter guide independently when they are wondering how to form a letter. Adults may also use such a guide when they want to print for children using a consistent format.

➤ Make letter sounds with children as they write.

In Chapter 3 we discussed phonological awareness—being aware of the various sounds in our language. The activities suggested in that chapter primarily involve *oral,* not written, language. However, before children can learn to read, they need to discover the alphabetic principle—that there is a relationship between the sounds we speak (phonemes) and the letters we write (graphemes). This understanding grows gradually; children need many experiences with both sounds and letters. When children "get it," it will show in their attempts at sounding out words they want to read ("Hey, this says 'Mom,' I see the *M*!") and in their writing, when they begin to write words based on sounds they hear:

"Teachers are concerned—and with good reason—that if they regularly provide formal and direct instruction [in handwriting] to preschool and kindergarten classes, children's interest in writing may be undermined. Nevertheless, the thoughtful teacher takes advantage of opportunities to demonstrate writing and help individual children if the need arises."

—Judith Schickedanz (1999, p. 109)

"LV" = "love"

"OPN" = "open"

"IWGOTDBS" = "I will go to the beach."

Helping children to learn letter sounds is not difficult. Letter names often contain the sound typically represented by the letter—*dee, eff, jay, em, tee,* etc.—so children already have a clue to most of them. (Notable exceptions are the letters *h, w,* and *y.*) Rather than teaching isolated lessons on letter-sound relationships, it is more effective to point out these relationships in "the context of meaningful reading experiences, taking children's dictation and reading it back, and supporting them in their efforts to read and write" (Neuman et al., 2000, p. 90).

On pages 111 and 112 are phoneme charts (adapted from Moats, 2000) to help you make the correct sounds with children. The first table shows 25 consonant phonemes (in American English) and the most common letters or letter combinations that represent them (their graphemes). When making the sounds for children, you should keep the first seven starred (*) phonemes short, trying *not* to include a vowel sound (this is difficult to do). For example, /b/ is not "buh," but the sound at the end of the word *tub.* The remaining consonants (and all of the vowel phonemes) may be drawn out (or sssstrrreeetched), a useful technique when helping children to hear the sounds in the words they are trying to write (see Chapter 5).

The next table shows 15 vowel phonemes (in American English) and their graphemes. (Regional variations in word pronunciation are usually due to differences in vowel pronunciation—so these examples may not "fit" everyone's dialect.)

The information on these charts is obviously more than any preschooler needs to know, but the adults who work with them should be aware of what each phoneme in our language sounds like. When helping preschool writers to sound out words, you'll know when to give them a regular sound—like /b/—and when to tell them the letters that are "irregular"—like "ough."

Consonant Phonemes

Phonic Symbol		Examples	Graphemes for spelling
*	/b/	tub, bit	b
*	/d/	mud, die, loved	d, ed
*	/g/	peg, girl, ghost	g, gh
*	/j/	jump, wage, judge	j, ge, dge
*	/k/	kite, crib, tack, chord, walk, quit	k, c, ck, ch, lk, q
*	/p/	stop, pet	p
*	/t/	at, top, mitt, sipped	t, tt, ed
	/f/	fluff, rough, phone, calf	f, ff, gh, ph, lf
	/h/	house, rehearse	h
	/l/	look, meal, all, single	l, ll, le
	/m/	mitt, hum, comb, hymn	m, mb, mn
	/n/	no, hen, knee, gnat	n, kn, gn
	/r/	rat, wrap, her, bird, turn	r, wr, er/ir/ur
	/s/	sit, fuss, scene, cent, psychic	s, ss, sc, c, ps
	/v/	van, have	v, ve
	/w/	win, shower, queen	w, (q)u
	/y/	yes, you, onion, use, feud	y, i, u, eu
	/z/	zoo, buzz, cheese, xylophone	z, zz, s, x
	/ng/	sing, sink	ng, n
	/ch/	teach, chin, etch, future	ch, tch, t
	/sh/	shoe, sure, mission, charade, conscience	sh, s, ss, ch, sc
	/th/	thin, breath	th
	/th/	this, breathe	th
	/wh/	where, when	wh
	/zh/	measure, azure	s, z

Note. From *Speech to Print: Language Essentials for Teachers* (p. 93), by Louisa Cook Moats, 2000, Baltimore: Paul H. Brookes Publishing Co. Copyright 2000 by Paul H. Brookes Co. Adapted with permission.

* When making letter sounds for children, keep these starred phonemes short, trying not to include a vowel sound (this is difficult). For example, /b/ is not "buh," but the sound at the end of the word *tub*.

Vowel Phonemes

Phonic Symbol	Examples	Graphemes for spelling
/ā/	table, make, rain, play, great, eight, they	a, a_e, ai, ay, ea, eigh, ey
/ă/	at, mad	a
/ē/	me, these, eat, see, either, key, chief, baby	e, e_e, ea, ee, ei, ey, ie, y
/ĕ/	pet, head	e, ea
/ī/	rifle, time, pie, right, heist, buy, by	i, i_e, ie, igh, ei, uy, y
/ĭ/	sit, gym	i, y
/ō/	go, old, vote, boat, doe, snow, though	o, o_e, oa, oe, ow, ough
/ŏ/	fox, bottle, father, palm	o, a
/ŭ/	cup, cover, flood, tough, among	u, o, oo, ou
/o͝o/	took, could, put	oo, ou, u
/o͞o/	tube, blue, chew, moo, suit, through	u, u_e, ue, ew, oo, ui, ough
/oi/, /oy/	oil, boy	oi, oy
/ou/, /ow/	out, cow, bough	ou, ow, ough
/aw/	water, all, pause, daughter, saw, bought	a, au, augh, aw, ough
/ə/ [schwa]	alone, elect, definition, lesson, circus [Usually in unaccented syllables, the schwa sound is in between "eh" and "uh"]	a, e, i, o, u (in some unaccented syllables)

Note. From *Speech to Print: Language Essentials for Teachers* (p. 94), by Louisa Cook Moats, 2000, Baltimore: Paul H. Brookes Publishing Co. Copyright 2000 by Paul H. Brookes Co. Adapted with permission.

➤ Plan and support playful experiences with the alphabet throughout the daily routine.

Adults can find many natural and playful ways, both planned and spontaneous, to support children's letter learning throughout the day. Some examples have already been described in the section on alphabet materials. More are described next. Discussions about letters can happen any time, anywhere, as children become aware of and interested in the letters in their environment, and as adults build on this interest. Conversations about letters may occur when children are playing with specific literacy-building materials such as letter or word manipulatives, or with any materials that

"Because young children vary a great deal in their preparation and readiness for learning letters, it is important to expose them to the alphabet in ways that allow for success but do not allow for failure. In other words, young children should be exposed to letters in a natural, playful way rather than in a way that requires mastery (which develops later)."

—Barbara Wasik
(2001, p. 37)

include print. Using children's own names in various activities is a good way to start building interest in letters: these are usually the letters children learn first. The letter-learning suggestions that follow are organized by each segment of the daily routine.

Greeting time

Children may spontaneously notice (and comment on) letters on the message board:

> *As he watched his teacher write the words "Julie is out sick" beneath the symbols, Steven said, "Hey, that's for Steven—S is for me!" The adult replied, "Wow, Steven found one of the words that starts with the same letter as his name! Let's try to find words in the room today that begin with the letters in our names, too."*

In a guessing game at the message board, one letter is uncovered at a time to reveal a child's name. That child then gets to choose a song.

At other times, adults may casually draw children's attention to letters on the board:

> *"Look at this—we wrote, 'Corin brought cookies' on the message board, and* Corin *and* cookies *both begin with a C!" Later, at snack time, the teacher took a bite out of her cookie (to make it look like the letter C) and showed the children her "C-cookie."*

Planning/recall time

When children are planning for work time, occasionally use three-dimensional letters as planning props. For example, children could choose the first letters of their names, and place them on the large cards that represent the areas of the room where they plan to play. At recall time,

At recall time, the teacher slowly pulls the name of a play area out of an envelope, giving the children time to guess which area it is. Then the children who played in that area talk about what they did.

you could start by taking the *S, M,* and *J* letters that were on the house area card, ask who those children were, then invite them to talk about what they did there (or elsewhere).

Work time

Children may choose to work with the letters and letter-related materials in the classroom in a variety of ways. For example, in the computer area, children may choose to work with letters in a word-processing program or play with appropriate software programs that focus on letters. In the block area, a child could build with ABC blocks or arrange the blocks to form words. Storing some alphabet materials in each area of the room (see pp. 106 and 108 for ideas) is one way to encourage their use during work time; this way, even children who never choose to play in the writing area are still exposed to the letters in the block and house areas, for example. Be prepared for children who use the materials in creative ways: Rafael may try to spell out a "naughty" word with the magnetic letters, while Teresa may use them to make "vegetable soup"!

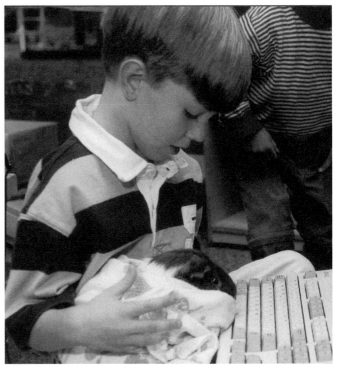

This child helps a class pet "read" the letters on an old computer keyboard.

Small-group time

Here are some letter-related small-group-time ideas:

- **Give each child a basket with three-dimensional letters**—include some letters in his or her own name, plus other letters the child recognizes and some he or she doesn't. Listen to individual children's conversations about the letters; observe what they do with them. Jot down notes about their levels of letter knowledge to help you plan the next letter activity.

- Play this name game: Give individual children a **card with their own name printed on it** and a three-dimensional letter—their name's first letter. Together, go from area to area in search of similar letters, for example, Leslie may find her *L* on the Lego basket in the toy area, and Tonio may find his *T* on the Trix cereal box in the house area. If Yvonne can't find her initial letter written anywhere, help her find another letter in her name.

- Point out a **letter in the title of a book** you are reading to your small group. See if they can find more of that letter—in the story, in their names, in signs and labels throughout the room.

- Begin work on a **class alphabet book** (after sharing many commercially produced ABC books). The first pages you complete with children might be those for the letters that your children's names begin with (you could include their labeled photos on "their" letter page). Magazine photos, familiar product labels, and children's drawings can also be included.

Large-group time

This part of the day is another opportunity for teacher-planned alphabet experiences such as the following:

- Sing the **ABC song** together.
- When doing movement activities, occasionally include **"forming letters with your bodies"** as a suggestion (this works best with older preschoolers; it may be too abstract for three- and four-year-olds):

    "How can you move up high? Show me how you can move down low. Who can make their body be the letter **T**? *Who can be a* **C**? *Can two people be an* **O**? *See what other letters you can make with your bodies."*

In a small-group activity, a teacher helps a child find his initial in a book so he can form the letter with a pipe cleaner.

Waiting times

Play the "alphabet clue game" (Schickedanz, 1999, p. 110) when children have to wait for something: Draw one line of a letter at a time, asking them to guess which letter it will be. Answer with comments as in the following steps for guessing *R*.:

1. ⊢—*(Draw the straight vertical line.)* "Well, this could be an **L** because **L** has a tall straight line, too, …but I'm thinking of a different letter."
2. P—*(Next, draw the curved segment at the top.)* "This sure looks like a **P**, doesn't it?…but I'm not done making the letter I'm thinking of….Yes, Brad, it could be a **B**, if I made another curved line down here, just like the top one…but I'm thinking of a different letter."
3. R—*"I'll draw one more short line, right here."* (Draw bottom diagonal line.) *"Can you tell what it is now?"*

This can be a fun game, if it is not overused! You may even find children playing it with one another on their own.

"The most critical understanding for young children to develop is that of the function of alphabet letters in writing. Alphabet books, as well as authentic writing experiences, help children learn the alphabet in this comprehensive way."

—Judith Schickedanz (1999, p. 149)

Various times of the day

Look for opportunities to work with and talk about letters throughout the day:

- Forming letters and talking about them can occur while using all sorts of materials, indoors and out: **Letters can be constructed** out of curved and straight wooden blocks, train-track sections, Lego blocks, cooked spaghetti noodles, yarn, ribbon, pipe cleaners, paper strips, popsicle sticks, play dough, twigs and leaves, pebbles, buttons. Letters can be drawn with fingers or sticks in finger paint, shaving cream, sand, or dirt; in water on sidewalks, in the steam on windows.

- Anytime children need to **choose partners,** you may use this activity: Prepare a basket with half as many letters as there are children in your group, then add a duplicate of each letter. For example, if you have 10 children, you might put in two *C*'s, two *F*'s, two *O*'s, two *T*'s, and two *V*'s. Ask the children to each take one letter, then find someone whose letter looks just like theirs.

The alphabet is the symbolic code that enables us to turn our spoken language into a written language, and learning to read involves "cracking the code." Preschool children can begin learning to do this, in developmentally appropriate, playful ways. Rather than using drill or rote memorization techniques, adults can surround children with meaningful print, make three-dimensional letters and other alphabet materials available to them, talk about the names and sounds of letters, and provide children with many opportunities for writing. In this way, children will acquire the *familiarity with letters* that they need to become successful readers.

7

Reading in Various Ways

The process of reading (like listening) involves *interpreting messages,* in contrast to writing and speaking, which involve *creating messages.* This chapter discusses early or *emergent* reading, the kind of reading that most preschoolers engage in (and the kind of reading referred to in *reading in various ways,* the fifth language and literacy key experience in High/Scope's early childhood approach).

Before exploring the many forms of early reading, let's first define *conventional reading*—the kind of reading you are doing right now as you read this text.

Components of Conventional Reading: Decoding and Comprehension

Learning to read conventionally involves two abilities. The first is **decoding,** or converting written words into their spoken form—for example, turning the written word *dictionary* into the word that is pronounced **"dik**-shun-air-ee." When encountering new words, children (and adults as well) use various methods, known as *decoding strategies,* to make the conversion from print to speech. These strategies include

- **Sight:** retrieving known words from memory.
- **Phonics:** sounding out letters and blending the sounds into words.
- **Analogy:** using known words with similar spelling patterns to figure out new words. (A child who knows the name *Frank* and has a repertoire of initial letter sounds can also read *bank, sank, tank,* etc.).

Talking about the pictures and words in a story while reading with an adult is a form of early or emergent reading, one of many steps young children take toward conventional reading.

- **Structural analysis:** looking for smaller chunks and words within long words, as in the word *mis-under-stand-ing.*

- **Context clues:** This strategy for figuring out an unrecognized word involves focusing on the meaning—asking, What word makes sense here? For beginning readers, the context clue is very often found in a picture ("Arthur is eating a _____ ice cream cone"). For more advanced readers, the rest of the sentence may be the context clue ("He hopped on his _____ and rode away"). And even adults use context clues to decide how to pronounce some words (as in "The pencil *lead* broke" versus "She wanted to *lead* the parade").

The second ability necessary to conventional reading is **understanding the meaning** of words, whether they are standing alone or used in phrases and sentences. For example, understanding that a *dictionary* is a book where you can find out what words mean and how they are spelled, or knowing what "look it up" means, involve this comprehension process. Comprehension skills are acquired in the course of children's oral language development and are supported by the child's background knowledge of the way the world (and language) works.

Children typically begin to exhibit this conventional reading ability—observable when they can read unfamiliar text and derive meaning from it—between the ages of five and seven years (Snow et al., 1998). As they get better at conventional reading, between kindergarten and third grade, children in the various stages are often referred to as *beginning, transitional,* and then *fluent* (or independent) readers.

Early or Emergent Reading

Long before they learn how to read conventionally, however, young children in a supportive literacy environment engage in what has been variously named *early, emergent, practice,* or *approximate* reading. At the same time, they are developing the knowledge, skills, and attitudes that lay the foundation for conventional reading—the eight key dimensions of literacy learning (Neuman et al., 2000) that have been discussed in previous chapters:

- As discussed in Chapter 1, a child's literacy journey actually begins in infancy, with **oral** language development. Children learn that language carries messages, and that the spoken words they hear represent (are symbols for) the people, objects, actions, and events in their lives. They learn how to use language, and by the time they come to preschool, most children have learned to speak and understand many words.

- As they explore and manipulate objects and have various experiences in the world around them, children are constantly building **background knowledge,** which helps their **comprehension** of what they hear now and what they'll one day be reading about.

- When their **literate environment** includes exposure to books and hearing stories being read aloud, children become familiar with the sounds of written language, the language of books, and how stories work.

- As adults read stories aloud, as well as other kinds of text (poems, notes, lists, letters, etc.), children learn about the various **types of text** and their uses.

- Children also begin to learn something about the **purpose, power, and pleasure of reading** from their very first days of hearing stories being read aloud, and as they see adults read for their own enjoyment and to retrieve information.

- Children are exposed to and gradually acquire **knowledge of print** in their world from the books, toys, and environmental print they encounter.

- As they explore print and begin discovering its importance, children start learning about individual **letters and words.**

- Children play with the sounds of language (as well as with meaning) and, with adult support, they increasingly develop **phonological** and then **phonemic awareness.**

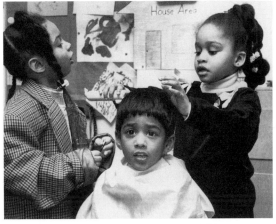

After a class trip to a barbershop, the children's pretending and conversation about barbershops expands. Such experiences build children's background knowledge, providing a foundation for reading comprehension.

Print Awareness

These last three dimensions—print awareness, letter knowledge, and phonemic awareness—seem to be crucial in the process of learning how to decode. We have already discussed letter knowledge (Chapter 6) and phonemic awareness (Chapter 3); now let's take a look at **print awareness.**

Print awareness involves a cluster of interrelated and simultaneously developing concepts about the functions of print, how books work, and the conventions of reading. A broad definition would include the following things that children are learning about print:

- That reading has various purposes: to gain information, receive a message, or enjoy a story.
- That the print is what we read, although it may be supplemented or illustrated by the pictures.
- That written text is made up of sentences, which are made up of words, which are made up of individual letters.
- That spaces are left between individual words.

- That a period signifies the end of a sentence.
- That books are held right-side up.
- That books have a "front," a "back," and a "cover."
- That directionality is important in reading: We read words and sentences from left to right and books from front to back. At the end of a line of print, our eyes sweep down and back to the beginning of the next line. We read from the top of a page to the bottom. We read the left-hand page before the right-hand page, then turn the right-hand page and begin reading the next left-hand page.

When preschoolers page through a book independently, they are showing us that they already understand a lot about how books work, even if they can't decode the words.

Early Reading Behaviors

We now know that reading is not an all-or-nothing skill: even the terms *nonreaders* and *prereaders* have fallen out of favor, to be replaced by the term *emergent readers,* which better reflects how children become, over their first five or six years, increasingly competent at the various behaviors that will lead eventually to conventional reading ability. Neuman and Roskos (1998) argue that even the terms *emergent* and *conventional* don't accurately reflect the developmental literacy continuum—that there is really no beginning or end point, that literacy development begins at birth and continues for a lifetime. They prefer to use the term *early literacy* instead. In this chapter, we will use both the terms *early* and *emergent* readers to refer to children in this early stage of literacy.

> *"[The development of print awareness] does not occur in a vacuum. It depends on growing up in an environment where print is important. It depends on an environment where interactions with print are a source of social and intellectual pleasure for the individual children and the people who surround them. It thrives on pride and affection and develops only through extensive experience."*
>
> —Marilyn Jager Adams
> (1990, p. 336)

While there is a fairly definable continuum of early writing behaviors (see Chapter 5), it is more difficult to place early reading behaviors on such a scale. Reading involves multiple skills and abilities, such as book handling behaviors, understanding of pictures and stories, concepts about print, letter knowledge, and phonemic awareness. Each component has its own developmental continuum. In addition, children take many different paths to conventional reading. Any group of preschool children may exhibit some of the same reading behaviors, but in a different order, at different ages, and for various lengths of time. As discussed in Chapter 1, understanding this individual variation in literacy development is extremely important for teachers of young children—if we are to build on their individual strengths and meet them where they are on their different paths to literacy, we need to provide a wide variety of materials, strategies, and levels of support for the children in our classroom. One size will *not* fit all!

The "Developmental Accomplishments" charts, published by the National Research Council (Snow, Burns, & Griffin, 1998), and reprinted in Appendix C of this book, represent the most useful early literacy continuum available. The International Reading Association and the National Association for the Education of Young Children based the continuum in their joint position statement (2000) on these charts. As any preschool classroom can have children ranging developmentally over a four- or five-year spread, it behooves all adults working in early childhood environments to be familiar with this literacy continuum.

While early reading development is too variable to be defined sequentially, what is readily observable is *how* young children go about their reading: whether of pictures, signs, symbols, environmental print, their own writing, or books. Children in an active learning environment can be seen engaging in two kinds of "practice" reading in their first six or seven years, shared reading and independent practice reading (Schickedanz, 1999).

Shared reading is what children do when they read with an adult, and participate in the process (talk about pictures, chime in with rhyming words, etc.). Over time, adult support can decrease as child contributions increase. (See page 135 in this chapter for more about shared reading.)

Independent practice reading is what children do when they read by themselves. In its earliest form, this can be observed as "book babbling," in which toddlers sound like they are reading a familiar book, even though real words aren't involved. Elizabeth Sulzby (1985) describes various ways of reading storybooks that young children (ages two to six years) are able to engage in independently with familiar, favorite books. These include

In shared or scaffolded reading, the adult assists as the child reads in his or her own way.

- Labeling or making comments about the pictures on each page

- Making up or retelling a story from the pictures, which may involve

    Retelling the story in one's own words

    or

    Retelling the story, using more formal "book language" ("Once upon a time..."), either *looking at the print* (and perhaps pointing to it) while retelling or *not looking at the print*

Children are engaged in independent practice reading when they look at a book by themselves, or read it to a stuffed animal, an adult, or another child. They are also practice-reading independently when they interpret photos, drawings, and other pictures ("This is me and my grandma"); when they interpret symbols and signs ("That means 'No trucks allowed here'"); and when they interpret any form of their own writing ("I made a list for the store: it says get milk and hot dogs and chips"). Sometimes practice reading occurs for a functional purpose (such as reading the symbols on the shelf to figure out where the basket of cookie cutters should be stored or reading a helper chart to see who should feed the fish); sometimes it occurs in the course of dramatic play (such as pretending to read a cookbook in the house area at work time).

Following are some "snapshots" of what early reading may look like. Notice that some of these examples illustrate shared reading, and that some illustrate independent practice reading.

- *Ben (6 months old), on the floor, plays with his vinyl book of animal pictures—he looks at it, pats it with his hand, and sucks on the edges.*
- *Keisha (13 months old), sitting on her father's lap, looks at the pictures of* Baby Faces *as her father reads the words. Later, holding the board book upside down, Keisha babbles as she looks at some of the pictures by herself.*
- *Jackson (18 months old) chimes in with words and hand motions as his aunt reads (and rereads)* Hand, Hand, Fingers, Thumb *to him.*
- *Mollie (2 years old), randomly turns the pages of* When Mama Comes Home Tonight. *She points to and names the pictures that she knows: Mama, car, etc.*
- *Roberto (2½ years old), riding in a car with his mother, points to the sign at the intersection and says, "Stop, Mommy—that say 'STOP'!"*
- *Dylan (3 years old), sitting in the book area with his mother, pages slowly through* Caps for Sale *(one of his favorite books), and retells the familiar story in his own words, as he looks at each picture.*
- *Jessica (3½ years old) reads her shopping list (a series of squiggly lines) at recall time: "It says, 'sugar, powder, chicken, and cake.' Me and Andy bought 'em to make supper."*
- *Brian (3½ years old) looks at the daily routine chart on his classroom wall and says, "After nap time is outdoor time, and then Mommy comes."*
- *Callie (4 years old), sitting all her stuffed animals in a row, reads* I Love Trucks *to them from memory.*
- *Nicholas (4 years old), paging through a library book about insects, looks closely at the pictures of the life cycle of the monarch butterfly.*
- *Jeremy (4½ years old) points to the new box of cereal and says, "Hey, here's a T like in Terra's name…does it say 'toy'? I think there's a toy inside!"*
- *Deanna (4½ years old), following the words with her finger, reads from memory*

Where the Wild Things Are *(a story she has heard many times) to her teacher at work time.*

Using Marie Clay's definition of reading—"a message-getting, problem-solving activity which increases in power and flexibility the more it is practiced" (1991, p. 6)—we can safely say that these young children are already engaging in early reading behavior.

Suggestions for Adult Support

Based upon this understanding of the wide range of behaviors that constitute reading in young children, following are ideas for encouraging preschoolers to read. These suggestions build on those already published in High/Scope curriculum materials (see Hohmann & Weikart, 2002, pp. 366–370).

➤ Continue to provide a symbol- and print-rich environment.

Because children in a preschool classroom are reading at a variety of developmental levels, we want to make sure their environment is filled with some things that each child can read. Therefore, use photos, drawings, signs, and symbols in conjunction with the written word: on classroom area signs, on containers and shelves where materials are kept, on the daily routine chart, on the message board. That way, *all* children can experience success at reading from the very beginning. (See pp. 102–103 in Chapter 6 for specific ideas for incorporating print in each area of the room.)

Environmental print has been found by researchers and practitioners alike to be extremely beneficial in helping emergent readers (Lonigan, Burgess, & Anthony, 2000)—but it does no good if children don't *notice* it. This is one reason we want the print throughout the classroom to be meaningful to the children and functional in their daily lives. Labels on every piece of furniture don't really serve a purpose; labels showing where the crayons and blocks are stored do. Throughout the day, find reasons to **refer children to the print in their surroundings**—suggesting to Raven that she go read the daily routine chart when she asks you when it will be time to go outside, for example.

➤ Provide each child with a nametag and personal symbol or letter link.

Giving each child a unique "personal symbol" (such as a heart for Mary, a truck for Jack) to identify with and to use as a label next to their name (on cubbies, sign-in lists, helper charts, etc.), is a strategy that has been used for years in diverse preschool settings. Children who come to preschool not yet able to recognize their own name can very quickly recognize their own symbol, especially if they have chosen it themselves. Even for children who know their own name, it is much easier to recognize (and read) their class-

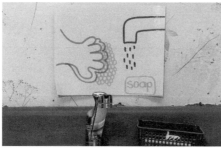

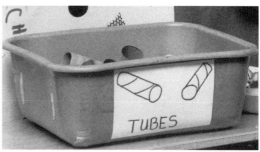

A setting for preschoolers should be filled with symbols and words that they can read, on classroom area signs, labels for materials, daily routine charts, attendance charts, child-friendly recipes, and so forth.

"Young children's learning environment should be rich in print. But more doesn't always mean better. In a room cluttered with print for print's sake, letters and words become just so much wallpaper....Put labels, captions, and other print in the places that count: where they catch children's attention and where they serve a purpose."

—Susan Neuman et al. (2000, p. 38)

mates' names—wherever they are displayed—when each name is accompanied by a symbol they have come to associate with that person. (This is especially helpful when two or more children have the same first name.) Pictorial symbols are more concrete, more distinguishable, and therefore easier for young children to remember and read, than the letter symbols that make up our written language. A relatively new way of using personal symbols is to link children's symbols to the letter and sound of their first name (Hohmann & DeBruin-Parecki, 2003). Rather than randomly chosen symbols, each child is given an image or "letter link" for a word that begins with the same letter and sound as his or her first name. So Max might have a motorcycle for his letter link, Lindsay a leaf, and Shawn a shoe. Whenever possible, the child's pictorial image is always shown with the first letter and used with the child's nametag. This strategy can help children begin to understand the alphabetic principle—that the sounds in spoken words are linked to the letters in written words—in a very functional way.

Personal symbols are used as identifiers throughout the classroom, as on this small-group name chart, right, and on children's coat hooks, above.

During his first day at school, Christopher chose a crane as his letter link. The crane was one of several letter-linked images (others were a crab, a cradle, and a crown) teachers had offered as possible choices. Christopher soon knew which cubby was his (by the label), which small group he was in (by the list posted on the wall near his small-group's table), and when it was his turn to feed the fish (by the sign next to the fish tank). Because his name was always written first, followed by the crane image, he would see both at the same time—and he was very soon able to pick out his name even if the crane was not included. The adults in his classroom labeled his artwork and other creations with his name and the crane. Other places that Christopher encoun-

A letter link is a type of personal symbol. It includes a child's nametag (Lee's) with a linked picture of something that starts with the same word sound and letter (lion).

tered his name and letter-linked picture were on his lunch box, his cot, and the family photo wall. When Christopher first wrote his name, he used scribbles and then letterlike forms. By the end of the year, he was writing all the letters in his name.

Using children's names along with personal symbols or letter-linked images in the preschool setting is a way to help young children feel successful as readers almost instantly. You may decide to discontinue the images towards the end of the year, if every child is able to recognize all the other children's names. If, however, there are children in your class who have not reached that stage, continue to use both picture and name to support these "picture-readers."

➤ Provide books (and other text) that children will be able to read.

In Chapter 4, we discussed the many different kinds of books that adults should read *to* children. The following list includes the kinds of books that emerging and beginning readers can feel successful at, as they read them *by themselves.* (For suggestions of particular books in each category, see Appendix D.)

"One of the beauties of wordless books is that children themselves become the storytellers. Each time a child goes through such a book, she tells the story somewhat differently. She uses her developing vocabulary, creativity, and knowledge of narratives to elaborate, explore, and refine the story."

—Susan Neuman et al. (2000, p. 54)

Books

- **Wordless books** can be read by children at an early age; they can interpret the pictures and create or retell a story to go with them.

- **Predictable books and familiar books with simple text (including big books)** allow children to feel and behave like readers, as they can quickly memorize the text or parts of it.

- **Decodable texts** with controlled vocabulary ("The fat cat sat on the mat") would be deadly if these were all there were to read. However, for some children, this kind of text

An evening pajama party attended by children and their families is an opportunity for independent and shared story reading and a kick-off for the classroom lending library.

brings a degree of success that soon motivates them to tackle the more difficult (irregular) words used in quality children's literature. Readers learn to read by reading!

- **Picture dictionaries, nature guides, and other reference books** help children see what words mean, in pictures they can understand.

Other text

- **Environmental print** that holds meaning for children—packaging on products they use, signs on places they visit, labels on materials they play with—is familiar and inviting to children. Often these words are among the first sight words preschoolers learn.
- **What children themselves have written** is perfect reading material, because children usually begin writing quite early and can be encouraged to read (interpret) their own drawings, scribbles, or letter approximations long before they are writing real words.
- **What they themselves have dictated** (see Chapter 8) is easier for children to read because the text is their own words, in their own natural language patterns.

➤ Encourage children to read in various ways throughout the day—to themselves, to one another, to an adult.

When opportunities to read occur throughout the day, children learn firsthand about the purposes, pleasures, and skills of reading. Here are some ideas for encouraging reading during every part of the routine.

Arrival

A regular daily event that encourages children's reading is to have children gather in the book area as they arrive in the morning. At least one adult should be there with them, ready to read books on request. Parents or caregivers who accompany children to school are welcome to join in, to increase the number of laps and available readers. Because the materials available for use during this brief time of day are limited to books (and sometimes puzzles), children will usually either look at books themselves or with a friend, listen to a book being read by an adult, or engage in conversation—all of which contribute to early literacy.

"To learn to read, a child must learn first what it means to read and that he or she would like to be able to do so. Our class-rooms, from preschool on up, must be designed with this in mind."

—Marilyn Jager Adams (1990, p. 411)

The sign-in sheet described in Chapter 5 (p. 89) is another way to encourage reading as children arrive. This requires children to read (recognize) their own name and/or symbol in order to "sign in" each morning.

At greeting circle children read the message board. Messages: 1. New computer games on computers 1, 2, and 3; 2. Gregory is here to take pictures; 3. Owen and his Dad will share a special activity with the class; and as a result, 4. Large-group time will trade places with snack time on the schedule.

Greeting time

Using a message board, encourage children to read the daily messages, written with picture-symbols and some words. This board could be a dry-erase board, chart or easel paper, or the blackboard. Locating it in the book area helps to create a smooth transition in the morning from reading books upon arrival, to putting the books away, to reading the message board together.

Adults usually write two or three meaningful messages on the board each day about events of the day or week ahead, new materials added to the room, who will be absent that day, and any other changes in the daily routine.

The message board fulfills two vital functions: First, by preparing young children for changes in their routine or environment, it helps them feel more secure and in control; second, because messages are written in pictorial symbols that even very young children can understand, the message board is a powerful literacy tool. Children can read these messages long before they can read the print that often accompanies them, and they are often motivated to write their own messages as well.

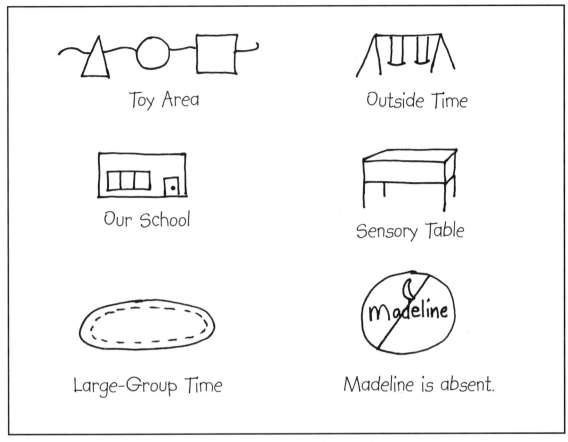

Here are some examples of symbols used on the message board in one classroom.

The pictorial symbols used on the message board may include

- Children's personal symbols (sometimes teachers also have their own symbols)
- Stick figures to represent adults (teachers are drawn with an identifying characteristic: for example, one adult wears glasses, the other has long, curly hair)
- Area symbols (crayon = art area; block = block area; beads on string = toy area, etc.)
- Symbols for the daily routine (swing set = outside, oval rug = large-group time, etc.)
- Photos
- Occasionally, real objects (balloon, ribbon, note written by child)
- Other symbols and pictures as needed: ? ♫ ☺

The symbols are consistently drawn the same way, so that once children learn what a symbol stands for, they can successfully interpret it (in much the same way that they will soon learn that the letters *c-a-t* always mean "cat"). In addition to these pictorial symbols, the message board always includes some words written beneath some of the symbols or pictures.

Planning and recall time

For **planning time,** occasionally use planning sheets or charts that contain both symbols and words. (See photos, p. 93 and p. 131.) Children read the sheets or charts as they make their plans, and can read them again at recall time as they talk about what they actually did.

At **recall time,** when children have written something (in any form of emergent writing) during work time, encourage them to show and read it to the others. This is a good time to talk about the fact that what you can write down, you (and others) can read later.

Work time

During work time, encourage children to read during their play whenever it seems appropriate and natural—your suggestion to write should build on what children are doing without disrupting the flow of their play. You may encourage them to pretend-read or at other times to actually read pictures, symbols, signs, words, or books (according to their ability). For example, as a participant in children's play, you may make suggestions like

- [House area] *"Well, I'll call the doctor, but I don't remember her phone number—Jeremy, could you look it up in the phone book and read it to me?"*
- [Block area] *"If we're going to catch the train to Miami, somebody should read the schedule over there to see what time it leaves."*

At other times you encourage reading in your role as a supportive adult:

- [Music area] *"Freddie asked to hear the CD with marching music—who can read the CD covers to find that one?"*
- [Book area] *"I wonder if anyone wants to read to **me** today?"*
- [Computer area] *"Remember, we started a turn-taking list yesterday, Douglas. Could you go read the list to see how many more names before it's your turn?"*

Building on any of the above suggestions, you can also encourage children to read things to one another. Refer to the children often as readers, as they truly are.

Here are some ideas for making materials that encourage children to read at work time:

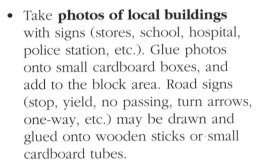

Laminated tags with children's names and other common words have many uses. At left two boys read through the tags together. At right a child puts her nametag in the pocket of a planning chart to indicate her plan to play in the block area.

- Take **photos of local buildings** with signs (stores, school, hospital, police station, etc.). Glue photos onto small cardboard boxes, and add to the block area. Road signs (stop, yield, no passing, turn arrows, one-way, etc.) may be drawn and glued onto wooden sticks or small cardboard tubes.

- Make a set of **laminated name cards,** and store them in the book area (perhaps on a ring). Children's first sight words often include their own and their class-mates' names. On one side of each card include the child's symbol and name; on the other, the name only.

- Another readable teacher-made material that is usually a big hit in the classroom is a **photo album** of the children. On the first pages, attach individual photos of all the children, labeled with their names. Then add several pages with family or group shots and appropriate captions: "Kevin's family," "Maria y su abuela [grand-ma]" "Our party," "At the zoo."

- Gather **labels of products** you know are familiar to the children: from cereal boxes, toothpaste packaging, other foods and household products, fast-food restaurants, toys, movies or television, shows, etc. Make a set of laminated cards with these labels, or compile them as a book in a three-ring binder. (This may be the first "book" that many of the children can read independently.)

Cleanup time

Let children know that they are reading labels when they put away materials:

- *"Karla, could you hand me the empty can that says 'skinny markers'?"*
- *"Adam, ask Troy to help you read the labels on the toy shelf to see where those new farm animals belong."*

Small-group time

Here are some ideas for incorporating reading into your small-group-time plans:

- Assemble **familiar books and stuffed animals or dolls** as the materials for a small-group-time activity. Ask children to choose a book and read it to an animal, doll, or another child. Hold this small-group time in the book area, or after gathering materials, move with the children to a shady tree outside or a similar cozy spot.
- Provide each child with a folded piece of paper, with **"My Book"** and his or her name and symbol written on the front cover. After children create their own books by writing in various ways (see Chapter 5), they read them to one another. Some may read just by naming something on each page, while others may actually create a story. If any children say they can't read their book, encourage them to talk about what they drew or the marks they made. (Remind them that talking about pictures is one of the ways preschoolers read.) Encourage children to read their books to their families when they take them home.
- Read a **favorite story in big-book format** (commercial or homemade). Finger-point as you read it to the children in your small group. If they want, let them take turns being the teacher and pointing to the words.
- When using **paper bags** filled with materials or sheets of papers for an activity, pre-label them with the children's symbols and names, and hand them to different children to pass out. Children will read the symbols and names as they pass the bags or papers to the appropriate person.
- Play **"Goin' on a Word Hunt"**: Give each child a blank "workbook" (several sheets of blank paper stapled together) or a small clipboard. Ask them to go on a word hunt, and "collect" words they find on classroom signs and labels. They figure out what the word means (by looking at the material it labels, for instance), then write it (in various ways, see Chapter 5) in their workbooks. Have them share what they found with the group afterwards.

- Engage children in **making books** of their own. Ahead of time, prepare and collect a variety of labels that the children will recognize. These may include classroom labels, such as reproductions of area signs, children's personal symbols, and shelf or toy labels, as well as logos and signs (with or without words) from familiar restaurants, stores, and food containers (cereal boxes, toothpaste box, soup labels, etc.). Give each child a basket containing their name and symbol written on a strip of paper, plus several labels that they will recognize. Invite them to read their cards and labels to a partner. Set out the remaining labels, so that each child can reach and read some. When everyone has an assortment of labels, give a blank book to each child, and set out tape or glue. Children tape their labels into their books. Some children may want to add words that they can write and read as well. (Magazine pictures could be used for back-up materials.)

This child has just chosen the next song for the group by paging through the class song book. (Each page has a song title and a picture.)

Large-group time

Here are ideas for teacher-made materials that children may read at large-group times:

- Make a set of **song cards.** On a sheet of sturdy paper, draw a symbol or picture that symbolizes the song (a star for "Twinkle Twinkle Little Star," a sheep for "Mary Had a Little Lamb") and write the song title below it. (You could also write the words to the song on the back, as an aid to other adults working in the room who may not know the song.) When choosing songs to sing at large-group time, you could lay four or five cards on the rug, and let different children turn each one over and read what the next song will be.

- Take a favorite, familiar song, and prepare a **song chart** on easel paper to display when singing. Some children may actually be able to read the words as you finger-point to them while singing: others will already know the song and may look at the words as they sing it.

- Make a set of **movement cards:** on each large card, draw a stick figure engaging in a specific action: marching, swinging arms, bending and straightening, stretching on tiptoes, etc. Write the word for the movement on each card, laminate the cards, and put them on a ring. Ask children to read them and "follow the directions" for a large-group-time activity. Leave them out for children's use during work time as well.

Outside time

Point out **outdoor print** wherever you find it: on or near the playground, on walks, and when you take the class on field trips. Road signs are fun to read: many children already know the word *STOP,* and other signs often have a symbol to go with the words (turns, no parking, one way, etc.). Take photos of the road, store, and restaurant signs you encounter to add to the block area (see work-time ideas, above).

You might also consider taking an **outdoor message board** to the playground when you go outside (or installing one under a shelter if you have it). Messages might include things such as

- *"There are books under the tree."*

- *"The scooter is broken."*

- *"New buckets and shovels in the sandbox!"*

Snack or meal time

Prepare a helper chart to designate who will pass out cups, napkins, etc., at snacks or meals. Children read the names and symbols each day to determine whose turn it is to help.

A child reads the snack chart to see which job she wants to do, then writes her name in the appropriate space.

Bring the **empty food containers** you used (juice can, cracker box, peanut butter jar, soup can, etc.) to the table occasionally. Let the children pass them around and talk about the words and letters they see. Save these containers for use in the house area afterwards, or cut out the labels for use in a small-group activity or as a book (see ideas above).

➤ Read *to* and *with* children regularly.

Read and reread the books that children love, and then leave them out for children to explore and read. Also, help children to *notice* print throughout the day—look for things to read to and with them.

Four types of reading that children participate in are listed below, from modeled reading (where the adult does all the work) to independent reading (where the child does all the work). As children progress along the continuum of early reading, they need less and less adult support or scaffolding.

Modeled reading (reading aloud)

In *modeled reading,* the adult does all the work, demonstrating what reading looks and sounds like by reading a book (or other print) aloud *to* the child. When reading text aloud to an older preschooler, you could occasionally also "think aloud"—demonstrating what you do when you encounter a word you don't know. For example, you might refer back to the accompanying picture, or say the sentence with a blank to see what makes sense, or look at the first letter of the word and try different words that might make sense, or try to sound it out, or see if it contains smaller words that you already know. In so doing, you are modeling what usually happens in the mind of a reader, demonstrating different decoding strategies that children will eventually learn.

Remember to read other types of texts as well as books—let them see and hear you reading notes, lists, messages and letters, recipes, and directions.

Shared reading

When the adult invites the child to participate in reading (using an enlarged text when doing this with a small group of children) we call this *shared reading*. This may be done (as suggested in Chapter 4) by encouraging the child to talk about the pictures or to make predictions, by pausing for the child to fill in rhyming words or to chant a refrain, by talking about individual letters or words, by pointing to the words as you read, etc. Or, as the child's reading skills increase, he may read a word, a sentence, and eventually even alternate pages as the adult reads the rest. With shared reading, the child develops the identity of being a reader, which contributes to the intrinsic motivation so necessary for learning (and wanting) to read independently. Shared reading also facilitates the development of phonics and other reading strategies in an authentic context.

Guided reading

If the child does most of the work of reading, with help from the adult when needed, the term *guided reading* applies. Although typically children are in the early elementary grades when they need this minimal level of support, you may occasionally have children in your preschool classroom who are beginning readers. If they need help decoding or understanding some of the words, an adult can help them figure out which strategy to use.

Independent reading

The term *independent reading* (as opposed to *independent **practice** reading*) usually refers to children reading conventionally on their own, to themselves or with partners, in need of little or no adult assistance.

"Research shows a correlation between a child's willingness to take risks (and make mistakes) and the ability to read and write. The children most willing to take risks are those who understand process, who thus see that a mistake is something you learn from."

—Marlene Barron
(1995, p. 5–6)

➤ Encourage children to write, and to read back what they write.

For many children, writing *is* the path to reading—once they begin to figure out the alphabetic principle, and start writing words phonetically, they often begin to sound out words that *others* have written. See Chapter 5 for a full discussion of children's writing.

➤ Provide an environment that is safe for risk taking.

As they go about learning anything new, children need to know that it's okay to make mistakes—otherwise, why bother trying? When babies are taking their first

Reading back one's own writing affirms the connections between print and spoken language.

steps, they fall down a lot...and we encourage them (with our open arms and excited voices) to get back up and do it again. When young children are learning to talk, we cheer and clap as they utter their first words and then phrases. When they're learning to ride a bike, we provide training wheels or run along supporting the bike until the child feels what "balance" is. And in the ideal environment for learning to read and write, a child is encouraged, cheered, and supported in much the same way—so that when the going gets rough, and he stumbles or stutters or falls down, he wants to hop right up and keep going.

Just as we share with children the different forms that writing can take over time (and call children writers as soon as they begin making marks on paper), so too we let young children know that they are *already* readers. We help them see that learning to read, like learning to write, is a process—that babies have baby ways of reading, toddlers read in toddler ways, and preschoolers have various preschool ways of reading. Likewise, when they are in elementary school they will read like first and second graders, and when they are grown-ups, they'll read like grown-ups read. If appropriate, help your children learn to answer the taunt of "You can't read!" with "Yes I can—I'm four and I read like a four-year-old."

"Children who are hung up about making a mistake rarely become efficient readers."

—Jane M. Healy
(1994, p. 235)

➤ Let children know you expect them to succeed at reading.

Your expectation that young children are already readers, who will continue to grow in their reading abilities, shows in all the ways that you support their early reading behavior:

"The evidence from the literature on self-esteem and expectations strongly indicates that the majority of failed readers have low expectations of themselves as readers and writers."

—Brian Cambourne
(2001, p. 785)

- By providing a symbol- and print-rich environment
- By providing each child with their own nametag and personal symbol or letter link
- By providing books that they are able to read in various ways
- By encouraging children to read throughout the day
- By reading to and with children regularly
- By encouraging children to write, and to read back what they write
- By providing an environment that is safe for risk taking

Learning how to read is a complex process. But the majority of children *do* learn how, and have already begun the journey by the time they come to our classrooms. As preschool teachers, we hold one of the keys to making sure not only that they continue that journey, but that it be such an enjoyable trip that our children will *choose* to continue reading long after their school days are over.

8

Dictation

Dictation—the process of adults writing down words that children say—is appropriately discussed after the language and literacy processes covered in earlier chapters—speaking, listening, reading, and writing—because it involves all of those processes. Dictation demonstrates to children that what is said can be written and what is written can be read. In this chapter we will discuss what dictation is, and how, when, and why to take it.

As we have already discussed, children are writers from a very young age, and it is important for them to see themselves as writers. Hohmann and Weikart (2002) explain that dictation "is probably most wisely used at the *children's* request. In general, it is more valuable for children to write and read their own writing than to have an adult take over this process for them" (p. 370). Nevertheless, while we encourage, value, and display lots and lots of children's *own* writing at all developmental levels, we also understand the value of modeling and demonstration as teaching tools. When we write in the presence of children, "we demonstrate more than we could ever dream possible about writing" (Calkins, 1997, p. 56).

When adults write down children's words, children learn that writing is a way to capture and share their own ideas, messages, and stories.

Therefore, when children ask us to write something for them, for any reason, we respect that request and write down their words, their ideas, and their stories—and find many occasions to read those words back to them and to others with whom they want to communicate. Dictation is an important experience for developing literacy skills. As such, it is the sixth language and literacy key experience—*dictating stories*—in High/Scope's preschool approach.

Let's take a closer look now at the various forms dictation can take and how children benefit from it.

What Is Dictation?

Dictation is actually a form of *scaffolding*—doing for children today what they will be able to do for themselves tomorrow (see Chapter 1). It is a temporary learning method, as once children are independent writers they no longer need someone else to write for them.

Dictation may be teacher-initiated or taken at a child's request, and it can be done with an individual child or with a whole group of children. The length of the dictation can vary from a single word to a detailed story. The person writing down the child's words—the scribe—could be any person literate in the language of the child (and prefer- ably one trained in appropriate dictation-taking strategies): a teacher, a family member, an older student, a senior citizen, or a community volunteer.

Dictation takes a variety of forms. When using **standard dictation,** often referred to as the language experience approach, an adult writes down a child's words, exactly as spoken, and then reads them back. This method can be used with children at any stage of emergent literacy, both individually and in groups.

After children have had many experiences with dictation, and as their writing knowl- edge and skills expand, standard dictation may gradually become **shared** or **interactive writing.** In this approach, children generate the words *and* start to share in the writing process itself: "Children contribute what they know about spelling and letter formation, and the teacher scaffolds their attempts by supplying spellings and other items of knowledge they lack" (Sipe, 2001, p. 269). Shared writing "not only models conventional reading and writing behavior, but also scaffolds children's participation in the process" (p. 270).

"Children will learn from these demonstra- tions only if they believe that what we're doing they can do, too. And so we want to include our children in the writing we do."

—Lucy Calkins
(1997, p. 57)

You might use shared writing with an individual preschooler who can write some or most of the letters of the alphabet and who has begun to associate sounds with the letters. For example, you might say, "You want me to write 'sunny day'—Let's see, sssssunny…what letter should I start that word with?….Okay, why don't you make the *s* and I'll write the next letter."

Scaffolded writing (as described in Bodrova, Leong, & Paynter, 1999) is another technique you might find useful with an individual preschooler—one who is already writing most letters, beginning to write words using developmental spelling, and want- ing to write sentences. Standard dictation does not meet this child in his or her *zone of proximal development* (ZPD). As the authors explain, "What children need at this stage is a technique that encourages their own writing, but still provides a significant amount of assistance—something in between dictating and independent writing" (p. 45).

In this approach, "a teacher 'takes dictation' by drawing lines, each line standing for one word in the child's message. The child then writes as much of each word on each line as he or she can, gradually developing the ability to write complete words and complete sentences" (p. 45). For example, Karina asks you to write "I love my mommy" on a piece of paper. As you repeat Karina's words to make sure you have the message right, you draw four lines, corresponding to the length of the words:

___ ____ ___ _____.

Then you and Karina say the message together, pointing to each line as you say the word it stands for. Karina then writes something on each line, perhaps something like

"<u>I</u> <u>LV</u> <u>M</u> <u>MOMY</u>."

Scaffolded writing has been found to increase the number of words children try to write, to increase the complexity of their written messages, to improve the correspondence between the written story and the re-reading of that story by the child, and to improve children's understanding of the concepts of *word* and *sentence* (Bodrova, Leong, Gregory, & Edgerton, 1999).

Why Take Children's Dictation?

Dictation is a valuable component of a preschool literacy program. It supports all eight dimensions of literacy learning discussed in *Learning to Read and Write* (Neuman et al., 2000):

1. Children feel the **power and pleasure of literacy** as they see their very own words and ideas transformed into print, into something permanent that can be read and re-read and enjoyed by others in a variety of ways. "Every time a child tells someone what to write on a blank piece of paper and watches her words become print, she learns about the power of language" (Decker Collins & Shaeffer 1997, p. 68).

2. Dictation enables children's own words to become part of the print-rich **literate environment,** as their captions, notes, signs, stories, and other messages are transcribed by adults and posted around the room.

3. Transcribing children's words supports their **language development** as well as their literacy development. Seeing their words captured in print often encourages children to talk more, to add details, to tell stories, to compose more rhymes and songs. Dictating "encourages children's descriptive language; when they know the teacher is writing down what they say, they often take extra pains to describe their thoughts and experiences" (High/Scope Educational Research Foundation, 2000, p. 25).

> *"Variations of the language experience approach offer yet another way to ease children into reading. The objective of this approach is to impart the understanding that anything that can be said can be written and vice versa. The basic method of the language experience approach thus consists of writing down what children say and then leading them to appreciate that what has been written is what they have said."*
>
> —Catherine Snow et al. (1998, pp. 182–83)

4. Sharing their various understandings of a common experience during group dictation can help build children's general **knowledge and comprehension.** As children represent their ideas in words and hear others' ideas about the same topic or experience, they also construct, internalize, and refine the concepts, information, and vocabulary they have encountered.

5. Dictation can enhance children's **knowledge of print,** when adults draw attention to the various features of print as they transcribe: directionality, spacing between words, punctuation, uppercase and lowercase letters, and the concept of letters, words, sentences, and paragraphs.

6. Children learn about various **types of text** as they dictate for different purposes, with adults formatting their words into letters, poems, stories, lists, invitations, signs, and so on.

7. As adults transcribe children's words, they stretch them out and emphasize the individual sounds (phonemes), thus helping children develop **phonological awareness.** "Watching one's words being written down and reading or hearing them read back is a natural and effective way for beginning language users to learn sound/spelling correspondences. The words have personal appeal because they belong to the learner" (Decker Collins, & Shaeffer, 1997, p. 67).

8. Children's knowledge of **letters and words** can be enhanced through dictation, as adults call attention to them while transcribing.

For all of these reasons, dictation is a worthwhile activity to include in any preschool classroom, where children follow many different paths to literacy. The remainder of this chapter will offer suggestions for how to use dictation in the classroom.

Suggestions for Adult Support

There is no "one right way" to take children's dictation. This can vary depending on the child or children involved, their developmental level, and the situation in which the dictation is occurring. The guidelines below can help you decide for which children and under what circumstances different types of dictation are appropriate.

➤ Take individual dictation at children's request.

Because we like to encourage children to do their own writing (and because we value all stages and forms of early writing), when a child asks us to write down her words, we may first ask something like "Wouldn't you like to write that in your own way, Angelica?" That may be enough to stimulate her to write whatever she wanted herself—perhaps a label, or a caption for her artwork. If, however, she wants to see her words in "grown-up writing," or if she has been writing and has tired of the process before she finished the message, or if she's in a hurry and knows an adult can write her message faster than she can, it is important to respect her request. Here are some tips for taking an individual child's dictation.

- When a child asks you to write something, find out if he or she wants your writing as the final product (say, a story the child has made up) or wants to copy it after you write it (in a birthday card for his or her mom, for example). This will help you determine *where* to write the child's words. In the second case, you would write them on a separate piece of paper for the child to copy from.

- If a child is dictating a caption or description of his or her artwork, write the words on a sticky note that can be attached to the back or posted below the picture (rather than writing directly on the artwork itself).

- As the child begins to tell you what he or she wants written, repeat the child's words to make sure you heard them correctly.

Children may dictate a label, a caption, a story, a message, or just need a few words added to their own writing.

Then write each word down as you say it again, enunciating clearly without correcting or editing grammar or word order. Mispronounced words, however, should be pronounced and spelled correctly (Morrow, 2001, p. 307).

> *A child says, "I wike pasketti wif meatballs. My brudder don't." The adult repeats this: "You want me to write, 'I like spaghetti with meatballs. My brother don't? Okay." Then the adult writes (while saying each word): "I...like...spa-ghett-i...with...meat-balls. My...bro-ther...don't."*

The reason we write the words exactly as the child says them is to make sure that the child understands the literal connection between the spoken and written word. For children to make this association, it must be *the same word they used,* not one that you have substituted because yours is grammatically correct.

- Ask genuine, open-ended questions during dictation to help children clarify their meaning, add details, and expand their thinking:

> *"I'm writing down Tim's plan: 'I'm going to make a boat.'...What will you use to make the boat, Tim?....[writing] 'with those white trays in the art center, and some other stuff.'"*

*"So I wrote down what you said, Alyssa—'Mix it all together.' Now you want me to write 'Put it in the oven.' Is there anything we need to do to the dough **before** it goes in the oven?"*

Schickedanz (1999) cautions us to use this questioning strategy sparingly, when it's necessary for the reading audience's understanding—for instance, when the child is dictating a recipe or thank-you card, but not when the child is dictating a story for his or her own pleasure. As in other adult-child interactions, "bombarding children with too many questions…is likely to discourage them from talking fully and freely" (Epstein, Hohmann, & Hohmann, 2001, p. 16).

- If any of the children speak a primary language that you do not know, ask for volunteers who *do* understand the language to work with these children so that they have many opportunities to see their own words written down. This strategy is supported by current research in bilingual learning showing that children are more successful when they learn to read the language in which they are orally proficient and then transfer those skills to English (Burns et al., 1999).

➤ Take group dictation.

Many of the suggestions listed above for taking dictation from individual children also apply to taking dictation in group situations. In addition, consider the following ideas for group dictations:

- The dictations may be planned ahead (asking for children's made-up endings to a story, perhaps) or arise spontaneously (several children want to create a group get-well card for another child). Dictations may take place in a small group or with the whole class.

- When taking dictation with a group, the paper should be positioned—and your lettering should be large enough—for all to see. An art easel or flip-chart stand works well for this, or you can tape the paper to a wall.

At left a child points out a word he recognizes in his own part of a group story. Below, the teacher reads back the whole story the group has dictated.

- The children may decide as a group what message they want to convey, and the sentences may be jointly created (as in a story or a thank-you letter), or each child may add his or her own idea (as in a list of favorite foods). Either way, make sure that every child has a chance to contribute to the final product (even if it is done over a period of time rather than at one sitting).

- When it is appropriate—when making a list, for example—be sure to include each child's name and symbol or letter link along with his or her contribution. For example, precede Hailey's sentence with "♥ Hailey says…," or add the child's name/symbol after the dictation. (See examples of children's contributions to group dictations, pp. 146 & 148.)

One day I saw a rainbow tree and it was big! Then I saw my babysitter and she had Henry. Then I asked my mom if I could go to my babysitter's house and she said, "Yes!" And then after I stayed for a little while my mom came to pick me and Henry up.

By: MADELIV

By typing Madeline's dictation into the computer, her teacher modeled a link between speech, literacy, and technology. Madeline signed her dictation in her own way.

What To Take As Dictation

As Snow et al. (1998) write, "The range of opportunities for capturing talk in writing is enormous" (p. 183). Some ideas for what to write for children are listed below; the children in your classroom will most likely come up with additional ideas.

Individual dictation (taken upon children's request)

Names—on a child's personal possessions, plans, and work products (This example is so obvious that we tend to forget it, yet children often ask adults to write their names on things. Since the letters in their names are often the first letters children learn, taking this type of dictation offers a primary learning experience for them.)

Labels (for a new area in the room, for classroom materials, for personal items)

Captions on children's artwork

Props for role playing and other work activities (such as menus, traffic signs, party invitations)

Child-authored and illustrated storybooks (Children might draw the pictures first and dictate the story afterwards, or vice versa.)

Notes on holiday cards they have made

Notes and messages to each other (A message center or post office encourages this.)

Songs, rhymes, and chants that an individual child makes up spontaneously

Group dictation

Songs, rhymes, and chants that children make up as a group

Stories they make up together

Rules for a game they've made up

Each child's favorite food or toys

Plans for (or recall of) work-time activities

Places they'd like to go on a class field trip

Shared experiences, with comments from each child ("Our train ride")

Children's expectations *before* a trip or experience ("What we want to do at the park")

Children's reactions *after* a trip or experience ("What we liked best about the farm")

Children's recollections at the end of the day ("What we did today")

Small-group problem-solving discussions ("How can we stop fighting over the red wagon?")

➤ Transcribe children's dictation on the computer.

Children's word-processing programs that use large letters, such as *KidWorks Deluxe* (Knowledge Adventure), *Dr. Peet's Talk/Writer* (Interest-Driven Learning, Inc.), and *Clicker 4* (Crick Software), are excellent for transcribing both individual and group-generated dictations. However, you can use any word-processing program to type in dictations; simply use a large font. When the text is printed out, you'll have pages that can be illustrated and made into child-authored books. Keep these books in the book area, and read them frequently to individual children and with small groups of children. You can make copies of these class-authored books to send home to parents as well.

When you type children's words and stories into the computer, you are not only demonstrating a link between speech, literacy, and technology, you are modeling another important skill (typing) that children will soon be doing for themselves.

➤ Take dictation throughout the daily routine.

Be alert for any opportunity to take dictation from children. Remember to read and re-read the things they have dictated, whenever it seems appropriate, so that their writing does not simply become part of the room decoration. Below are some ideas of what an individual or group dictation might look like during various times in the daily routine.

Arrival/greeting time

On a Monday morning when the children come in with lots of news to share about their weekend activities, write down a sentence from each child on a large sheet of paper:

> *"I stayed with Grandma," said Keisha.*
>
> *"We went to that place with rides," said Petie.*
>
> *"I watched cartoons," said Max.*
>
> *"My brother throwed up," said Tonio.*

Or, the children might want to dictate something to be added to the message board:

> *"Stephanie brought us a special treat for snack today. What would you like me to write about it on the message board, Stephanie?…Okay: 'Stephanie…has…cookies…for…us!'"*

You could also add symbols to this message, perhaps below the words:

> *Stephanie   has   cookies   for us!*

Planning and recall time

During planning time, write down children's plans for work time as they relate them to you. At recall time, read the plans back to them and add a sentence as children tell you what they actually did at work time (see box, below). They may want to contribute to the writing process as well.

Another recall strategy is to ask the children to draw a picture of what they did for recall, perhaps in a journal. Some of the children (like Myles, right) may want to dictate words as well as draw.

Work time; Outside time

At work time and outside time, you might take dictation at a child's request. A child may ask you to write a caption for his or her painting or to type a story on the computer. At outside time, you may be asked to make a traffic sign needed right away, or to write a note to someone's mother.

Small-group time

Take the easel outside one day for small-group time, and make a list of all the "nature things" children find on the playground. Be prepared for surprises as they show you their "finds" and make observations (see next page):

Myles's recall drawing of what he did at work time goes with the story he dictated: "This is what Dali and me played. This was Dali in our fighting costumes. This is the race track and Dali and me zoomed our car down the very big race track."

Dictation at Planning and Recall Time

What we plan to do	What we did at work time
Dylan: "I'm going to play in the block area with Eli and we're going to make a spaceship."	**Dylan** (drew a picture of two people, himself and Eli).
Eli: "I'm going with Dylan."	**Eli** (copied his name from a wall chart, and drew a block symbol and art symbol): "We went to the art area too, so we could make a shield to fight the bad guys."
Caroline: "Me and Ashanti want to paint, don't we?"	**Caroline:** "I painted the blue picture. See it over there?"
Ashanti: "Yep, we're painting on the easels."	**Ashanti:** "I worked on the computer and listened to tapes. And painted, too."
Evan: "I'm just thinking…"	**Evan:** "I was in the house area with Jenna and Jonah. We went to a wedding."

"There's spiders on the climber!"—Jamal

"I see lots of flowers."—Midori

"There's the garbage truck!"—Pablo

"I hear the train."—Carrie

"There's an airplane in the sky."—Kaitlyn

Large-group time

Before a visit to the local pet store, ask the children to help think of things to buy for the classroom, and write them down on a list:

guinea pig food

guinea pig treats

exercise ball

new toys

new fish

fish food

At the store, read the items and check them off as you get them.

After a field trip have the children dictate their comments as part of a thank-you letter. Remember to identify who said what so the children are recognized for their contributions.

➤ Encourage children to create stories for dictation.

Listening to children's stories—whether they tell them directly to you, as they talk to themselves, or as part of their play with others—is an excellent way to encourage *more* storytelling (see Chapter 4, pp. 78–80). Sometimes you may want to simply listen to a child's story; however, there may be times when you (or the child author) want to capture these stories in permanent form, either in writing or on audiotape. These methods are discussed below.

Recording dictated stories

Dictated stories may be recorded in several ways: directly transcribed by an adult as the child talks, tape-recorded and then transcribed later by an adult, or tape-recorded and not transcribed.

Adult-recorded dictation is really a one-on-one activity; as with lap-reading, classroom volunteers are invaluable in this situation! Parents, college students, community volunteers, older elementary students, anyone who will sit with a child and write down his or her story (in the child's exact words) can be a scribe. Teachers who do not have an assistant can take dictation themselves.

Here are some ideas for encouraging and recording dictated stories:

- **Retelling familiar stories.** After children are familiar with a story you have read many times *(The Three Billy Goats Gruff* or *Where the Wild Things Are,* for example), ask them to retell it, perhaps as a small-group activity, and transcribe their version.

- **Caption for a child's drawing.** When a child makes a drawing, ask if he or she would like to write or dictate a word or sentence about it. If so, you can say something like "Wow! This sounds like a story. I wonder what happens next?" Write down what the child says on another piece of paper, leaving room for the expanded story to be illustrated. If the child wishes, staple several blank pages to the first page for him or her to continue the story. Include a page for the book's cover. *Variation:* Use an interesting magazine picture, art print, post card, or photograph in place of the child's own drawing. Glue it onto a piece of plain paper and use as a story starter. Attach additional sheets of paper as the story grows.

- **Bookmaking.** Have "blank books" handy (pre-stapled sheets of paper) for children to draw a picture on each page and to dictate a story that goes with the pictures. *Variation:* If the child already has a story to tell you, he or she can illustrate it *after* dictating it to you. "When words are down *before* pictures are drawn, the illustrations are usually more directly linked to the sentences at the bottom of the page. That helps the child read the words later" (Drummond, 1997, p. 2). Try transcribing one idea or action per page.

- **Stories without pictures.** Children's made-up stories don't *have* to be illustrated, and they don't have to be long. Early stories are often only one sentence long. If asking children for a story draws a blank, ask them to tell you about an adventure or a dream instead (Clemens, cited in Drummond, 1997). Or, try prompting them with "Once upon a time…" as an opener. Holly, a four-year-old who loves the *Daisy* books, dictated this story one day:

  > *"Daisy found a giraffe and a mama. Daisy was chasing a butterfly and swimming away. When she gets closer to her mama she'll stay close because she found her."*

Another way to record stories is to have children **self-record** them at a time and place of their own choosing, using a tape recorder. This is often more appealing to a shy child than telling the story to an adult. It is wise to first establish a recording rule—when children are done recording, they press the "stop" button and *do not rewind* to listen to it. When everyone who wants to record has had a turn, you can listen to all the stories as a group. Check with children ahead of time to make sure it's okay to play back their story for the group. *Variation one:* Give children individual tapes to record on whenever they want. You'll have a progressive oral record of each child, and the tapes can be shared with families. *Variation two:* Transcribe the tape-recorded stories later so that they are in written format, and you can read them to the group the next day. Teagan, a four-year-old, recorded this story, and added "Once upon a time…" to the beginning when he heard it read aloud:

"The Fire Breathing Dinosaur

He went to a city and a town called Workville. He went to a tower called the Rescue Over Big Water. He blew his fire, that came from his mouth, and he tried to knock over the tower. All the people were scared and there was a truck called the 'lookout truck'—it was really called the 'Working Building Help Truck,' the 'lookout truck' was its nickname. All the knights captured him and put him in the dinosaur prison. He didn't know how to get out. All the guards watched him. The End"

Acting out dictated stories

You may find that some children are not all that interested in dictating stories. One way to encourage them is to have them create stories for the group to act out. Vivian Paley (1981) found that many children, especially boys, showed no interest in dictating stories to her until the class started acting them out.

Many young children are accustomed to acting out informal stories in their pretend play: "You be the dad, you be the baby, and I'm the mommy. We gotta go now—here comes the bus." And they often act out parts of stories they know from familiar movies, television shows, and books. With a little encouragement, children will be able to act out the stories they create themselves.

When you introduce story enactment, read children's dictated stories during

At the adult's suggestion, a child and her teacher reenact a story the child dictated to the adult earlier.

large-group time and ask who wants to have their stories acted out with the group. Or, you might choose one day a week as Story Day. Post a list of several names ahead of time of children who want to act out their stories, then meet with them individually during work time on Story Day to write down their stories. Authors can choose the actors and direct the enactment of their stories later that day. Characters can be both animate and inanimate, and many children can play the same part. For example, an ocean could be played by 10–15 children. Help the author/director decide where each character will be placed, and then begin to read the story, slowly, pausing for the action (if any) to occur.

As Drummond suggests, "Clap and cheer at the end. Hooray! It is marvelous to write a story, no matter how rudimental the first attempts may be. Really be enthusiastic and the children will be, too" (1997, p. 2).

As we take dictation for children, we are clearly demonstrating the link between speaking, listening, writing, and reading. Seeing their spoken words being turned into print—whether it be in stories, sentences, or single words—is one more way that young children learn what this "reading and writing stuff" is all about.

9

Language and Literacy Assessment in Preschool Settings

The preceding chapters have delineated the development of young children's emerging language and literacy while providing many suggestions for supporting children in preschool settings. How is a teacher to decide which of these ideas to use with which children? The answer—assessment points the way.

Assessment and instruction are closely tied; they are actually complementary processes. We assess to find out what we want children to learn in our programs, how individual children are doing, and how we can improve both their learning and our teaching. At the same time, we plan learning opportunities for children in whatever areas our assessment process indicates they are ready for next. This is not the same as "teaching to the test"—it is finding out where each child is developmentally in order to plan appropriate instruction based on curriculum goals.

Assessment is closely tied to teaching—it draws upon daily observations and indicates which learning opportunities children are ready for next.

While this chapter focuses on the assessment of language and literacy, it is important to keep in mind two things: First, we assess *all areas* of children's development, not just their language and literacy. We don't want to lose sight of the importance of the other cognitive areas, or of children's social, emotional, and physical development. Second, all these areas are interwoven. Language and literacy learning does not occur in a vacuum; it both depends upon and influences children's development in other areas.

With that in mind, let's look at some definitions related to assessment in general:

- **Screening** is a brief, one-time procedure, often conducted upon the child's enrollment. It is used to identify the need for special services; if results indicate a cause for concern, the child is then referred for a more in-depth evaluation.

- **Assessment,** as defined in the 1990 joint position statement of NAEYC and NAECS/SDE (reprinted in Bredekamp & Rosegrant, 1992, p. 10), is "the process of observing, recording, and otherwise documenting the work children do and how they do it, as a basis for a variety of educational decisions that affect the child"—in other words, collecting the data that will inform instructional planning for children.

- **Evaluation** is the process of summarizing, interpreting, and reflecting upon that data. Data may be examined at the level of the individual child, the classroom, or of a larger unit, such as all the programs in a center or agency.

As we discuss assessment in this chapter, we will be referring to the second and third definitions: the ongoing collection of data on the children and what we do with that data after we collect it.

When discussing the literacy assessment of young children, it is useful to keep some guiding principles in mind (Neuman et al., 2000, p. 104):

Literacy assessment

- "Should support children's development and literacy learning"

- "Should take many different forms"

- "Must avoid cultural bias"

- "Should encourage children to observe and reflect on their own learning progress"

- "Should shed light on what children are able to do as well as the areas where they need further work"

"Teachers, administrators, parents, policymakers—all of us need to keep in mind that language and literacy assessment is a means and not an end in itself. As such, it must be undertaken and conducted by responsible and informed adults for children's benefit, with the ultimate goal of assisting them to become lifelong literacy learners."

—Susan B. Neuman et al. (2000, p. 110)

Reasons for Assessing Language and Literacy

Why assess language and literacy? When classroom language and literacy assessments are authentic and developmentally appropriate, everyone concerned benefits:

- **Teachers** become more familiar with the developmental language and literacy continuum as they participate in the assessment process. In so doing, they also become more focused on the appropriate materials and experiences that support children's language and literacy learning.

- **Children** receive the appropriate support, materials, and experiences for their emerging skills and knowledge. They become aware of their own growth and progress over time, and see themselves as readers and writers from the beginning.
- **Parents** learn about their own children's abilities, what behaviors might be expected at each stage of development, and how they can support their children's language and literacy development at home.
- **Administrators** get feedback on what the program is accomplishing and what kinds of ongoing resources staff need to continue supporting children's development.
- **Researchers** learn about the factors that affect children's development and can interpret this information to help administrators and practitioners design the most effective early literacy experiences.
- **Policymakers** and **funders** get valid information about where to direct resources to emphasize language and literacy within a comprehensive child development program.

Assessment of young children has multiple **purposes,** which include

- Planning appropriate instruction to support children's learning
- Informing parents about their children's progress
- Identifying children in need of special services
- Evaluating programs and their effectiveness
- Holding students, teachers, and/or programs accountable (often tied to funding)

The main focus of this chapter is on the first two purposes: assessing children's language and literacy development in order to plan support for further learning and communicate with parents about their children's progress. When these individual and classroom data are collected for groups of children and combined with other relevant information, they can be used to address the last two purposes, program evaluation and accountability. The third purpose of assessment, identifying children in need of special services, is typically met, as already mentioned, with the use of screening and diagnostic procedures.

How to Assess Language and Literacy: Four Steps

There are both formal and informal procedures that can be used to assess children's development in language and literacy. Formal assessment procedures, such as standardized tests, are widely considered to be inappropriate for preschool-age children, for a variety of reasons (Shepard, Kagen, & Wurtz, 1998; NAEYC & NAECS/SDE, 2001). Informal types of assessment (sometimes called "authentic assessment") are considered to be the most appropriate for preschoolers. Children perform better when they are in a familiar, safe environment, engaged in familiar routines, and working with adults they know and trust. Assessments that are done by the child's own teacher in the natural course of daily activities are therefore more indicative of their true capabilities. Note, however, that *informal* does not mean subjective or unsystematic. As described below, informal assessments should be objective, and conducted on a regular basis, in order to be valid indicators of children's progress.

For teachers, the assessment process involves four steps. You will need to **(1) collect evidence or data; (2) select the data** you will use; **(3) compile the data** into a manageable format; and **(4) evaluate the data,** to make sense of it for yourself and the child's parents.

Fountas and Pinnell (1996) caution that "assessment is a difficult organizational task and teachers should be careful not to load themselves down with too many forms or formal procedures" (p. 84). So we will look at only two types of language and literacy data to collect, **anecdotes** and **artifacts.** Following is a synopsis of each step in the process. Note: While there are various ways to compile and evaluate anecdotes, in the following chart and throughout this chapter we have chosen to use the Preschool Child Observation Record (COR), Second Edition (High/Scope Educational Research Foundation, 2003), to illustrate this process. (See opposite for a description of the COR.) Other validated instruments might be considered for this purpose. (For example, see The Work Sampling System, Fourth Edition, 2001, developed by S. Meisels, J. Jablon, P. Marsden, M. Dichtelmiller, & A. Dorfman.)

> *"Among literacy researchers, there is considerable support for the necessity of 'informal' assessment, and very little support for 'formal' measures of early literacy."*
>
> —Peter H. Johnston and Rebecca Rogers (2001, p. 381)

Step 1: Collect data: multiple types, from multiple sources, over time.

Four sources of data yield much valuable information for assessing each child in your program—what you observe the child doing and saying in the classroom, samples or "artifacts" of the child's work, information from the child's family (both observations and

Four Steps in Assessment

1. Collect Data	2. Select Data	3. Compile Data	4. Evaluate Data
Observe child; record **anecdotes**.	Choose one or two* anecdotes for each Preschool COR item.	Complete and score the Preschool COR, several times a year.	Write up (or print out) summary report.
Collect **artifacts**.	Choose some artifacts that illustrate child's development.	Compile into portfolio, album, or scrapbook.	Reflect on child's work and briefly summarize progress.

Note. The Preschool Child Observation Record (COR) is used here to illustrate the assessment process. Other instruments may be used.
*Depending on version of COR being used.

artifacts), and the child's own self-reflections. The following section describes each of these four sources of data.

Classroom observations

Observations of children's language and literacy should be an ongoing part of daily teaching. You should observe children throughout the day, in different circumstances: during both child-initiated and teacher-initiated times, and as children work and play both individually and in small and large groups. You may observe by watching children silently or by engaging them in conversation and then noting their responses. Pulling children out of their routine to "test" them on specific skills is never recommended. Instead, you may at times set up certain situations in order to see how children respond—for instance, a small-group activity using three-dimensional letters, a rhyming game during large-group time, or a one-on-one conversation with a child during work time. These situations can yield valuable information if you are observant.

About the Preschool COR

The Preschool Child Observation Record, Second Edition, is an observational assessment tool for children aged 2½ to 6 years, developed by the High/Scope Educational Research Foundation (2003). An infant-toddler version of the COR is also available.

The Preschool COR is designed to measure children's progress in all early childhood programs (not just those using the High/Scope educational approach). It looks at children's development in 32 key dimensions of learning, in six broad categories critical for school success: *initiative, social relations, creative representation, movement and music, language and literacy,* and *mathematics and science.* (See pp. 164–165 for COR items in the *language and literacy* category.)

The COR is designed to be "teacher-friendly": easily used by teachers and caregivers because it is closely tied to the curriculum goals and teaching approaches of preschool programs with a child development orientation. Teaching staff gather information to complete the COR in the course of everyday program activities, so COR assessment is seamlessly integrated with early childhood teaching and planning. The results provide detailed information on each child's development, as well as a variety of group reports analyzing children's progress for various audiences.

High/Scope offers a selection of forms and teaching aids for those using the COR. These include booklets for recording child anecdotes in the COR developmental categories (*Child Anecdotes* booklets), forms for reporting COR results both for individuals and the group, literature to introduce the COR to parents, family report forms, a teaching guide to help teachers use COR results in planning daily experiences, instruction manuals, and posters.

In addition to the printed COR, software and online versions are offered; these enable teachers to store COR anecdotes on the computer and generate COR reports automatically. A software program, the *COR–Head Start Outcomes Reporter,* is also available to help Head Start programs use COR results in generating reports based on the Head Start Child Outcomes Framework. For more information on the COR, see the High/Scope Web site, *www.highscope.org.*

Observing, however, is just half of this data collection process; what you see and hear also needs to be *recorded*. In preschool classrooms, one way to do this is to write **anecdotal notes** (also called anecdotes). An anecdote is a brief report on a developmentally significant child behavior you have observed. It describes what a child did or said in concrete, objective terms, giving the specific place and time the incident occurred. It is best to record anecdotes in all domains of children's development, not just in language and literacy. (See pp. 161 & 162 for sample anecdotes and Appendix F for anecdote-writing instructions.) Anecdotes are used in two time-frames; first, you and other members of your teaching team record and discuss them each day, referring to them as you develop the next day's plans. Later, when many anecdotes have been collected for each child over a period of several months, you "score" the anecdotes, using the Preschool COR (or other instrument) to identify the child's developmental level on each aspect of behavior rated by the instrument.

"Literacy is a continuously evolving and situation-specific endeavor for each child. No single set of indicators can accommodate its variability; no single assessment approach can capture its ever-changing status within individuals."

—Kathleen A. Roskos and Susan B. Neuman (1994, p. 85)

In some preschool programs, teachers use literacy **checklists** based on the program's standards or performance indicators to guide their observations. In other settings, teachers make up their own checklists. Checklists can be a useful aid to observation, especially if you create them yourself, with behaviors you want to notice and support. A combination of checklist and anecdotal notes is much more complete then either alone, and can be a real timesaver. The checklist serves as a reminder of what to look for; the anecdotes can either be written in spaces provided on the checklist or on blank sticky notes attached to a clipboard holding the checklist. A checklist format can also be useful as a summary report; see pp. 165–166.

Classroom artifacts (products and recordings)

Artifacts, a second source of data about the children, are actual samples you collect of what individual children have done, including both their behaviors and the products they have created. You can collect children's actual creations (or copies of them); or you may sample children's work by using photos, audiotape, or videotape to record the child's constructions, words, and/or actions. The latter are often referred to as "performance samplings" or "work samplings." **Child-created artifacts** may include

- Drawings with dictated stories; self-portraits
- Other dictations
- Writing in any form: name-writing attempts, special scribble messages (invitations, letters, lists)
- Books made by the child
- Work done on the computer by the child
- Printed copy of text that the child has read (or names of books that the child can read)

158

Recordings may include

- Photographs of block constructions or models made of clay, dough, or other materials (with child comments); photos of child reading, writing, or involved in dramatic play

- Audiotape or videotape recordings of child's conversations (with peers and adults); taped examples of child's storytelling, emergent storybook reading, story retellings and reenactments, other dramatic play, singing, planning and recalling

While artifacts are often child-initiated creations, you may occasionally suggest that children create them. For instance, as you open a small-group activity, you might suggest: "Draw a picture of yourself, and sign your name like artists do, in any way that you want." If you do this at the beginning, middle, and end of the year (or even more often), you will have a record of how this particular aspect of literacy is progressing for each child.

One potential problem with artifacts is that occasionally there are children who do not want to save their work at school—they either want to take it home or they throw it away. Making photocopies (if appropriate) of drawings or writings the child wants to take home immediately is one solution for this problem. Showing all the children what you are going to do with their work also helps: for instance, you may be able to show the children another child's album of work samples from a previous year, telling the children that they will get to take their own albums home at the end of the year. (See pp. 162–163 for more on creating and using albums and portfolios.)

> *"Kidwatching answers the question, How does what children say and do show us what they know about oral and written language? Kidwatchers talk with children and listen to them speak and read. They ask children to explain what they are doing with language, interview them in an open-ended fashion, and closely observe reading and writing activities."*
>
> —Kathryn F. Whitmore and Yetta M. Goodman (1995, p. 163)

Contributions from families

At the beginning of the year (or whenever a child enrolls in your classroom), the child's family can be another valuable source of data on the child's developing literacy. Some teachers conduct home visits; others interview the parents or have informal conversations when the child starts in the program. Some schools have a standard questionnaire for families to fill out. Useful information for you to seek at this time includes the child's language development to date (in both first and second languages); special words the child may use (comfort words, names of family members, personal needs, etc.); what the child's interests are, what kinds of stories he or she likes to hear, what opportunities he or she has for writing at home, etc. All of the information you get from the child's family helps you to informally assess where the child is now in literacy development and to plan appropriate experiences for him or her.

Throughout the year, encourage parents to send or bring in anecdotes, samples of their child's writing, and lists of the child's favorite books, authors, words, etc. During the first meeting with parents, you may want to give them a list of suggested items. This will make them more informed observers—and help them view their child as an emergent reader and writer. And it will give you even more evidence of the child's capabilities.

Self-reflections from the child

A fourth source of data is the children themselves: what they think of themselves as readers, writers, and language users. A positive self-image is essential to literacy learning (as it is to all learning); preschoolers are not too young to begin thinking of themselves as already belonging to the "literacy club." When children, throughout the year, see parents and teachers collecting evidence of their emergent reading and writing, feelings of "I can't read" or "I can't write" are far less common. Children see that literacy learning is a process, and that three- and four-year-olds read and write in ways that are different (but no less valued) than the ways adults read and write.

Below are some possible questions to ask children and record their answers to during informal interviews:

- Do you like to read/look at books? Who do you like to read with? When is your favorite time to read/look at books? What do you like to read about? Tell me one of your favorite books or stories.

- Do you like to write/draw? Is there anyone you like to write to? What kinds of things do you write? When do you write when you're at home?

Storing the data collected

Anecdotes can be stored several ways: in Preschool COR *Child Anecdotes* booklets, in computer files created with the software or online versions of the COR, in a three-ring binder, or in individual file folders.

Collecting all this "artifact stuff" from 20 children in a classroom could be overwhelming. Some teachers use **pizza boxes** for individual storage containers; others use **three-ring binders** or folders. A method that works well in some settings is to have a box of **hanging file folders** in the classroom (accessible to the children) with a date stamp nearby. The folders are labeled and alphabetized by children's first names. When children want to put something in their folder, they stamp the date on the back and put it in their file. (Younger preschoolers may need assistance with this.) Of course, the teachers

Children look over samples of their own work stored in a box of file folders in the classroom. Some of these samples will be selected for children's portfolios.

add items as well, including photos. Parents may add anecdotal notes and samples of their child's work from home. This is the initial *collection* step; step 2, below, helps to narrow the amount of data collected.

Step 2: Select the data that you want to use.

Using the Preschool COR assessment process on a daily basis, as many early childhood programs do, is an excellent way to organize, select, and interpret your anecdotes. To select data for assessing literacy with the Preschool COR, you would gather all the anecdotes you have collected in the COR **language and literacy** category and for each item on the COR find either one or two anecdotes that support one of the five developmental levels. (The number of anecdotes depends on the COR version you are using.) For instance, Danny's teacher selected these two anecdotes, among many others, to illustrate COR item *U. Demonstrating knowledge about books:*

10/4   *In the book area at greeting time, D and A paged through* The Napping House. *Looking at the pictures on each page, D told the story to A.*

11/9   *At small-group time, D chose a wordless book* (Rosie's Walk), *and read it to his stuffed animal, making up a story that matched the pictures.*

Both of these anecdotes are evidence of book knowledge at level 4—*Looking at the pictures in a book, child tells the story or makes up a story related to the pictures.*

(Note: Teachers using the computerized COR have an advantage here—they have already entered the anecdotes into the computer, scoring each one as they did so. When they print out the report, the computer makes the selection for them, choosing the highest level for which there is at least one anecdote). For details on using the COR to interpret and score anecdotal notes, see the Preschool COR *User Guide,* Second Edition (High/Scope Educational Research Foundation, 2003).

You'll also need to select artifacts to document children's progress. Several times a year (prior to parent conferences is a logical time), go through each child's file, folder, or pizza box and pick out those items that are significant because they show understanding or illustrate progress. It is beneficial to involve children in this process—letting children know you are making a special "album" or "portfolio" (see next section) to show their progress and letting them help you choose prized items to include. (You can even record on a sticky note why a child considers a particular item special, and attach that note to the item.) Any items that are not going into the album or portfolio should be sent home.

Step 3: Compile the data.

Periodically, it is necessary to compile the data that has been selected into a manageable format. Teachers who are using the Preschool COR process are already organizing their anecdotes into developmental categories, and probably also scoring them, as they go along. Just as the COR provides a reliable, valid tool for compiling and scoring anecdotes, a **portfolio** or **album** format is a systematic way to organize the artifacts.

Portfolios are designed for compiling selected artifacts—both products and experiences. Some teachers leave the items they have selected loose (in a box or folder), making sure they are in chronological order; others bind two-dimensional items into a book format. You could use three-ring binders, or commercial or homemade scrapbooks. Roskos and Neuman (1994) refer to these as "literacy albums," and have written, "Unlike

---

Sample Excerpt from a Family Report Form

V. Language and Literacy

Developmental Summary:
When listening to a story, rhyme, or narrative, Anaya comments on or asks a question about it. She uses two or more words to describe something. Anaya uses two or more simple sentences in a row and says two words that begin with the same sound. Looking at pictures in a book, she tells the story or makes up a story related to the pictures. Anaya names 10 or more letters over time. She recognizes a written word and she writes a string of letters and reads them or asks to have them read.

Supporting Anecdotes:
10/19 At snack time when her teacher read the Pizza book, Anaya said, "My Gram made me pizza last night!"

11/13 At work time on the rocking boat, Anaya said, "I'm going fishing. This is the water!" as she pointed to the blue carpet.

11/29 During morning arrival, Anaya told the story Rosie's Walk to J.R. and J.R.'s bear. She held the book, turned the pages, and described what she saw, while J.R. sat close to her, holding his bear and leaning close to look at the pictures.

12/14 During work time, Anaya painted "OMCRI" on paper at the easel. Then she asked Ms. Ray, "What did I write?"

Parent Observations:
2/03 Anaya's mom said Anaya often asks to "read" when she [mom] is reading books to her. Anaya has memorized some of her favorite stories and enjoys reciting parts of them and turning the pages as they read together.

more traditional forms of assessment (such as inventories and scales), albums have the capability to accommodate the great variability in young children's literacy learning, as well as their diverse and often concrete ways of expressing what they know" (p. 79). One advantage to the album or scrapbook format is that the books can be made available to the children to look at throughout the year, giving them an opportunity to see their own progress. (Audio- and videotapes may need to be stored separately.)

"Portfolios are not just educational scrapbooks; they are systematic collections of similar products constructed at regular intervals that can be compared to assess children's progress over time."

—Tynette W. Hills (1992, p. 60)

Step 4: Evaluate the data.

Compiling the anecdotes and artifacts isn't the end of the assessment process; the data also need to be reflected upon and summarized, making the information more useful to you and parents alike.

When COR anecdotes are scored with computer versions of the COR, a summary of the language and literacy behaviors that they encompass is automatically generated by the program. If you are using the print version of the Preschool COR, you write your own summaries based on the wording of the COR levels. A sample of such a summary statement may be seen on the excerpt from a Preschool COR family report, opposite (the report also includes some of the anecdotes that support that summary statement).

For the portfolios, you can create a summary, either in a narrative format (similar to the summary on the family report) or a checklist format (see pp. 165–166), to capture whatever else you want to document about the language and literacy development of the child.

What to Assess: The Content

We have looked at why and how we assess children's language and literacy development; now let's look at what it is we're assessing—the content. Since assessment should be tied to the curriculum, what you assess should be aligned with what you want the children to learn.

Some behaviors on a preschool assessment (those related to prior experience, for example, such as knowledge about books) are the same as those on an early elementary assessment. Other behaviors (those related to cognitive development) are not. For instance, phonological awareness for most preschoolers is at the level of words and syllables, rhymes, and initial sounds, but not at the level of identifying, blending, and segmenting individual phonemes—items that might be found on a kindergarten or first-grade phonemic awareness assessment.

On the updated Preschool COR (2003) the following are the items in the language and literacy category. Each item has five developmental levels of observable behavior.

Items from the Preschool
COR, Second Edition

Language items

Q. Listening to and understanding speech

1. Child responds with actions or words to a suggestion, request, or question.
2. When listening to a story, rhyme, or narrative, child anticipates and fills in a word or phrase.
3. When listening to a story, rhyme, or narrative, child comments on or asks a question about it.
4. Child contributes to an ongoing conversation.
5. Child sustains a dialogue by taking three or more conversational turns.

A developmental scale or checklist helps teachers evaluate and summarize children's accomplishments.

R. Using vocabulary

1. Child talks about people or objects close at hand.
2. Child talks about absent people or objects.
3. Child uses vocabulary related to a particular subject.
4. Child uses two or more words to describe something.
5. Child asks about the meaning of a word.

S. Using complex patterns of speech

1. Child uses words and phrases.
2. Child uses a sentence of four or more words.
3. Child uses two or more simple sentences in a row.
4. Child uses a compound subject or object in a sentence.
5. Child uses a clause that starts with "when," "if," "because," or "since" in a sentence.

T. Showing awareness of sounds in words

1. During play, child makes the sound of an animal or vehicle, or some other environmental sound.
2. Child joins in saying or repeating a rhyme or a series of words that start with the same sound.
3. Child rhymes one word with another or makes up a phrase or sentence that includes a rhyme.
4. Child says that two words begin with the same sound.
5. Child creates a pair or series of words that start with the same sound.

Literacy items

U. Demonstrating knowledge about books

    1. Child shows interest when a book is read aloud.

    2. Child holds a book right-side up, turns the pages, and looks at them.

    3. Child asks another person to read a book to him or her.

    4. Looking at the pictures in a book, child tells the story or makes up a story related to the pictures.

    5. Child points to the words in a book or follows a line of text while telling or reading the story.

V. Using letter names and sounds

    1. Child says or sings some letters.

    2. Child names three or more alphabet letters he or she is holding, looking at, typing, or making.

    3. Child makes the sound of a letter in a word he or she is looking at, writing, or typing.

    4. Child names 10 or more letters over time.

    5. Child says a word and identifies the beginning letter or sound.

W. Reading

    1. Child uses the same word to name more than one object.

    2. Child says what a picture or symbol represents.

    3. Child calls attention to print.

    4. Child recognizes a written word.

    5. Child reads aloud a simple phrase or sentence.

X. Writing

    1. Child writes using pictures, squiggles, or letterlike forms.

    2. Child uses clay, wire, or sticks to make a recognizable letter.

    3. Child writes two or more recognizable letters.

    4. Child writes a string of letters and reads them or asks to have them read.

    5. Child writes a phrase or sentence of two or more words.

Other aspects of literacy to assess

The Preschool COR is a comprehensive tool that assesses behaviors in *all* of the developmental domains; it does not, therefore, encompass every single aspect of language and literacy. Teachers need to decide what other literary behaviors (if any) they want to look for and document, either with anecdotes or artifacts, and add those items to their **summary checklist.** In addition to the COR items, these behaviors might include

Print and book awareness

1. Child understands directionality (where to start reading, where to go next).
2. Child recognizes punctuation marks (period, question mark, quotes).
3. Child knows reading terminology: letter, word, front/back of book, cover, title, author, illustrator

Sense of story

1. Child follows plot when listening to story, can make predictions about plot.
2. Child retells a familiar story.
3. Child tells stories with a beginning, middle, and end.

Alphabet knowledge

1. Child recognizes uppercase, lowercase letters.
2. Child is beginning to recognize letter-sound correspondences.

Name knowledge

1. Child recognizes own name.
2. Child forms own name (with three-D letters, stamps, keyboard, etc.).
3. Child writes own name.

Early writing

1. Child uses emergent writing (identify child's stage: drawing, scribble-writing, letterlike forms, writing actual letters, writing words).
2. Child "writes" with a purpose in mind.
3. Child writes with directionality (left to right, top to bottom).
4. Child uses spaces to indicate breaks between "words."
5. Child uses developmental (preconventional) spelling (identify child's spelling stage: prephonemic, early phonemic, later phonemic, conventional).

Early reading

1. Child reads from pictures, symbols.
2. Child reads from memory.
3. Child reads some sight words.
4. Child is beginning to sound out words.

What to Do With the Results of Assessment

As discussed earlier, the two primary reasons for classroom teachers to assess young children are to inform instruction and to communicate with parents. Once you have a good grasp of the development of language and literacy, and an understanding of where each child is on the various continua, you are then able to help the child take the next step on his or her literacy journey. Essentially, this means you are using assessment on a daily basis, as you observe and interact with individual children.

Your formal communications with parents about assessment will possibly occur about two or three times a year (at parent conferences), but sometimes more often in informal conversations. Parents who have been involved in collecting the assessment data are usually more interested in knowing the results. They are also often interested in knowing how they can support their child at home. (See Chapter 10 for more on family involvement.)

By following the recommendations in this chapter for systematically documenting each child's progress in literacy development, teachers will gain the information they need to make their teaching and communications with parents more focused, meaningful, and effective. It's also important for teachers to remember that the data they collect can be brought together with data from other groups of children and used to provide valuable information to administrators, researchers, policymakers, and funding agencies. By engaging in these authentic assessment procedures, practitioners are contributing to a wider body of knowledge and helping to promote effective language and literacy programs for all young children.

Teachers share the results of their assessment of a child's literacy development in regular parent conferences.

10

Parent Involvement in Children's Early Literacy

Parents* are the first teachers of their children, and the most important.

What happens in a child's first five years, before formal schooling, sets the stage for all that follows. Parents (and families) are involved in their children's education long before they have any kind of involvement with their children's preschool program, child care center, or school. They are teaching their children about the world and how it works, in all sorts of ways, implicitly and explicitly, from the day they are born. And, as we saw in Chapter 2, one of the most important things children learn about from their parents is *language,* both spoken and written.

Parent or family involvement goes by various names, and can mean a variety of things. The chapter begins by briefly discussing the benefits of and barriers to parents' participation in their children's early learning in general. Then it focuses on how early childhood teachers can facilitate and encourage parent involvement in their children's literacy development—at home, at school, and in tandem with the community.

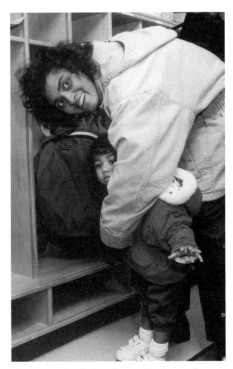

Parents who feel welcome in the early childhood center are likelier to participate.

---

*"Parent" in this chapter refers to any adult who plays a significant role in a young child's upbringing—whether it be a parent, a grandparent or other close relative, a guardian, or other full-time caregiver.

Benefits of Parent Involvement

Much has been written about parent involvement (for resources, see Appendix E). The research (as summarized in White-Clark & Decker, 1996; DiNatale, 2002; and the Iowa Department of Education, n.d.) shows that when families and schools work in partnership, everyone involved benefits—the children, the families, the teachers and schools:

"The values, attitudes, and expectations held by parents and other caregivers with respect to literacy are likely to have a lasting effect on a child's attitude about learning to read."

—Catherine E. Snow et al. (1998, p. 138)

- **Children** benefit by increased self-esteem, motivation, and academic achievement. They develop attitudes that are essential for achievement and school success. They have a better relationship with their parents, and a more positive attitude toward teachers and school. Students whose parents continue to be involved in their education also have a lower high-school dropout rate.

- **Parents** also increase their self-esteem as a result of greater involvement with their child's school. They develop more confidence in helping their children learn at home and more understanding of how the school system works. As their feelings about teachers and schools become more positive, they often enroll in continuing education. As parents feel more supported, they become more supportive of their children, and parent-child relationships improve.

- **Teachers and schools** benefit from the parents' more positive feelings about them. Teacher morale improves as a result, and as the children become more successful, the school climate improves, as well as the school's reputation in the community.

At this center parents are encouraged to spend a few minutes doing puzzles or reading with their child before leaving for work.

Establishing a strong connection between home and school during the preschool years can have the added benefit of keeping parents interested and involved in their children's education when they begin more formal schooling. As Porche (2001) has noted, "Just as the quality of early schooling...may affect children's ability to learn, the quality of early parent-teacher interactions and programmatic attention to parents of children in early childhood programs may influence the quality of later parent involvement" (p. 291).

Overcoming Barriers to Parent Involvement

The importance of family participation in the education of their young children can not be overstated. There are, however, many barriers that make it difficult to establish a good home-school connection—and teachers should know what these barriers are, in order to work around them. Some barriers involve parent-related issues; some involve teacher-related issues. As you work with families, keep in mind these common barriers.

Parents may…

- Have low self-esteem
- Have had negative experiences with schools; feel intimidated by teachers and administrators
- Be unsure of how to help their children learn
- Not feel welcome at school
- Not understand the system
- Face severe economic problems that take precedence over school involvement
- Be working or unavailable when events are scheduled
- Lack transportation and/or child care
- Not speak or understand English well
- Not be able to read or understand written school communications
- Have a different perspective on the roles that schools and parents should play in children's education

Teachers may…

- Fail to ask parents for help
- Fail to give parents materials or information they can use to help children
- Unintentionally discourage participation
- Organize events for staff (rather than family) convenience
- Have low expectations for poor or at-risk children
- Think parents don't care about education
- Not value cultural and linguistic diversity
- Have limited time for home visits and talking with parents
- Lack training in how to communicate with and involve parents
- Be unable to communicate with non–English-speaking parents

While you may find this a daunting list, the good news is that these barriers are not insurmountable; many programs have found ways to overcome them. The key is to make every effort to communicate with parents. Aim for *two-way* communication as much as possible; let parents know how valuable their input is. You can communicate with parents in a variety of ways: formally (in regular parent conferences) and informally (by chatting with parents before or after school, at social events, etc.). Contacts with family members can take place at school and in their homes; one-on-one and in small groups; through face-to-face conversations, telephone calls, written material, or audiotapes and videotapes. You can create opportunities to strengthen relationships by planning regular social events that involve parents in fun, relaxed family-school activities. For parents who have difficulty coming to meetings, parent conferences, or school social events, consider providing transportation and/or child care, scheduling the meeting for a more convenient time, or meeting at a location other than the school.

Holding the last segment of the day outdoors makes it easier to chat with parents as they pick up their children.

Inform parents about your program and classroom. Provide parents with a handbook or statement of school/center policies and procedures; hold an orientation meeting at the beginning of every year to explain them. Make family members feel welcome in your classroom, whether they are volunteering, just staying a few minutes to read a story to their child at drop-off time, or joining their child for lunch time. Invite parents to visit the classroom at any time.

Get to know the families of your children, their communities and cultures. Survey parents to find out their interests, skills, and talents and how they might like to be involved with the school during the year. Acknowledge family contributions both privately and publicly; hold a "parent appreciation" party.

When you have parents who do not speak English, communicate whenever possible in their language, making use of translators if possible. When you have low-literacy parents (or parents who don't read in English), make sure any written information sent home is available to them in another form, such as audiotape cassettes, personal visits or phone calls, or a translation, if appropriate.

Parent and Family Involvement With Literacy

In addition to strengthening relationships with parents through the general ways described previously, you also need to target some of your parent involvement efforts to focus specifically on children's language and literacy. There are many ways parents can be involved in the process of helping children develop language and literacy skills. This involvement may occur at home, at school, or at other locations in the community. It can be initiated and/or carried out by the teacher, by the parent, or jointly. Parents may be involved by working with their own child, with other children, with other adults, or by working alone. In encouraging parent involvement, you may focus on school literacy learning (for example, explaining to parents how and why the class does group dictation following a field trip) or on home literacy learning (encouraging parents to let their child help write a grocery list).

Offer parents and families a wide selection of literacy-related activities to choose from, with varying levels of participation. Some programs hold a meeting early in the school year for parents and teachers to brainstorm ways that the parents can choose to be involved. When parents are part of the process of creating such options, they usually feel more ownership and consequently have a higher degree of participation.

In the following pages, we discuss what teachers can do to facilitate parent and family involvement in literacy learning, at home, at school, and working within the community.

Encouraging parent involvement with literacy at home

To know how best to encourage parents to provide literacy experiences for their children, teachers need to get to know program families and the ways they are currently approaching family literacy. One way to find out about each family's literacy experiences is to conduct an informational home visit when children enter the program. During the home visit, ask parents about family literacy activities: their child's reading and writing activities at home, family trips to the library, and so forth. You may ask one simple question, such as "Tell me about your child as a reader and a writer," or you may ask a variety of questions to help you get to know the child (and family) better. *A Path to Follow: Learning to Listen to Parents* (Edwards, 1999) is a helpful resource to guide talks with parents. As you seek information, avoid making assumptions about families' abilities to contribute to children's literacy. To understand how much literacy goes on in families that you might consider "impoverished," "disadvantaged," or "not interested in education," refer to *Family Literacy* (Taylor, 1998) and/or *Many Families, Many Literacies* (Taylor, 1997).

Home visits

In addition to the informational home visits you make when families enter the program, some parents—those with low literacy levels or who speak a language other than English—might benefit from extra visits. You could plan one or more home visits to show them ways they can support their child's language and literacy development regardless of language differences or reading limitations. For example, you might suggest that they

- Tell stories to their child.
- Read books in their home language.
- Look at picture books together and talk about the pictures.
- Listen to their child read (the pictures) or tell the story.

- Model literacy for children by engaging in adult literacy events: looking at pictures in magazines, reading in their home language, laughing at wordless picture books, listening to books on tape.

Home visits with any of your families are a good opportunity to model interactive reading with a child and to demonstrate other learning activities to do at home—creating a family message board, for instance, using words and pictures.

Parent workshops

Holding a series of literacy-focused parent workshops throughout the year is another option for reaching parents. For example, workshops are an excellent way to

- Explain the developmental processes of learning to read and write. When parents understand that their children *are* showing signs of developing literacy, they are more likely to provide appropriate help.
- Show how everyday home activities can support language and literacy learning.
- Demonstrate and explain the value of using various kinds of "extended discourse" in talking with preschoolers.

For other workshop ideas, you might distribute a questionnaire or take a poll (by phone or during home visits) to find out about literacy-related workshop topics that would be of interest to families. In addition, the following are good resources for planning workshops:

The Essential Parent Workshop Resource (Graves, 2000)

Getting Involved: Workshops for Parents (Frede, 1984)

In all the workshops you conduct (in fact, in all your contacts with parents about literacy), be sure to let parents know about the many things they are *already* doing that contribute to children's learning how to read. By first affirming their strengths as supporters of their child's learning, you will increase their confidence and interest in learning additional ways to nurture children's speaking, listening, reading, and writing abilities.

Materials to send home

Home visits and parent workshops involve teachers interacting *directly* with parents about children's literacy. Such direct communication may also take place over the telephone, in casual conversations, at parent conferences, at school social events, as well as in newsletters, monthly calendars, journals, and short notes.

An *indirect* way to involve parents is to send home with the children specific materials that facilitate parent-child literacy experiences. (See suggestions in box, opposite). Some of these materials may need to be accompanied by a note (or other communication), explaining how to use them.

Materials That Encourage Parent-Child Literacy Experiences

- Audiotapes of favorite stories and songs, to accompany books or song sheets
- Videotapes that model reading aloud and story discussions
- Regular newsletters that tell what literacy events have recently occurred in the classroom
- Monthly calendars with suggestions for literacy activities to do at home
- Monthly two-page activity handouts that tie classroom learning to familiar home routines and activities (Simmons, 2002)
- Short lists of good read-aloud books for various ages (infant, toddler, preschool, and elementary)
- A home-school journal, in which teachers write an anecdote or note about the child's progress, and parents are asked to respond
- A family literacy journal, sent home with a child-selected book to share. The child reads the pictures to his parents, and parents read the text back to the child. Parents are invited to comment on how the interaction went, and the teacher responds, asks questions, etc. (Harding, 1996).
- Exploration kits: videos, books, or games, plus index cards with activity ideas on a particular topic

- Books for children to borrow and take home to read with their parents. Other materials that can be added to a lending library include toys, games, audio- and videotapes, dramatic play materials, puppets and other book-related props.
- Teddy bear (or other stuffed animal) with backpack, crayons, and a diary. The child dictates what the bear did while visiting his or her family (over the weekend perhaps), and parents write it in the diary. The child may illustrate it, and share it with the class later.
- Book backpacks: 20 backpacks, each containing several related books, a parenting book, a composition "comment book," and an inventory card. Possible topics: travel, monsters, water, folk and fairy tales, health, families, favorite authors, buildings, post office, grandparents, ecology, birthday. Children keep the pack for one week, then take home a different one. A parent volunteer inventories them (Cohen, 1997).
- Literacy suitcases filled with writing materials: paper, fancy pencil, alphabet chart, name cards of all the children in the class, note to parents, note to child (Moomaw & Hieronymus, 2001)

Resources for educating parents about home literacy learning

Various books and print materials are available to help you educate parents about everyday activities at home that support children's literacy. You may want to create a parent resource room or library stocked with books, pamphlets, magazines, audiotapes, videotapes, and brochures covering children's literacy and other topics that may be of interest to your families. One useful resource available from High/Scope Press is a booklet written specifically for parents, *Helping Your Preschool Child Become a Reader* (Epstein, 2002). A Spanish version is also available. In addition, the following parent information sheet, "Learning to Read: What You Can Do at Home to Help Your Child," gives parents a sense of what to expect from their child along the road to reading, and specific strategies for each stage of language and reading development. (You can distribute this entire list as a handout to parents. However, since it is a lot of information for parents to digest

Learning to Read: What You Can Do at Home to Help Your Child

While there are many, many things you can do to help your child learn to read (see below), they basically fall into two categories of experiences: one category is experiences with **language** (spoken language), the other is experiences with **print** (written language). These experiences begin the day you bring your child home from the hospital.

Birth to age three years

- Talk to your baby, about anything; the sounds of language are what is important in the early months.
- Listen to the sounds your baby makes and repeat them back.
- Talk to your toddler about the "here and now"; toddlers learn words best when adults speak to them about people and objects in their immediate environment. That way they can link what they see with the words they hear (mommy, cup, fall down, kiss you). Describing what the child is doing is called parallel talk ("You kicked the ball!"); describing our own actions is called self talk ("Mommy is cutting the apple"). Both kinds of talk help your child learn new words.
- Listen to what your toddler tries to communicate to you, and respond with the words that convey his or her meaning.

    Toddler babbles and points to his cup. You say, "Oh, you'd like some more juice in that cup? Okay, let's pour you some more juice."

- Sing songs; recite poems and nursery rhymes; move to rhythmic chants.
- Read aloud to your baby or toddler, *at least* once a day.

Ages three to five years

In general:

- Provide new experiences, go to interesting places, and talk about these experiences. This helps to build your child's background knowledge and vocabulary.
- Have high expectations for your child.
- Provide a literacy-rich environment in your home, with a variety of printed materials, such as books, magazines, newspapers, lists, mail, posters, packaging with print, etc.
- Limit the amount of time your child watches television or uses the computer.
- Watch shows such as *Sesame Street* and *Between the Lions* with your child.
- Write down "anecdotes" of what your child does and says that show the progress he or she is making in language or beginning reading and writing. For example,

    6/12/03 T. scribbled some marks on a piece of paper, gave it to me, and said, "Send this to Pop-Pop. It say, 'I love you.'"

You can share anecdotes like this with your child's teacher in various ways: in parent conferences, in a journal that goes between home and school, or in your child's literacy portfolio at school.

Talking and listening:

- Talk with and listen to your child; have *extended conversations* daily. While preschoolers still need to converse about their immediate experiences, they also benefit from talk that is *not* about the "here and now," as well as from talk that involves several turns. This includes *explanatory talk, narrative talk,* and the *talk of pretend play.* Next are some examples of what adults might say as they participate with children in these types of extended conversations:

▶

This information sheet can be used as the basis for a series of parent handouts or newsletter articles.

Explanatory talk: making connections between objects, events, concepts, or conclusions; defining words or describing objects.

> *"Running with socks on this floor is dangerous, Katie. I just waxed it, and the wax makes it slippery. You might fall and hurt yourself."*

Narrative talk: telling about past or future events.

> *"Aunt Julia and your cousin Toby are coming to visit this weekend. We'll pick them up at the station tomorrow night, after supper. Toby can sleep with you, Joey, and Aunt Julia will sleep on the couch."*

Pretend play: talking about things that aren't real or visible.

> *"Oh, I see that your bus is ready to leave, Darren. Can I buy a ticket? How much money will that cost? Okay, and I want to take this suitcase with me, too."*

- Encourage pretend play; play with your child, and follow his or her lead.
- Use new words with your child, in ways that help him or her to understand the meaning. Introduce new words while playing with toys, during mealtimes, while reading books, and when visiting new places.
- Play with sounds, and play with words.
- Play rhyming games together.
- Tell family stories to your child.
- Encourage your child to tell stories to you.

Writing—Early forms

- Refer to your child as a writer, and encourage whatever developmental stage of writing he or she is in:

Scribble-writing

Drawing

Real Letters

Mock Letters

- When your child starts putting letters together to make words, know that spelling, too, is a developmental process:
  1. The first words that young children write with real letters (written singly or in strings) may have no relationship to sounds (this is often called *prephonemic spelling*). Example: *KTRRFO* (Child: "This says, 'Everybody watch out!'")
  2. As children become aware of the *sounds* in words, they begin to use initial and sometimes final consonants in the words they write by themselves: *HB2D* ("Happy birthday to Daddy"); *KM HR* ("Come here").
  3. As children hear more and more of the sounds, they begin to add more letters to their words: *Hpe birfda*.
  4. In the early elementary years, children's developmental spellings gradually give way to conventional spellings. ▶

Learning to Read (cont.)

Writing—More ideas:

- Provide your child with a place to write and writing materials: markers, pencils, paper, envelopes and stamps from junk mail, and so forth.
- Let your child help you make a grocery list, and then go shopping together.
- Read letters from family and friends out loud; encourage your child to add his or her own kind of writing to the letters you write.
- Write together at home with your preschooler and other family members:

  Keep a **family journal** (of trips, gardening, nature walks).

  Write **letters** (to family friends, relatives).

  Write **notes** to one another (on a white board, in a lunch box, on a door, a mirror, a bed).
- Keep a set of magnetic letters on the refrigerator; spell out family names, short messages.
- Use a message board to write messages to one another.
- Display examples of all stages of child's writing at home.
- Save and add anecdotes and writing examples to the portfolios (folders with samples of each child's work) kept at school.

Reading:

- Refer to your child as a reader, meaning whatever stage he or she is in: "You're reading the pictures to me—that's how three-year-olds read!"
- Encourage your child at all stages of early reading: looking at and listening to books; noticing environmental print; interpreting pictures, signs, and symbols; showing interest in letters and words; retelling favorite stories, and so on.
- Have a positive attitude toward books and reading.

- Model reading in your daily activities, for information and for pleasure.
- Read with your child every day (making it a warm, cozy experience).
- Read favorite books over and over again.
- As you read, vary your voice tone and use different voices for different characters.
- Talk about the books before, during, and after reading them.
- Make connections between books and your child's own experiences.
- Point to illustrations as you are reading to aid your child's understanding.
- Encourage your child to read books to you (by "reading" the pictures or telling the story).
- Choose a variety of types of children's books.
- Carry books wherever you go, so your child can read or be read to whenever there is a wait—on car or bus trips, when eating out, shopping, visiting, etc.
- Point out and read environmental print (stop signs, exit signs, store and restaurant names, etc.).
- Let your child help you cook: you read the recipe, your child pours and stirs.
- Go to the library regularly with your child; see if there is a preschool story hour that fits your schedule.
- Buy books for your child to own: at bookstores, yard sales, library sales, resale stores, through school book clubs.
- Ask for books as gifts for your child.
- Provide your child with a bedside reading lamp, a bookshelf, and time for looking at books before bedtime.
- Sing the ABC song together.
- Name the letters of the alphabet when your child shows an interest in them; talk about their sounds.
- Play matching games with letters.

at once, you may prefer to break it into sections to use in parent newsletter articles, workshop handouts, etc. Depending on the needs of your group of parents, some of the guidelines listed may require further examples or explanations.)

Encouraging parent involvement with literacy at school

Parents as curriculum volunteers

As well as encouraging parents to support children's literacy development at home, it's also important to let parents know they can contribute to the actual curriculum at school. Invite parents (as well as grandparents, students, and other community members) to be classroom literacy volunteers. Provide (or arrange) orientation and training for literacy volunteers, in which you explain their classroom role, which may include

"The most important aspect of any effort to facilitate parent involvement would seem to be to establish mechanisms for teachers to communicate clearly to parents about the sorts of activities that are most beneficial to children's learning."

—Michelle V. Porche
(2001, p. 311)

- Sharing books with children
- Telling stories
- Engaging in one-on-one conversations
- Listening to children read
- Taking dictation

Remind parents that they don't have to work with students directly to be a literacy volunteer; they can help to contribute to the center or classroom in other ways, such as helping to maintain the classroom lending library. Another way they can help is to make or collect literacy-related materials at home to add to the classroom or center. For example, they can

- Make "welcome" signs for the classroom or center, in each language spoken by families in the program
- Collect food packaging labels and other environmental print for the teacher to use in making classroom "label books"
- Make blank books for the classroom writing center
- Make literacy manipulatives (with the teacher supplying materials and directions)

A parent volunteer reads a big book with a child.

- Record stories and songs on audiotape
- Collect clothing and other props to donate to the classroom dramatic play center

Parents as participants in child assessment

Assessment is another area where parents can play a direct part in the educational program. During home visits, parent meetings, or in parent newsletters, explain the process used in the classroom to document and assess child progress. As discussed in Chapter 9, you should inform parents about your anecdotal note-taking and child portfolios, and invite them to contribute their own notes or portfolio items reflecting children's actions and language. At periodic parent conferences, discuss their child's progress in literacy, referring to the anecdotal notes, portfolios, and other records, and encourage parents to contribute additional observations and child creations from home.

Encouraging families to participate in community literacy efforts

Community efforts in support of early literacy are springing up all over, at an ever increasing rate. From local book drives to community reading centers to bedtime story nights, from policemen distributing books to kids on the streets to inmates taping stories for their children to pediatricians giving read-aloud "prescriptions" to new parents, individuals and organizations in many cities, towns, and villages are joining together to help today's parents raise a generation of children who will grow up as able and enthusiastic readers. By encouraging your program families to connect with these community efforts you can support your own families while also contributing to the community at large. Here are some examples of how early childhood programs can tie into these community services and literacy-related efforts.

Literacy Celebrations Throughout the Year

Many literacy events are celebrated locally and nationally. Find out when each of the following special days or weeks is celebrated in your area (the associated Web site usually includes dates), and then find a way to involve children, families, and your community.

March

Read Across America Day
   (*www.nea.org/readacross*)
Dr. Seuss's birthday, March 2

April

National Library Week (*ala.org/pio/nlw*)
TV-Turnoff Week (*www.tvturnoff.org*)

May

Reading is Fun Week (*rif.org*)
The Read In! (*readin.org*)
Get Caught Reading Month
   (*getcaughtreading.org*)

September

Library Card Sign-up Month
   (*ala.org/pio/librarycard*)
International Literacy Day (*reading.org*)

November

National Family Literacy Day (*famlit.org*)
National Young Readers Day
National Children's Book Week
   (*cbcbooks.org*)

- Distribute information on literacy-related community resources and services to your families: library and bookmobile locations and hours, for instance.
- Encourage community members (college students, senior citizens, etc.) to be literacy volunteers in your classroom. [Ask program parents if they know anyone that might make a good volunteer, and enlist veteran parent volunteers to train the volunteers from the community.]
- Locate bilingual community members who can assist as translators for communicating with families and helping you locate books and other resources in families' home languages.
- If some families don't feel comfortable coming to the school, use community buildings (churches, community centers, etc.) for parent meetings, literacy workshops, and social events.
- Coordinate resources and services for families with community agencies, businesses and other organizations.
- Help to organize special school-community events, such as a Saturday "read-in" at the local mall.

A parent reads to children at an evening pajama party at the school, part of a community-wide literacy effort.

When it comes to literacy, it is highly likely that all of us—parents and families, educators, and community members—want the same thing for the young children in our lives. We want them to be successful at learning to read and write, so that they can be successful in school (and throughout life), where those skills are so necessary. As the first adults that young children encounter on their journey to literacy, parents and other family members can do so much to make that journey a pleasant one. As this chapter has shown, early childhood educators can encourage and facilitate parents' involvement in their children's early literacy development in many ways.

Appendix A: Interest Areas and the Daily Routine in High/Scope Programs

This section provides additional information on two aspects of the High/Scope Curriculum: classroom play spaces (interest areas) and parts of the daily routine for children. These structural elements of the High/Scope program create a secure and stimulating learning environment that encourages the children's overall development, including language and literacy abilities.

Interest Areas

A High/Scope classroom is divided into several specific interest areas, which encourage different types of play. These interest areas have defined physical boundaries, such as low shelves or other pieces of furniture, carpeting, or tape on the floor.

Some essential interest areas are included in all High/Scope early childhood classrooms: the **art, block, house,** and **toy areas,** as well as an **outdoor area.** Most settings also have a **book area,** sometimes with a separate **writing area** nearby. Other teachers store all the materials for drawing and writing in the art area. Many classrooms include a **computer area** (with several computers); most have a **sand and water area.** Some teachers create a **woodworking area** as well. Each of these areas and the materials stored in them provide many opportunities for language and literacy to flourish.

Each area is stocked with a variety of materials that are interesting to the children and that reflect the diversity of their family lives. Materials are stored in consistent, logical locations, with a **labeling system** that is geared for all levels of development. This labeling system (besides facilitating cleanup time for children and adults alike) encourages an early stage of reading—connecting symbols and pictures with the things they stand for (see photos, next page).

Some materials are labeled in very concrete ways, with the object itself. The counting bears, for instance, may be stored in a basket, with a bear attached to both the basket and the edge of the shelf where the basket belongs. Some labels may be a little more abstract, using symbols such as photos or drawings. The box of rubber animals may have a picture of some of the animals for its label, and the unit blocks may be stored on top of labels made by tracing their outlines.

A written word is also a symbol, standing for its spoken equivalent, and words are used on the signs that designate the interest areas, along with simple pictures (such as a paintbrush for the art area). In classrooms where children are beginning to notice and be interested in letters and words, words are included on some of the labels for materials as well. Because the graphic representation of an area and its materials is paired with the written word, children are exposed very early to the idea of written language as a symbol system. They begin by "reading" the symbol and eventually read the word with which it is always associated.

Each child's personal things are stored in a place that is labeled with his or her own name, often with a photo or unique symbol attached to it. In this way, children become familiar with the idea that symbols can stand for objects and for names, which will eventually help them understand, as they learn to read, that letter-symbols can stand for the sounds in all the words we speak. (Refer to *Letter Links: Alphabet Learning With Children's Names,* DeBruin & Hohmann, 2003, for a unique system that pairs a child's printed nametag with a picture of an object that starts with the same letter and sound. A photo of a letter link in use appears on p. 125.)

Signs to identify the interest areas contain both the name of the area and a simple picture.

The lists of classroom materials included in this book are by no means complete lists of all the materials you would find in a High/Scope preschool classroom, as this book's focus is on language and literacy. See *Educating Young Children* (Hohmann & Weikart, 2002) for a complete description of interest areas and the variety of materials that can be provided in each.

The Daily Routine

The High/Scope daily routine is a consistent sequence of events, made up of the segments that are described below. The particular sequence varies from classroom to classroom; all of the following components are included in half-day as well as whole-day programs. Language- and literacy-related experiences may occur during any of these times.

Greeting time functions as a transition between home and school. The children gather together with the teachers, talk informally with one another and with the adults, look at books and listen to stories, and find out something about the day by reading a "message board" that

To accommodate children at various levels, labels on storage places for materials may include a picture, an outline of the material, an actual sample of what is stored (e.g., a small block), and sometimes the word for the material.

may include pictures, symbols, and words. Parents whose schedules permit often stay for greeting time to share the language, literacy, and social experiences of this part of the day with the children.

Small-group time allows each teacher to work with a part of the class, usually 5–10 children. They may explore materials, create things, read books, listen to stories, work on a project, or solve a problem. Children talk about what they are doing with one another and with the adult.

Large-group time enables all the children and teachers to gather together for enjoyable shared experiences. Large-group activities can involve singing songs, making music, playing rhythm instruments, dancing and moving to music, telling and reenacting stories, playing group games, or working on a joint project.

Plan-do-review is the largest portion of the High/Scope daily routine. It consists of the following consecutive segments:

- **Planning time:** Children indicate (through gestures, actions, talking, drawing, or writing in various ways) what their intentions are for work time.

- **Work time:** For about 45–60 minutes, children carry out their plans, playing and working throughout the room. They may carry out the plan they described at planning time or initiate new plans. The adults play as partners with the children, listen to and converse with them, observe and take notes, and assist in problem solving. Work time is followed by **cleanup time,** when everyone puts the materials back where they are stored, and helps to clean up the room.

- **Recall time:** Children are encouraged to remember something they did during work time, and share it in various ways—through gestures, talking about it, showing something they made, drawing, or writing about it.

Outside time enables children to play energetically outdoors, use their large muscles, and be in contact with the natural world.

Snack and meal times provide an opportunity for relaxed conversations, and sometimes the sharing of stories, between small groups of children and an adult.

(For more information on the High/Scope daily routine or other aspects of the curriculum, see Hohmann & Weikart, 2002).

Appendix B: Glossary

alliteration: Repetition of the beginning sound in a group of words: "big bad baboon," "cheddar cheese," "cute kitty cats."

alphabetic principle: Sound-symbol correspondence; the concept that every spoken sound of our language can be represented by a letter or group of letters.

beginning reader: A child in the early stage of conventional reading, who can decode and understand some previously unencountered text.

big books: Oversized picture books that can be read to and with a group of children.

child-directed talk: Also referred to as "motherese," "parentese," and "baby talk"; the way many adults intuitively speak to babies.

communication: The exchange of information; the sending and receiving of messages.

decodable text: Text that contains a large proportion of phonetically regular words, such as "The fat cat sat on the mat."

decoding: The ability to figure out printed words by translating the alphabet letters into recognizable speech sounds.

decontextualized talk: Talk about the past or future, about things that are not observable when speaking about them; talk about the "there and then." Also referred to as **nonimmediate** or **nonpresent talk.**

developmental spelling: A beginning writer's attempt to write words, matching the letters he knows how to write with the sounds he hears in the words. Also referred to as **invented** or **temporary** spelling.

dictation: The process of writing down the words that a child says, reading them back, and sometimes encouraging the child to read back what was just written.

early (or emergent) literacy: The emerging understandings and behaviors of young children in the process of becoming literate; precedes conventional writing and reading.

environmental print: Words found in the child's everyday environment, such as on product labels, store and street signs, etc.

expressive language: See **language.**

extended discourse: Talk that requires the use of several utterances, such as in explanations and narratives.

graphemes: Written symbols (single letters or groups of letters) that represent spoken sounds.

invented spelling: See **developmental spelling.**

language: A shared system of communication used by a group of people; it can be spoken, signed, communicated nonverbally, or written. Language can be **expressive** (sharing information with others) or **receptive** (understanding information expressed by others).

letter knowledge: The ability to identify the letters of the alphabet, in any of a variety of ways.

letter-sound correspondence: The link between discrete phonemes (sounds) and individual graphemes (letters).

literacy: The mastery of language in its written forms.

metalinguistic awareness: The ability to think and talk about language itself.

morphology: The aspect of language that involves word formation—the structure of words.

onset. See **onset and rime.**

onset and rime: The division of words into units that are smaller than syllables. The **onset** is all the sounds of a word that come before the first vowel (e.g., /str/ in *straight*); the **rime** is the first vowel in a word and all the sounds that follow (e.g., /aight/ in *straight*)

phonemes: The smallest units of sound, which are combined to form syllables and words.

phonemic awareness: The understanding that every spoken word is made up of a sequence of individual speech sounds (phonemes); the ability to identify (perceive) and manipulate those sounds.

phonics: The relationship between letters and sounds in written words. The term also refers to an instructional method that teaches children these connections, as well as a strategy children use to sound words out.

phonological awareness (a broader notion than phonemic awareness): The ability to perceive and manipulate various units of sound in language, including words, syllables, parts of syllables (onsets and rimes), and phonemes.

phonology: The aspect of language that deals with speech sounds.

pragmatics: The aspect of language that involves its social uses (rather than its structure).

predictable books: Picture books with regular rhythm, repeated sentences or lines, familiar stories or sequences, or a close match between illustrations and text.

print awareness: Awareness of the conventions and characteristics of letters, words, and text.

receptive language: See **language.**

rhyme: Repetition of the ending sound in two or more words.

rime: See **onset and rime.**

scaffolding: A process whereby temporary assistance is provided to a child working on a task that at that point in time he or she cannot do independently.

semantics: The aspect of language that deals with the meaning of words, phrases, and sentences.

shared reading: Adult and child (or group of children) read a book together, using context and picture clues.

shared (interactive) writing: Adult and child (or group of children) write something together, with the child doing as much as he or she can and the adult adding whatever words are requested.

syntax: The aspect of language that determines word order; the structure of phrases and sentences.

temporary spelling: See **developmental spelling.**

zone of proximal development (ZPD): The gap between what children can do independently and what they can do with assistance.

Appendix C: Developmental Accomplishments of Literacy Acquisition

Birth to Three-Year-Old Accomplishments

- Recognizes specific books by cover.
- Pretends to read books.
- Understands that books are handled in particular ways.
- Enters into a book-sharing routine with primary caregivers.
- Vocalization play in crib gives way to enjoyment of rhyming language, nonsense word play, etc.
- Labels objects in books.
- Comments on characters in books.
- Looks at picture in book and realizes it is a symbol for real object.
- Listens to stories.
- Requests/commands adult to read or write.
- May begin attending to specific print such as letters in names.
- Uses increasingly purposive scribbling.
- Occasionally seems to distinguish between drawing and writing.
- Produces some letter-like forms and scribbles with some features of English writing.

Three- and Four-Year-Old Accomplishments

- Knows that alphabet letters are a special category of visual graphics that can be individually named.
- Recognizes local environmental print.
- Knows that it is the print that is read in stories.
- Understands that different text forms are used for different functions of print (e.g., list for groceries).
- Pays attention to separable and repeating sounds in language (e.g., *Peter, Peter, Pumpkin Eater, Peter Eater.*)
- Uses new vocabulary and grammatical constructions in own speech.
- Understands and follows oral directions.
- Is sensitive to some sequences of events in stories.
- Shows an interest in books and reading.

- When being read a story, connects information and events to life experiences.
- Questions and comments demonstrate understanding of literal meaning of story being told.
- Displays reading and writing attempts, calling attention to self: "Look at my story."
- Can identify 10 alphabet letters, especially those from own name.
- "Writes" (scribbles) message as part of playful activity.
- May begin to attend to beginning or rhyming sound in salient words.

Kindergarten Accomplishments

- Knows the parts of a book and their functions.
- Begins to track print when listening to a familiar text being read or when rereading own writing.
- "Reads" familiar text emergently, i.e., not necessarily verbatim from the print alone.
- Recognizes and can name all uppercase and lowercase letters.
- Understands that the sequence of letters in a written word represents the sequence of sounds (phonemes) in a spoken word (alphabetic principle).
- Learns many, though not all, one-to-one letter-sound correspondences.
- Recognizes some words by sight, including a few very common ones (*a, the, I, my, you, is, are*).
- Uses new vocabulary and grammatical constructions in own speech.
- Makes appropriate switches from oral to written language situations.
- Notices when simple sentences fail to make sense.
- Connects information and events in texts to life and life to text experiences.
- Retells, reenacts, or dramatizes stories or parts of stories.
- Listens attentively to books teacher reads to class.
- Can name some book titles and authors.
- Demonstrates familiarity with a number of types or genres of text (e.g., storybooks, expository texts, poems, newspapers, and everyday print such as signs, notices, labels).
- Correctly answers questions about stories read aloud.
- Makes predictions based on illustrations or portions of stories.
- Demonstrates understanding that spoken words consist of sequences of phonemes.
- Given spoken sets like "dan, dan, den" can identify the first two as being the same and the third as different.
- Given spoken sets like "dak, pat, zen" can identify the first two as sharing a same sound.
- Given spoken segments can merge them into a meaningful target word.
- Given a spoken word can produce another word that rhymes with it.
- Independently writes many uppercase and lowercase letters.
- Uses phonemic awareness and letter knowledge to spell independently (invented or creative spelling).

- Writes (unconventionally) to express own meaning.
- Builds a repertoire of some conventionally spelled words.
- Shows awareness of distinction between "kid writing" and conventional orthography.
- Writes own name (first and last) and the first names of some friends or classmates.
- Can write most letters and some words when they are dictated.

Note. From *Preventing Reading Difficulties in Young Children* (pp. 61, 80), Catherine E. Snow, M. Susan Burns, and Peg Griffin (Eds.), 1998, Washington, DC: National Academy Press. Copyright 1998 by the National Academy of Sciences. Reprinted with permssion.

Appendix D: Children's Books

No sooner does one create a list of good children's books than it is quickly outdated. Almost 5000 new children's books are published each year, and many books go out of print and become difficult to find. Therefore, the lists below are just a sampling of the many books available in each category. For more book lists, check out the resources at the end of this appendix.

Books Using Rhyme and/or Alliteration

Aardema, V. *Bringing the Rain to Kapiti Plain*

Alda, A. *Sheep, Sheep, Sheep, Help me Fall Asleep; Pig, Horse, Cow, Don't Wake Me Now*

Bayer, J. *A My Name is ALice*

Brown, M. W. *Goodnight Moon*

Carter, D. *More Bugs in Boxes*

Degen, B. *Jamberry*

Fleming, D. *In the Tall, Tall Grass; In the Small, Small Pond; Barnyard Banter*

Fox, M. *Time for Bed*

Wood, A. *Silly Sally*

Ziefert, H., & Brown, H. *What Rhymes with Eel?*

Predictable Books

Alborough, J. *Duck in the Truck*

Carle, E. *The Very Hungry Caterpillar; The Very Busy Spider*

Cowley, J., & Melser, J. *Mrs. Wishy-Washy*

Fox, M. *Hattie and the Fox*

Galdone, P. *The Gingerbread Boy*

Hutchins, P. *Good-Night Owl; The Wind Blew*

Martin, B. *Brown Bear, Brown Bear*

Numeroff, L. *If You Give a Mouse a Cookie; If You Give a Pig a Pancake; If You Give a Moose a Muffin*

Wadell, M. *Owl Babies*

Wood, A. *King Bidgood's in the Bathtub; The Napping House*

Multicultural Books

Bryan, A. *What a Wonderful World* (Multiethnic)

Heo, Y. *One Afternoon* (Asian-Pacific American)

Palacio Jaramillo, N. *Grandmother's Nursery Rhymes / Las Nanas de Abuelita* (Latino)

Reiser, L. *Margaret and Margarita / Margarita y Margaret* (Latino)

Steptoe, J. *Baby Says* (African-American)

Tarpley, N. *I Love My Hair!* (African-American)

Te Ata. *Baby Rattlesnake* (American Indian)

Thomas, J. *You Are My Perfect Baby* (African-American)

Thong, R. *Round Is a Mooncake: A Book of Shapes* (Asian-Pacific American)

Wheeler, B. *Where Did You Get Your Moccasins?* (American Indian)

Williams, V. *"More, More, More," Said the Baby: Three Love Stories* (Multiethnic)

Zolotow, C. *Do You Know What I'll Do?* (African-American)

Note: For lists of more multicultural books for ages five and up, see the Web site of the Cooperative Children's Book Center at the School of Education, University of Wisconsin-Madison: *http://www.soemadison. wisc.edu/ccbc/50mult.htm*. Other online resources: the Web sites of the National Education Association (*http://www.nea.org*) and the American Library Association (*http://www.ala.org*).

Wordless Books

Blake, Q. *Clown*

Chesworth, M. *Rainy Day Dream*

Collington, P. *The Midnight Circus; The Angel and the Soldier Boy*

Day, A. *Good Dog, Carl; Carl Goes to Daycare*

dePaola, T. *Pancakes for Breakfast; The Hunter and the Animals*

Hutchins, P. *Rosie's Walk; Changes, Changes*

Mayer, M. *Frog, Where Are You?; Frog Goes to Dinner; Ah-Choo!*

Ormerod, J. *Moonlight; Sunshine*

Rohmann, E. *Time Flies*

Spier, P. *Dreams; Noah's Ark; Peter Spier's Rain*

Turkle, B. *Deep in the Forest*

Alphabet Books

Ehlert, L. *Eating the Alphabet*

Hague, M. *Alphabears*

Martin, B. *Chicka Chicka Boom Boom*

Miranda, A. *Pignic: An Alphabet Book in Rhymes*

Pallota, J. *The Frog Alphabet Book*

Sendak, M. *Alligators All Around*

Seuss, Dr. *Dr. Seuss's ABC's*

So, S. *C is for China*

Van Allsburg, C. *The Z was Zapped*

Note: Look for alphabet books written by authors in your area; these books will often have pictures of animals or objects that are more familiar to your children.

Poetry Books

Bennett, J. *Noisy Poems*

Cousins, L. (illus.). *The Lucy Cousins Book of Nursery Rhymes*

deRegniers, B. *Poems Children Will Sit Still For; Sing a Song of Popcorn*

Hopkins, L. *Side by Side: Poems to Read Together*

Prelutsky, J. *The New Kid on the Block; Poems of A. Nonny Mouse; The Random House Book of Poetry for Children; Read-aloud Rhymes for the Very Young*

Schwartz, A. *And the Green Grass Grew All Around: Folk Poetry from Everyone*

Silverstein, S. *Where the Sidewalk Ends*

Wright, B. F. *The Real Mother Goose*

Song Picture Books

Aliki. *Hush, Little Baby; Go Tell Aunt Rhody*

Berry, H. *Old Macdonald Had a Farm*

Hague, M. *Twinkle, Twinkle Little Star*

Hurd, T. *Mama Don't Allow*

Keats, E. *Over in the Meadow*

Raffi. *Down by the Bay; Shake My Sillies Out; Wheels on the Bus*

Slavin, B., & Tucker, K. *The Cat Came Back*

Spier, P. *London Bridge is Falling Down*

Trapini, I. *The Itsy Bitsy Spider*

Weiss, N. *If You're Happy and You Know It*

Where to Find Lists of Good Children's Books

(See Reference List for more information on each title.)

Adams, M. J., et al. (1998), *Phonemic Awareness in Young Children: A Classroom Curriculum*. Annotated bibliography of rhyming stories (pp. 159–169).

Bishop, A., et al. (2002), *Ready for Reading: A Handbook for Parents of Preschoolers*. Sixty "book-sharing experiences" to use with preschool-age children; activities to do before, during, and after the reading of each book (with additional related titles suggested for each).

Burns, M. S., et al. (1999), *Starting Out Right: A Guide to Promoting Children's Reading Success*. A list of "100 Great Picture Books" compiled by the New York Public Library (pp. 38–41); a list of all 42 Dr. Seuss books (p. 154).

Calkins, L. (2001), *The Art of Teaching Reading*. Examples of leveled reading books (Appendix A); read-aloud books for children ages five and up (Appendix B).

Fountas, I. C., & Pinnell, G. S. (1996), *Guided Reading: Good First Teaching for All Children*. Books listed by reading level. (Levels A–C, books appropriate for beginning readers, are on pp. 339–350.)

Hall, S. L., & Moats, L. C. (1999), *Straight Talk About Reading: How Parents Can Make a Difference During the Early Years*. Lists of books to read aloud (grouped by infants and toddlers; preschool and kindergarten; first, second, and third grades) and books for beginning readers, first through third grade (in Appendix 3).

Kropp, P. (2000), *How to Make Your Child a Reader for Life*. Short lists of "must-have" books for very young children, for beginning readers, and for older readers.

Maehr, J. (1991), *Language and Literacy*. Lists of read-aloud books, poetry, wordless books, books with predictable language (repetition and rhyme), and sing-along books (in Appendix A).

McGee, L. M., & Richgels, D. J. (2000), *Literacy's Beginnings: Supporting Young Readers and Writers*. Extensive lists of books for very young children, including alphabet books, wordless books, predictable books, language play books, and multicultural books (in the Appendix).

Moomaw, S., & Hieronymous, B. (2001), *More Than Letters: Literacy Activities for Preschool, Kindergarten, and First Grade*. List of predictable books (in Appendix A); excellent section on selecting, making, and using big books; also, suggestions for related books to accompany each of the many literacy-related activities.

Neuman, S. B., Copple, C., & Bredekamp, S. (2000), *Learning to Read and Write: Developmentally Appropriate Practices for Young Children*. List of wordless books (p. 54).

Neuman, S. B., & Roskos, K. A. (1997), *Language and Literacy Learning in the Early Years: An Integrated Approach*. Lists of activity books, alphabet books, concept books, informational books, predictable books, and story books, as well as magazines, literacy-related software, toys, videos, and Web sites; compiled by Lehart (pp. 275–300).

Schickedanz, J. A. (1999), *Much More Than the ABCs: The Early Stages of Reading and Writing*. Lists of good books for preschoolers, including fiction, nonfiction, verse, and alphabet books (pp. 68–70); list of predictable books (pp. 77–78).

Schiller, P. B. (2001), *Creating Readers*. Lists of books focusing on listening, sounds, rhymes, alliteration; wordless books; books that inspire dramatic play; predictable books; and books for each letter of the alphabet.

Strickland, D. S., & Morrow, L. M. (2000), *Beginning Reading and Writing*. A list of authors who write culturally diverse books compiled by Galda & Cullinan (pp. 134–142) (as well as criteria for selecting multicultural literature).

Trelease, J. *The Read-Aloud Handbook* (2001). A "giant treasury of great read-aloud books"; annotated bibliography includes lists of wordless books, predictable books, reference books; suggested age levels (preschool and up) are included in the lists of picture books, short and full-length novels, poetry, anthologies, and fairy and folk tales. (This book is revised every four or five years, and new books are listed on the author's Web site, *www.trelease-on-reading.com*).

Appendix E: Resources

There is a wealth of information on early literacy "out there"—one just needs to know where to look. This appendix is designed to be a starting place; searching online can bring up many more recent resources as well.

Videos

Building Literacy Competencies in Early Childhood, with Elena Bodrova and Deborah J. Leong, 2000, 30 minutes. Order from Davidson Films: 888-437-4200, *http://www.davidsonfilms.com.*

Early Book Stages, produced by Roxanna Holguin, 1995, 24 minutes. Available in both English and Spanish. Order from Roxanna Holguin: 520-377-9616.

Language and Literacy (High/Scope Preschool Key Experiences series), 2000, 60 minutes. Order from High/Scope Press: 800-407-7377, *http://www.highscope.org.*

Language is the Key video set: 1. *Talking and Books,* 20 minutes, 2. *Talking and Play,* 23 minutes; with Linda Kennedy, 1998. Set is available in six languages (not dubbed): English, Spanish, Mandarin Chinese, Korean, Vietnamese, Tagalog; or with English or Chinese subtitles. Order from Washington Research Institute, 206-285-9317, *http://www.wri-edu.org.*

Nourishing Language Development in the Early Years, with Alice Sterling Honig, 1996, 31 minutes. Order from Davidson Films: 888-437-4200, *http://www.davidsonfilms.com.*

Ready to Learn, with LeVar Burton and Jamie Lee Curtis (English version) or Edward James Olmos (Spanish version), 2001, 24 minutes. Order from the I Am Your Child Foundation: 888-447-3400, *http://www.iamyourchild.org.*

Web Sites

Web sites come and go with alarming frequency. At the time of publication, the following were among the current early literacy resources. Most sites have a "search this site" button; entering terms such as "early literacy," "preschool," "reading," "phonological awareness," etc., often results in a listing of all the relevant pages. You can also search those terms in a general search engine like *http://google.com.*

A to Z Kids Stuff
http://www.atozkidsstuff.com
Articles about and activities for toddlers, preschoolers, and school-age children.

ABC Teach
http://www.abcteach.com
Thousands of free printable pages, more if you join as a member.

The American Federation of Teachers
http://www.aft.org
Includes an "educational issues" department, as well as a parent page, with links to various literacy-related articles.

American Library Association
http://ala.org

American Psychological Association
http://www.apa.org

Association for Supervision and Curriculum Development
http://www.ascd.org

Building Blocks
http://www.blocks4reading.com/buildingblocks
Web site that describes "Building Blocks," the "FourBlocks" framework for kindergarten classrooms.

Carol Hurst
http://www.carolhurst.com
Children's literature site, maintained by Carol Otis Hurst, a nationally-known storyteller, lecturer, author and language arts consultant. Includes a listing of recommended children's books, that can be accessed by grade level (starting with preK). For each book listed, includes a short review; and for featured books, discussion topics, activities, related books, and related Web sites.

Center for the Improvement of Early Reading Achievement
http://www.ciera.org

Children's Literacy Initiative
http://www.cliontheweb.org
Information for teachers, parents, and administrators; the organization also provides literacy training and classroom literacy materials.

The Children's Literature Web Guide
http://www.acs.ucalgary.ca/~dkbrown
Internet resources related to books for children and young adults; by David K. Brown, University of Calgary.

Children's Software Revue
http://www/childrensoftware.com

DIBELS: Dynamic Indicators of Basic Early Literacy Skills
http://dibels.uoregon.edu
Provides access to a set of standardized, individually administered measures of early literacy development, used in kindergartens and primary grades. Also provides links to Web sites appropriate for assessing development of infants, toddlers, and preschool-age children at
http://dibels.uoregon.edu/youngerchildren.php

Early Childhood Research and Practice
http://ecrp.uiuc.edu
Internet journal on the development, care, and education of young children; edited by Lilian G. Katz, University of Illinois (Urbana-Champaign).

Early Literacy
http://www.earlyliterature.ecsd.net
A compilation of research, strategies, and resources for teachers and parents.

Family Education
http://www.familyeducation.com
Web site created by parents for parents.

The Horn Book

http://www.hbook.com

Publications about books for children and young adults; includes a hilarious article by author Jon Scieszka on the correct pronunciation of authors' names (at *http://www.hbook.com/exhibit/article_scieszka.html*).

International Reading Association

http://www.readingonline.org

Professional organization Web site providing access to articles, research, book reviews; includes an extensive online bookstore.

Jim Trelease

http://www.trelease-on-reading.com

Web site of author Jim Trelease (*The Read-Aloud Handbook*); includes author profiles, book excerpts, book lists, articles, and directions for installing rain gutters on classroom walls in order to display books!

The Kindergarten Connection

http://www.kconnect.com

Geared for kindergarten teachers; many ideas useful for preschool teachers as well. Includes teaching tips, lesson plans, book reviews, and links to other relevant sites.

The Knowledge Loom

http://knowledgeloom.org

Web site developed and maintained by The Education Alliance at Brown University; includes links to relevant early literacy information, as well as an ongoing panel discussion with educators on successful early literacy programs.

LD Online

http://www.ldonline.org

Web site on learning disabilities, for parents, teachers, and other professionals. Click on "LD In Depth" button for list of numerous articles under such topics as ADD, bilingual, reading, speech and language, etc.

Learning First Alliance

http://www.learningfirst.org

Web site of a "partnership of twelve leading education associations, dedicated to improving student learning in America's public schools"; includes access to the online publications of "Every Child Reading," "Top Ten Reading Tips for Parents," "Reading Tips for Teachers," and "Reading Tips for Schools."

Learning to Read

http://www.toread.com

Web site by John Nemes; "a clearinghouse for the dissemination of reading research"; includes links to over a hundred online resources which address some aspect of balanced literacy.

The Literacy Web, University of Connecticut

http://www.literacy.uconn.edu

Includes a preschool literacy home page, with many relevant links.

Mid-Continent Research for Education and Learning
http://www.mcrel.org
Links to articles, materials, and workshops related to early literacy.

National Association for the Education of Young Children
http://www.naeyc.org
Includes access to the joint position statement of NAEYC and the International Reading Association (IRA), "Learning to Read and Write."

National Center for Early Development and Learning
http://www.fpg.unc.edu/~ncedl
Web site of a national early childhood research project that focuses on enhancing the cognitive, social, and emotional development of children from birth through age eight.

National Center for Hearing Assessment and Management
http://www.infanthearing.org
Links to resources for families who have a child who is deaf or hard of hearing.

National Center for Learning Disabilities
http://www.getreadytoread.org
Early literacy information for educators, parents, healthcare professionals, and child advocates. "Get Ready to Read!" is a 20-question screening tool designed for parents to use with their four-year-olds.

National Child Care Information Center
http://nccic.org/pubs/literacy
Many links to information on literacy in early childhood settings, including state and local literacy initiatives, curriculum models, book distribution programs, etc.

National Council of Teachers
http://www.ncte.org
Articles and links to research relevant to early literacy.

National Institute for Literacy
http://nifl.gov
Access to several early literacy-related documents, among them "A Child Becomes a Reader" and "Put Reading First."

National Research Center on English Learning and Achievement
http://cela.albany.edu

North Central Regional Educational Laboratory
http://www.ncrel.org/litweb
NCREL's Center for Literacy Web site; provides links to many literacy-related articles and resources.

Northwest Regional Educational Laboratory
http://www.nwrel.org
Includes access to online publications, such as "Tips for parents about reading," available in both English and Spanish.

Parenthoodweb

http://www.parenthoodweb.com

Web site for parents, with numerous articles relevant to early literacy; click on topics such as imaginary play, reading, speech development, and writing.

Phi Delta Kappa

http://www.pdkintl.org/kappan/kappan.htm

International association for professional educators, providing online access to many relevant articles from their monthly print journal, the *Phi Delta Kappan*.

Planet Esme

http://www.planetesme.com

A children's literature Web site by author Esme Raji Codell (*How to Get Your Child to Love Reading*); includes book lists, links to Web sites for teachers, directions for special reading programs (like "Books for Breakfast") and author/illustrator studies.

Public Broadcasting Service

http://www.pbs.org

A variety of literacy-related information for teachers, parents, and children.

Reading Rockets

http://www.readingrockets.org

Updated *daily!* Information for educators, parents, child care providers, children, and policy-makers; includes information on learning to read, daily headlines on reading news from around the country, recommended books, interviews with children's book authors. Subscriptions available to their monthly online newsletter. Sponsor of the Web site for Spanish-speaking parents, at *http://www.colorincolorado.org*.

Resources for Reading

http://www.abcstuff.com

A company that offers a wide variety of materials and supplies for Reading Recovery and early literacy teachers—manipulative letters, charts and posters, magnetic boards, and more.

Scholastic

http://scholastic.com

Children's publishing company Web site with pages for teachers, parents, and children.

Schwab Learning

http://www.schwablearning.org

Funded by the Charles and Helen Schwab Foundation, "a parent's guide to helping kids with learning difficulties."

Scientific Learning

http://www.brainconnection.com

A variety of pertinent articles accessed through "Library Topics," which include early reading, bilingual education, child development.

Southwest Educational Development Laboratory

http://www.sedl.org/reading/topics.html

Includes papers on various topics in early literacy.

Teachers College, Columbia Unversity

http://www.tcrecord.org

Links to articles, journals, books, organizations, discussion groups on early childhood issues.

Teachers.net

http://teachers.net

Preschool teacher discussion boards, lesson plans, articles, a monthly gazette, and more.

Texas Education Agency

http://www.tea.state.tx.us/reading/sitemap.html

Links to numerous articles and online publications related to early literacy.

U.S. Department of Education

http://www.ed.gov

Links to resources for parents, teachers, and administrators; information on online access to many government publications related to early literacy.

Washington Research Institute

http://www.wri-edu.org

Web site of a nonprofit organization that conducts research, development, and training in education and the human services, focusing on the needs of children and families.

WestEd

http://www.wested.org

Access to online publications such as "Understanding Young Readers: The Role of Early Literacy Assessment."

Zero to Three

http://www.zerotothree.org/begin.html

Web site of the National Center for Infants, Toddlers and Families; includes articles and resources for parents and professionals, pertaining to a child's first three years.

Published Workbooks (Preschool and Kindergarten Level)

Some workbooks (those published by Scholastic, for instance) are geared for teachers, and the pages may be photocopied, attached to poster board, and laminated, cut out, colored, to create various manipulatives (such as word wheels, dominoes, picture-word mini-puzzles). These may be placed in a box in the writing area; where children may choose to use them during work time.

Other workbooks are geared for parents to buy for their children to use at home. Available in many department, discount, and grocery stores, these workbooks are usually inexpensive (often between $2 and $3), and vary greatly in quality: publishers include Fisher-Price, Sesame Street, as well as many lesser-known names. Some of these workbooks have one letter per page: they may include the uppercase and lowercase letter, key words and pictures that begin with the most common sound of that letter, how to write the letter, etc.

The workbooks can be used in a variety of ways. You may dismantle the entire workbook, and laminate each page (or even parts of the page) separately. Buying two copies of the same workbook enables you to use both sides of each page; mount the page on construction paper or poster board before laminating.

Appendix F: Writing Anecdotes to Document Child Observations

An anecdote is a brief statement about a child's actions and/or language that highlights his or her growth or development. It is a verbal "snapshot" that captures what a child is doing at a particular moment in time. By gathering together many such anecdotes and using them in conjunction with a developmental assessment instrument such as the Preschool Child Observation Record (COR; High/Scope, 2003), you can create a complete and accurate portrait of each child's development.

Guidelines for Anecdote Writing

The process of writing anecdotes starts with taking notes during the course of children's activities. When you notice a child doing something significant, you can capture the moment by writing down a few key details of what happened and the date.

The level of detail required in your anecdotal notes varies depending on when and how you plan on entering the notes. For most people, recording notes is a two-stage process; they usually jot down a few notes at the time of the episode, then expand on these later when they write a final version of the anecdote, either in computer files, in a notebook, or on a written form (such as those in the Preschool COR *Child Anecdotes* booklet).

If you enter anecdotes daily, you are likely to remember most of the details needed to write your anecdote; in this case jotting down just a few words and the child's initials may be all that is needed to prompt your memory. If you are not able to enter anecdotes daily, then your initial notes will have to be more detailed; otherwise you are likely to forget, overlook, or confuse pertinent details.

An anecdotal note might start out as a telegraphic message to yourself alone, looking like this:

2/21 Tony—SGT—to Sue—"This T goes with my name." "See, there's my T."

Later, you would enter the anecdote in expanded form wherever you write your anecdotes—in a notebook, on a prepared form, or in computer files. For example, if you are using the *Child Anecdotes* booklet, the Preschool COR computer program, or the online COR, you would enter Tony's anecdote in the *language and literacy* category. The expanded anecdote might read something like this:

> *2/21 During small-group time, Tony worked with some wooden letters, glue, and straws. He found a T among the letters and placed it in front of him, saying to Vinnie, "This T goes with my name." He then took a straw and cut a piece off the end; gluing one straw piece on the paper and then gluing the second piece perpendicular to it, Tony looked at Sue [a teacher], pointed at the straws he glued, and said, "See, there's my T."*

Here is a sample of another anecdote highlighting emergent writing and reading:

> *5/14 On a piece of paper, Kenneth wrote some scribbles on note paper and gave it to Callie. Then he "read" it: "I'll get you a water baby and California Roller Blades."*

Helpful Hints

Learning to write informative anecdotes like these takes time and practice. Here are some hints to make the process easier and more effective:

- **Jot notes to yourself during the day as you interact with children.** Devise your own method, one that does not interfere with your primary role of interacting with children.

- **Keep paper for writing notes in various locations throughout the room** or in your pocket. Address labels, note cards, legal pads, and Post-it notes in particular work nicely for this purpose. Or simply tape a large piece of paper on a wall where you can write on it.

- **Date your entries.** Because you are watching for changes in a child over time, this step is essential. Failure to record the date may result in useless information. (Date entry is automatic in the online and computer versions of the Preschool COR.)

- **When? Where? With whom? What?** In addition to the date, note when in the daily routine, where in the room, with whom the activity took place, and what the child did or said.

- **Include all the necessary information.** Anecdotal notes should be short and concise, but be sure to include specific details. Notes should begin with a context for the behavior, then describe the behavior, and end with the outcome or the child's explanation of the behavior. An example of a note with these features is as follows:

    5/11 During work time [when], Hannah [who] pointed to the letters [what she did] on a box next to the terrarium [where] and said, "This says that it's turtle food." [child's explanation/outcome]

- **Stick to the facts.** Simply describe behaviors; do not interpret them. For example, use an objective statement, such as "Ted told Eileen in a loud voice, 'No, no, no!' when she tried to take away the fire truck," instead of a subjective statement, such as "Ted threw a huge fit when Eileen tried to take away his fire truck."

- **Keep the entries short.** It is unrealistic to try to write detailed entries about each child in your group in every aspect of development on a daily basis—the volume of the writing alone would be staggering. Develop a system for making your entries as brief as possible, including just enough detail to help you reconstruct what happened at some later time.

After you have taken anecdotes for a week or two, step back and reflect on all you have learned about some of the children in your class. You will be surprised at the richness of the details you have come away with.

References

Adams, M. J. (1996). *Beginning to read: Thinking and learning about print.* Cambridge, MA: The MIT Press.

Adams, M. J., Foorman, B. R., Lundberg, I., & Beeler, T. (1998). *Phonemic awareness in young children: A classroom curriculum.* Baltimore: Paul H. Brookes.

American Speech-Language-Hearing Association (ASHA). (n.d.). How does your child hear and talk? [Brochure]. Rockville, MD: Author.

Ansbach-Stahlsmith, U. (2001). Telling it tall: Effective storytelling. *High/Scope Extensions, 5*(6), 1–3.

Apel, K., & Masterson, J. J. (2001). *Beyond baby talk: From sounds to sentences—A parent's complete guide to language development.* Roseville, CA: Prima Publishing. [Sponsored by the American Speech-Language-Hearing Association]

Barron, M. (with Young, K. R.). (1995). *Ready, set, read and write.* New York: John Wiley & Sons.

Berk, L. E., & Winsler, A. (1995). *Scaffolding children's learning: Vygotsky and early childhood education.* Washington DC: NAEYC.

Bettelheim, B. (1989). *The uses of enchantment* (Reissue ed.). New York: Vintage Books.

Bishop, A., Yopp, R. H., & Yopp, H. K. (2000). *Ready for reading: A handbook for parents of preschoolers.* Boston: Allyn & Bacon.

Bodrova, E., Leong, D. J., Gregory, K., & Edgerton, S. (1999). *Scaffolded writing—A successful strategy for promoting children's writing in kindergarten.* Presentation at the NAEYC 1999 Annual Conference, New Orleans, LA. Retrieved November 11, 2003, from http://www.mcrel.org/PDF/EarlyChildhoodEducation/4006IR_NAEYC_Handout_Scaffolding.pdf

Bodrova, E., Leong, D. J., & Paynter, D. E. (1999, October). Literacy standards for preschool learners. *Educational Leadership, 57*(2), 42–46.

Bredekamp, S. (2000). *A commentary: What teachers need to know about language.* Retrieved November 11, 2003, from www.cal.org/ericcll/teachers/commentary.pdf [Center for Applied Linguistics Web site]

Bredekamp, S., & Rosegrant, T. (Eds.). (1992). *Reaching potentials: Vol. 1. Appropriate curriculum and assessment for young children.* Washington, DC: NAEYC.

Bredekamp, S., & Rosegrant, T. (Eds.). (1995). *Reaching potentials: Vol. 2. Transforming early childhood curriculum and assessment.* Washington, DC: NAEYC.

Brewer, J. A. (1998). Literacy development of young children in a multilingual setting. In R. Campbell (Ed.), *Facilitating preschool literacy* (pp. 119–130). Newark, DE: International Reading Association.

Bruner, J. (1983). *Child's talk: Learning to use language.* New York: Norton.

Burns, M. S., Griffin, P., & Snow, C. E. (Eds.) [National Research Council]. (1999). *Starting out right: A guide to promoting children's reading success.* Washington, DC: National Academy Press.

Calkins, L. M. (2001). *The art of teaching reading.* New York: Addison-Wesley Educational Publishers.

Calkins, L. (with Bellino, L.). (1997). *Raising lifelong learners: A parent's guide.* Cambridge, MA: Perseus Books.

Cambourne, B. (2001). Conditions for literacy learning: Why do some students fail to learn to read? *The Reading Teacher, 54*(8), 784–786.

Campbell, R. (Ed.). (1998). *Facilitating preschool literacy.* Newark, DE: International Reading Association.

Casbergue, R. M. (1998). How do we foster young children's writing development? In S. B. Neuman & K. A. Roskos (Eds.), *Children achieving: Best practices in early literacy* (pp. 199–222). Newark, DE: International Reading Association.

Children's Software Revue [Online newsletter]. Retrieved November 11, 2003, from http://www.childrenssoftware.com

Clay, M. M. (1991). *Becoming literate: The construction of inner control.* Portsmouth, NH: Heinemann.

Clay, M. M. (1998). *By different paths to common outcomes.* York, ME: Stenhouse.

Cohen, L. E. (1997). How I developed my kindergarten book backpack program. *Young Children, 52*(2), 69–71.

DeBruin-Parecki, A., & Hohmann, M. (2003). *Letter links: Alphabet learning with children's names.* Ypsilanti, MI: High/Scope Press.

Decker Collins, N. L., & Shaeffer, M. B. (1997). Look, listen, and learn to read. *Young Children, 52*(5), 65–68.

Dickinson, D. K. (2001). Large-group and free-play times: Conversational settings supporting language and literacy development. In D. K. Dickinson & P. O. Tabors (Eds.), *Beginning literacy with language* (pp. 223–255). Baltimore: Paul H. Brookes.

Dickinson, D. K., & Tabors, P. O. (Eds.). (2001). *Beginning literacy with language.* Baltimore: Paul H. Brookes.

DiNatale, L. (2002). Developing high-quality family involvement programs in early childhood settings. *Young Children, 57*(5), 90–95.

Drummond, T. (1997). *Writing and enacting stories in preschool.* Retrieved November 11, 2003, from the North Seattle Community College Web site: http://northonline.sccd.ctc.edu/eceprog/wrtng.html

Edwards, P. A. (with Pleasants, H. M., & Franklin, S. H.). (1999). *A path to follow: Learning to listen to parents.* Portsmouth, NH: Heinemann.

Eliot, L. (1999). *What's going on in there? How the brain and mind develop in the first five years of life.* New York: Bantam Books.

Engel, S. (1999). *The stories children tell.* New York: W. H. Freeman.

Epstein, A. S. (2002). *Helping your preschool child become a reader.* Ypsilanti, MI: High/Scope Press.

Epstein, A. S. (2003). *All about High/Scope.* Retrieved November 11, 2003, from http://www.highscope.org/About/allabout.htm

Epstein, A. S., Hohmann, C., & Hohmann, M. (2001). *How young children learn to read in High/Scope programs* [Position papers]. Ypsilanti, MI: High/Scope Press.

Fountas, I. C., & Pinnell, G. S. (1996). *Guided reading: Good first teaching for all children.* Portsmouth, NH: Heinemann.

Fox, M. (2001). *Reading magic: Why reading aloud to our children will change their lives forever.* San Diego, CA: Harcourt.

Frede, E. (1984). *Getting involved: Workshops for parents.* Ypsilanti, MI: High/Scope Press.

Golinkoff, R. M., & Hirsh-Pasek, K. (1999). *How babies talk: The magic and mystery of language in the first three years of life.* New York: Penguin Putnam.

Gopnick, A., Meltzoff, A. N., & Kuhl, P. K. (1999). *The scientist in the crib: Minds, brains, and how children learn.* New York: William Morrow.

Graves, M. F., Graves, B. B., & Braaten, S. (1996, February). Scaffolded reading experiences for inclusive classes. *Educational Leadership 53*(5), 14–16.

Graves, M. (2000). *The essential parent workshop resource: The teacher's idea book #4.* Ypsilanti, MI: High/Scope Press.

Grier, K. (1997). *Storytelling with preschool children: Making a start.* Retrieved November 11, 2003, from http://www.cfc-efc.ca/docs/cccf/00012_en.htm

Hall, N. (1998). Young children as storytellers. In R. Campbell (Ed.), *Facilitating preschool literacy* (pp. 84–99). Newark, DE: International Reading Association.

Hall, S. L., & Moats, L. C. (1999). *Straight talk about reading: How parents can make a difference during the early years.* Chicago: Contemporary Books.

Harding, N. (1996). Family journals: The bridge from school to home and back again. *Young Children, 51*(2), 27–30.

Hart, B., & Risley, T. R. (1995). *Meaningful differences in the everyday experience of young American children.* Baltimore: Paul H. Brookes.

Hart, B., & Risley, T. R. (1999). *The social world of children learning to talk.* Baltimore: Paul H. Brookes.

Healy, J. M. (1994). *Your child's growing mind: A guide to learning and brain development from birth to adolescence.* New York: Doubleday.

Healy, J. M. (1998). *Failure to connect: How computers affect our children's minds—For better and worse.* New York: Simon & Schuster.

High/Scope Educational Research Foundation. (2000). *Language and literacy (High/Scope Preschool Key Experiences* Series) [Booklet]. Ypsilanti, MI: High/Scope Press.

High/Scope Educational Research Foundation. (2003). *COR–Head Start Outcomes Reporter* (2nd ed.). Ypsilanti, MI: High/Scope Press.

High/Scope Educational Research Foundation. (2003). *Preschool Child Observation Record (COR)* (2nd ed.) [Components include *Child anecdotes* booklet, *Observation items, User guide*]. Ypsilanti, MI: High/Scope Press.

Hills, T. W. (1992). Reaching potentials through appropriate assessment. In S. Bredekamp & T. Rosegrant (Eds.), *Reaching potentials: Vol. 1. Appropriate curriculum and assessment for young children* (pp. 43–63). Washington, DC: NAEYC.

Hohmann, M. (2002). *Fee, fie, phonemic awareness: 130 prereading activities for preschoolers.* Ypsilanti, MI: High/Scope Press.

Hohmann, M. (2002). Recognizing letter sounds and names. *High/Scope Extensions, 16*(5), 4–5.

Hohmann, M., & Weikart, D. P. (2002). *Educating young children: Active learning practices for preschool and child care programs* (2nd ed.). Ypsilanti, MI: High/Scope Press.

Honig, B. (1996). *Teaching our children to read.* Thousand Oaks, CA: Corwin Press.

International Reading Association (IRA) & National Association for the Education of Young Children (NAEYC). (2000). The IRA/NAEYC position. In S. B. Neuman, C. Copple, & S. Bredekamp, *Learning to read and write: Developmentally appropriate practices for young children* (pp. 1–26). Newark, DE: International Reading Association. (Originally published 1998)

Johnston, P. H., & Rogers, R. (2001). Early literacy development: The case for "informed assessment." In S. B. Neuman & D. K. Dickinson (Eds.), *Handbook of early literacy research* (pp. 377–389). New York: Guilford Publications.

Krashen, S. (1993). *The power of reading: Insights from the research.* Englewood, CO: Libraries Unlimited.

Kropp, P. (2000). *How to make your child a reader for life.* New York: Broadway Books.

Lawrence, L. (1998). *Montessori read and write: A parent's guide to literacy for children.* New York: Three Rivers Press.

Learning First Alliance. (1998, June). *Every child reading: An action plan.* Retrieved November 11, 2003, from the Learning First Web site: http://www.learningfirst.org

Lonigan, C. J., Burgess, S. R., & Anthony, J. L. (2000). Development of emergent literacy and early reading skills in preschool children: Evidence from a latent-variable longitudinal study. *Developmental Psychology, 36*(5), 596–613.

Maehr, J. (1991). *Language and literacy (High/Scope K–3 Curriculum* series). Ypsilanti, MI: High/Scope Press.

McGee, L. M., & Richgels, D. J. (2000). *Literacy's beginnings: Supporting young readers and writers* (3rd ed.). Boston: Allyn & Bacon.

McLane, J. B., & McNamee, G. D. (2002). *The beginnings of literacy.* Retrieved November 11, 2003, from http://www.zerotothree.org/begin.html (Full version of article originally appeared in 1991 in *Zero to Three, 12*(1), pp. 1–8.)

Meisels, S., Jablon, J. R., Marsden, D. B., Dichtelmiller, M. L., & Dorfman, A. B. (2001). *The Work Sampling System* (4th ed.). Ann Arbor, MI: Rebus Planning Associates.

Moats, L. C. (2000). *Speech to print: Language essentials for teachers.* Baltimore: Paul H. Brookes.

Moomaw, S., & Hieronymus, B. (2001). *More than letters: Literacy activities for preschool, kindergarten, and first grade.* St. Paul, MN: Redleaf Press.

Morrow, L. M. (2001). *Literacy development in the early years* (4th ed.). Boston: Allyn & Bacon.

Morrow, L. M., & Gambrell, L. B. (2000). Literature-based reading instruction. In M. L. Kamil, P. B. Mosenthal, P. D. Pearson, & R. Barr (Eds.), *Handbook of reading research: Vol. III* (pp. 563–586). Mahwah, NJ: Lawrence Erlbaum.

National Association for the Education of Young Children (NAEYC) & National Association of Early Childhood Specialists in State Departments of Education (NAECS/SDE). (2001). NAEYC viewpoint: Standardized tests do not equal assessment or accountability! [Excerpts from NAEYC and NAECS/SDE 1990 position statement]. *Young Children, 56*(2), 18.

National Council of Teachers of English (NCTE). (1992). *Teaching storytelling: A position statement.* Urbana, IL: Author.

National Parent Involvement Network (NPIN). (n.d.). *Parent involvement in education: A resource for parents, educators, and communities.* Retrieved November 11, 2003, from http://npin.org/library/pre1998/n00321/n00321.html

National Reading Panel. (2000). *Teaching children to read.* Washington, DC: National Institute of Child Health and Human Development.

Neuman, S. B., Copple, C., & Bredekamp, S. (2000). *Learning to read and write: Developmentally appropriate practices for young children.* Washington, DC: NAEYC.

Neuman, S. B., & Dickinson, D. K. (Eds.). (2001). *Handbook of early literacy research.* New York: Guilford Publications.

Neuman, S. B., & Roskos, K. A. (1997). *Language and literacy learning in the early years: An integrated approach.* San Diego, CA: Singular Publishing.

Neuman, S. B., & Roskos, K. A. (Eds.). (1998). *Children achieving: Best practices in early literacy.* Newark, DE: International Reading Association.

Owocki, G. (1999). *Literacy through play.* Portsmouth, NH: Heinemann.

Paley, V. G. (1981). *Wally's stories.* Cambridge, MA: Harvard University Press.

Paley, V. G. (1990). *The boy who would be a helicopter: The uses of storytelling in the classroom.* Cambridge, MA: Harvard University Press.

Palincsar, A. S. (1998). Keeping the metaphor of scaffolding fresh. *Journal of Learning Disabilities, 31*(4), 370–373.

Porche, M. V. (2001). Parent involvement as a link between home and school. In D. K. Dickinson & P. O. Tabors (Eds.), *Beginning literacy with language* (pp. 291–312). Baltimore: Paul H. Brookes.

Rhoten, L., & Lane, M. (2001). More than the ABCs: The new alphabet books. *Young Children, 56*(1), 41–45.

Roskos, K. A., & Neuman, S. B. (1994). Of scribbles, schemas, and storybooks: Using literacy albums to document young children's literacy growth. *Young Children, 49*(2), 78–85.

Routman, R. (1994). *Invitations: Changing as teachers and learners K–12.* Portsmouth, NH: Heinemann.

Schickedanz, J. A. (1999). *Much more than the ABCs: The early stages of reading and writing.* Washington, DC: NAEYC.

Schiller, P. B. (2001). *Creating readers.* Beltsville, MD: Gryphon House.

Schweinhart, L. J. (1993). Observing young children in action: The key to early childhood assessment. *Young Children, 48*(5), 29–33.

Shepard, L., Kagan, S. L., & Wurtz, E. (Eds.). (1998). *Principles and recommendations for early childhood assessments.* Retrieved November 11, 2003, from http://www.negp.gov/Reports/prinrec.pdf

Sipe, L. R. (2001, November). Invention, convention, and intervention: Invented spelling and the teacher's role. *The Reading Teacher, 55*(3), 264–273.

Snow, C. E., Burns, M. S., & Griffin, P. (Eds.) [National Research Council]. (1998). *Preventing reading difficulties in young children.* Washington, DC: National Academy Press.

Strickland, D. S., & Morrow, L. M. (Eds.) (2000). *Beginning reading and writing (Language and literacy series).* New York: Teachers College Press.

Sulzby, E. (1985). Children's emergent reading of favorite storybooks: A developmental study. *Reading Research Quarterly, 20*(4), 458–481.

Tabors, P. O. (1997). *One child, two languages: A guide for preschool educators of children learning English as a second language.* Baltimore: Paul H. Brookes.

Tabors, P. O., Beals, D. E., & Weizman, Z. O. (2001). "You know what oxygen is?" Learning new words at home. In D. K. Dickinson & P. O. Tabors (Eds.), *Beginning literacy with language* (pp. 93–110). Baltimore: Paul H. Brookes.

Taylor, D. (Ed.). (1997). *Many families, many literacies.* Portsmouth, NH: Heinemann.

Taylor, D. (1998). *Family literacy: Young children learning to read and write.* Portsmouth, NH: Heinemann.

Teale, W. H., & Yakota, J. (2000). Beginning reading and writing: Perspectives on instruction. In D. S. Strickland & L. M. Morrow (Eds.), *Beginning reading and writing* (pp. 3–21). New York: Teachers College Press.

Torgerson, L. (1996, May). Starting with stories: Building a sense of community. *Child Care Information Exchange* (109), 55–58.

Trelease, J. (2001). *The read-aloud handbook* (5th ed.). New York: Penguin Books.

Vygotsky, L. (1987). *The collected works of L.S. Vygotsky: Vol. 1.* New York: Plenum.

Wasik, B. A. (2001). Teaching the alphabet to young children. *Young Children, 56*(1), 34–40.

Weaver, C., Gillmeister-Krause, L., & Vento-Zogby, G. (1996). *Creating support for effective literacy education.* Portsmouth, NH: Heinemann.

Weikart, P. S., & Carlton, E. B. (1995). *Foundations in elementary education: Movement*. Ypsilanti, MI: High/Scope Press.

White-Clark, R., & Decker, L. E. (1996). Benefits of parent involvement: What the research shows. In *The hard-to-reach parent: Old challenges, new insights*. Retrieved November 11, 2003, from http://eric-web.tc.columbia.edu/npinpdfs/hardtoreach.pdf

Whitehead, M. (1999). *Supporting language and literacy development in the early years*. Buckingham, UK: Open University Press.

Whitmore, K. F., & Goodman, Y. M. (1995). Transforming curriculum in language and literacy. In S. Bredekamp & T. Rosegrant (Eds.), *Reaching potentials: Vol. 2. Transforming early childhood curriculum and assessment* (pp. 145–166). Washington, DC: NAEYC.

Wood, D. J., Bruner, J. S., & Ross, G. (1976). The role of tutoring in problem solving. *Journal of Child Psychology and Psychiatry, 17*(2), 89–100.

Yopp, H. K. (1992). Developing phonemic awareness in young children. *The Reading Teacher, 45*(9), 696–703.

Yopp, H. K. (1995, September). A test for assessing phonemic awareness in young children. *The Reading Teacher, 49*(1), 20–29.

About the Author

Linda Weikel Ranweiler has been an early childhood consultant since 1994. While working for the High/Scope Educational Research Foundation, she conducted training projects for preschool teachers and trainers in the U.S., Canada, and Taiwan. As an independent consultant, she has continued to work on the development and improvement of High/Scope training materials.

Prior to working for High/Scope, Linda was involved with early childhood programs for 25 years, in a variety of roles: parent volunteer, student intern, classroom teacher (both preschool and kindergarten), and administrator. She has also been a child development specialist and home visitor for the "Parents as Teachers" program and a literacy tutor for the Boys and Girls Club. Her next project is training literacy volunteers to work one-on-one in elementary classrooms.

Believing that preschoolers are already readers and writers in their own way, Linda has written this book in the hope that teachers, parents, and administrators will agree, and will find many ways to support young children on their journey.

Index

A

Adams, Marilyn J., 28, 81, 120
Adult support strategies
  for building letter knowledge, 101–16
  for children reading, 123–37
  for dictation, 142–51
  for oral language, 23–36
  for reading aloud, 63–69
  for storytelling, 71–80, 148–151
  for word play, 43–57
  for writing, 87–98
Alliteration, 41
  books with, 50, 193
  games with, 47–49
  picture cards with, 49–50
  small-group activity with, 56–57
  songs with, 51–52, 55–56
Alphabet
  class book of, 115
  familiarity with, 100
  knowledge of, development of, 100–01
  letters and sounds, 41–43
  materials for learning, 103–09
  picture charts of, 106–09
"Alphabet clue game," 115
Alphabetic principle, 19, 41–42
American Sign Language, 18
Anecdotes, 156–158
  how to write, 205–206
Ansbach-Stahlsmith, Ursula, 74
Arrival time, literacy-related ideas for, 31–32, 89–90, 127, 146
Art area, literacy materials in, 88, 94, 102, 106
Artifacts, 158–59
Assessment of language and literacy
  checklists for, 166
  content of, 163–66

COR language and literacy items, 164–65
  data for, 156–60
  definition of, 154
  family contributions to, 159–60
  family report form for, 162
  guiding principles of, 154
  procedure for, 155–63
  rationale for, 154–55
  results of, 167

B

Barron, Marlene, 136
Beeler, T., 28
Bettelheim, Bruno, 76
Block area, literacy materials in, 88, 93, 102, 108, 131
Book area, literacy materials in, 65–66, 88, 102, 108
Books
  alphabet, 66, 194–95
  big books, 66, 126
  for emerging readers, 126–27
  learning about, 61
  lists of various types of, 193–95
  making, 132, 133, 149
  multicultural, 66, 194
  poetry, 195
  predictable, 65, 126, 193
  resources for more lists of, 196–97
  of rhyme and alliteration, 65, 193
  song, 195
  wordless, 66, 126, 194
Bredekamp, Sue, 5, 25
Brewer, J., 43
Bruner, J. S., 9
Burns, M. Susan, 17, 30, 86

C

Calkins, Lucy, 37, 65, 81
Cambourne, Brian, 137
Casbergue, Renée, 94
Child-directed talk, 25
Child Observation Record. *See* Preschool Child Observation Record
Chomsky, Noam, 22
Clay, Marie, 43, 59, 71, 79, 81, 97, 100, 104, 109, 123
Cleanup time, literacy-related ideas for, 55, 132
Communication, 16–17
Community literacy efforts, 180–81
Comprehension, 19, 118
Computer area, literacy materials in, 88, 103, 108
Conversation, 25, 32–34
  cognitively challenging, 26
  materials to stimulate, 35
Copple, Carol, 5
COR. *See* Preschool Child Observation Record
COR–Head Start Outcomes Reporter (software), 157

D

Daily routine, literacy-related ideas for
  alphabet learning, 112–16
  children reading, 127–35
  children writing, 89–95
  dictation, 146–48
  language development, 31–36
  reading aloud, 63–64
  word play, rhyme, alliteration, 54–57
Decoding, 117–18
Decontextualized talk, 26, 34

Whitmore, Kathryn F., 159
Wood, D. J., 9
Woodworking area, literacy materials in, 103
Word, concept of, 41
Word play, 37–38, 44–57
Words
  introduction of, 26, 32, 35
  and meaning, 40
  playing with, 37
  rare, 27, 33–34
  and sounds, 40
Work time, literacy-related ideas for, 34–35, 93–94, 114, 130, 147

Writing
  of alphabet letters, 108–09
  in daily routine, 89–95
  development of, 4, 82
  displaying samples of, 95
  and drawing, 91–92
  early forms (stages) of, 82–85
  encouraging, 108–9
  materials for, 87–89
  purpose of, 81
  and reading, 81
  responding to children's requests for help in, 96–97
  scaffolded, 140–41
  shared (interactive), 140
  and small-muscle development, 90–91
Writing aloud, 95
Writing area, literacy materials in, 87, 94, 106

Y

Yokota, Junko, 67
Yopp, Hallie Kay, 40

Z

Zone of proximal development, 9–13, 25, 140
ZPD. *See* Zone of proximal development